Scratchin' and Survivin'

The cover image of the book speaks to the larger theme of the text as a whole. Although Hollywood's system of awards is historically racially biased, a topic that exists outside the scope of this work, even the exclusion of these 1970s Black sitcom artists from Hollywood's Walk of Fame was met with resilience. The inclusion on the Hollywood Walk of Fame is one of the most enduring and honored symbols of celebrity around, but there is another, smaller, and all but forgotten monument to another group of celebrities simply etched into the cement outside of the former office building of Redd Foxx Productions. Although this "Redd Foxx Walk of Fame" is not officially recognized by any commemorative markers, in front of a modern office building at 933 North La Brea in West Hollywood, California, exists signatures, dates, and hand/footprints left by Foxx, Lynn Hamilton, LaWanda Page, and other Black actors and comedians popularized in the 1970s. In this 1987 *JET Magazine* image (repeated on the cover), ten years after the cancelation of *Sanford and Son*, Redd Foxx is seen holding the hand of his former costar LaWanda Page as she presses her feet into the wet cement and smiles at this momentous occasion.

Art: Johnson Publishing Company Archive. Courtesy J. Paul Getty Trust and Smithsonian National Museum of African American History and Culture. Made possible by the Ford Foundation, J. Paul Getty Trust, John D. and Catherine T. MacArthur Foundation, The Andrew W. Mellon Foundation and the Smithsonian Institution.

Scratchin' and Survivin'

Hustle Economics and the
Black Sitcoms of Tandem Productions

ADRIEN SEBRO

Rutgers University Press

New Brunswick, Camden, and Newark, New Jersey

London and Oxford

Rutgers University Press is a department of Rutgers, The State University of New Jersey, one of the leading public research universities in the nation. By publishing worldwide, it furthers the University's mission of dedication to excellence in teaching, scholarship, research, and clinical care.

Library of Congress Cataloging-in-Publication Data

Names: Sebro, Adrien, author.
Title: Scratchin' and survivin' : hustle economics and the Black sitcoms of Tandem Productions / Adrien Sebro.
Other titles: Scratching and surviving
Description: New Brunswick : Rutgers University Press, 2023. | Includes bibliographical references and index.
Identifiers: LCCN 2023009473 | ISBN 9781978834835 (paperback) | ISBN 9781978834842 (hardcover) | ISBN 9781978834859 (epub) | ISBN 9781978834873 (pdf)
Subjects: LCSH: African Americans on television. | Labor on television. | Situation comedies (Television programs)—United States. | Television programs—United States—History—20th century. | African American actors—United States. | African Americans in television broadcasting. | Tandem Productions—History. | Sanford and son (Television program) | Good times (Television program) | Jeffersons (Television program)
Classification: LCC PN1992.8.A34 S43 2023 | DDC 791.4508996073—dc23/eng/20230605
LC record available at https://lccn.loc.gov/2023009473

A British Cataloging-in-Publication record for this book is available from the British Library.

References to internet websites (URLs) were accurate at the time of writing. Neither the author nor Rutgers University Press is responsible for URLs that may have expired or changed since the manuscript was prepared.

rutgersuniversitypress.org

To my father, Michael. Thank you for teaching me how to hustle.

Contents

Publisher's Note

This book contains several instances of the word n-----. Rutgers University Press does not condone usage of this word and does not reprint it without careful thought. In this instance, the word is used in conveying archival materials from production notes and interviews pertaining to the Black sitcoms of Tandem Productions.

Scratchin' and Survivin'

Introduction

The Hustle

For as long as I can recall, watching television has always served as my escape. No matter the genre or intended audience, I've always found myself immersed in these imagined worlds, trying to understand every piece of their construction. Who created these worlds? Who chose these characters? Why are they popular? Questions like these have always occupied my mind, especially when I began to see myself, although scantly, reflected in the subject matter. I overwhelmingly saw myself and performances of Black culture in situational comedies (sitcoms). The production of all-Black-cast sitcoms (or Black sitcoms) has historically been a hard-fought battle in American network television. Throughout this book, the terms "Black sitcoms" or "all-Black-cast sitcoms" will be used interchangeably to define network television situation comedies that feature a majority Black cast and focus on a Black-lived experience that is culturally specific. Premiering in 2014, ABC's *Black-ish* (2014–2022) was the first broadcast sitcom in some time to feature an all-Black family as the primary cast.[1] In its season two finale, entitled "Good-ish Times," *Black-ish* paid tribute to the Tandem Productions' Black sitcom *Good Times* (1974–1979) by transporting the LA-based Johnson family back in time to inner-city Chicago portraying *Good Times* characters. In a *TV Guide* interview with *Black-ish* creator and showrunner, Kenya Barris (a Black man), he states that "forty years ago, the Evans family was *the* Black family on TV.... Creating this parallel was something I've always wanted to do."[2] The *Black-ish* cast, many of whom hadn't been alive during *Good Times'* original run, "binged episodes on YouTube" to understand the content and performance of these Black characters in the 1970s.[3] One young cast member even stated that they were "surprised to see how much it pulled on heartstrings and dealt with heavy issues, which is something that our show does too."[4] With *Black-ish*, what was once old has become new again, in regard to popular Black network sitcoms using comedy to address societal mores, race, politics, and economics. A large difference between these two shows is the creative freedom and authority to portray Black characters that was given to Tandem's Norman Lear and Bud Yorkin—two white men.

In 2018, Kenya Barris departed from *Black-ish* and ABC Studios due to creative differences. This departure is rumored to have happened in large part due to ABC indefinitely shelving an episode of *Black-ish* that he wrote and directed. The episode, "Please, Baby, Please," touched on current events, including the controversy over athletes kneeling during the national anthem and (of greater concern to ABC) criticism of former president Donald Trump.[5] These creative blockades to important social commentary on television pushed Barris to depart from network television to streaming services as he left ABC to sign with Netflix, effectively forcing him to resign from his position as co-showrunner on *Black-ish* to an executive producer role.

Half a century earlier, where the idea of a Black showrunner like Barris seemed mythic, escapist television fare that persisted throughout 1960s prime-time television made little reference to what was being reported on the news and in the popular press about the realities of Black life. That began to change in the late 1960s and early '70s as some shows began to reflect the Black cultural landscape. This new wave of redefined Black identities on-screen as a reflection of the political, social, and economic moment in the 1970s has been deemed the era of social relevance. This moment was constructed largely by Bud Yorkin and Norman Lear through their company, Tandem Productions. *Good Times*, like many of its television contemporaries of the 1970s, was the result of this era.

I came to write this book out of the curiosity of how shows like *Good Times* can be looked at and heralded through the lens of contemporary television like *Black-ish*. Although forty years apart in their production, they are both network sitcoms focusing on Blackness. However, the Black artists (creators, actors, writers, stand-ins, etc.) of the era of relevance are largely absent from discussions of groundbreaking auteurs of television fare. The battles to remain employed and to perform the unasked burden of representing their race in an industry that wasn't built for them called for Black artists to hustle by any means to leave an indelible impression on popular culture. Television had the potential and the promise to reverse centuries of unjust ridicule and antisocial images of Black people, both of which circulated throughout popular culture. Given that television was meant not only to be an entertainment medium but also to serve as a vehicle for social engagement, its potential role to encourage a more just society was crucial.[6] However, its early effects on the family and national viewing have been used to disseminate information widely and to identify authentically gendered, racial, and classed subjects.[7] In the transition from radio to television in early network shows like *Beulah* (1950–1952) and *Amos 'n' Andy* (1951–1953), Black people were portrayed as poverty-stricken and in comical or subservient terms, as sociologist Darnell Hunt puts it: "Either as buffoons unequipped for equal participation in society or as servants who seemed content to cater to the needs of their white masters."[8] While some may talk down to the roles that they were forced to portray to make their way into the television industry, actors like Hattie McDaniel, Louise Beavers, Ethel Waters, Spencer Williams Jr., Alvin Childress, and Tim Moore paved the way for Black television possibility by hustling through a new age of white-controlled and segregated visual communication that was rapidly shifting American culture. The term "hustle" has layered meanings. I am using it throughout this book to speak for the stakes in which Black artists had to tirelessly obtain and retain employment through aggressive action and negotiation. It was not until the relevance era of the 1970s that the television medium began to take form as a vehicle for radical social engagement, although the image of working class and poverty-stricken Black folks was still the norm.

I remember clearly the first time I was introduced to the era of social relevance. In middle school, my father complained that everything my siblings and I watched was "bad TV," and that each show was simply a pale recreation of television's past. He said to us, "Watch this if you want to see some good TV." *This* was a DVD of the sitcom *Sanford and Son* (1972–1977). The first episode I ever saw left me confused because of the historical references and the use of, then unfamiliar, Black vernacular. Nonetheless, I was engaged and tried to understand what exactly the main character, Fred Sanford, was saying about Black American culture in the 1970s *and* how he was saying it. The scene took place in a courthouse in Los Angeles, California. A thirtysomething Black man (Lamont Sanford) is challenging a twenty-five-dollar traffic ticket that he believes was given to him unlawfully as the result of the prejudice of a white police officer. Unable to afford a lawyer, Lamont attempts to represent himself in court, and at the first sight of struggle, his father (Fred Sanford), an elderly man in an old suit, rises to boastfully shout, "Your Honor, I am his counsel!" Now assuming the position of his lawyer, Fred addresses the white police officer and his prejudice. He stands over the officer sternly and asks, "What do you got against Black drivers?" The courthouse audience (all Black) cheers in support of the question. Maintaining order, the judge (a Black man), pounds his gavel and shouts, "Stick to the matter at hand!" In response, Fred states, "That's what's wrong with the court. A Black man ain't got no chance around here," but without hesitation, the judge counters, "I'm Black." Dismissive, Fred replies, "Well you the judge. That don't count." As the courthouse audience stands to applaud, the judge is again forced to regain order in the courtroom. Fred then reapproaches the officer asking why he doesn't arrest white drivers. When the officer claims that he does, Fred responds, "Well where are they? Look at all these Niggas in here. . . . Look around here; there's enough Niggas in here to make a Tarzan movie!" Fred asserts that a courtroom is where one goes to get justice and that he "demands justice!"[9]

My viewing of "Fred Sanford, Legal Eagle" came at an interesting time in my life when I was witnessing many of the young Black men that I had grown up with having to face the criminal justice system. Watching this episode at the time, I asked myself, Why must Fred demand justice? How is it that all these Black characters are acting in unison? Why do they not trust the judicial system? From then on, I became interested in investigating the sometimes broad and subtle political meanings that inform the comedy of Black sitcoms and how these translate to the realities of being Black and living in America. Since that first viewing of *Sanford and Son*, I realized that television in general and Black sitcoms in particular are much more than entertainment; they are windows through which to see the history, culture, and agency of Black performance both in real life and on-screen.

Black popular culture has always been a productive space that has introduced an element of difference in the complex struggle over cultural hegemony. Stuart Hall's "What Is This 'Black' in Black Popular Culture?" helps to understand this further.[10] As the United States emerged as a world power and center for cultural circulation, so did Black popular culture.[11] This emergence marks a "displacement and hegemonic shift in the definition of culture," moving away from the European model of the high culture aesthetic.[12] Black popular culture also marks an emergence of decolonized sensibilities and minds coupled with the impact of civil rights and Black struggles in the United States, specifically. This postmodern idea of culture betrays an extreme interest in "differences: a touch of ethnicity, a taste of the exotic, 'a bit of the other.'"[13] Cultural politics of difference, the struggles around difference, the production of new identities, and the appearance of new subjects on the political and cultural stage all demonstrate how Black popular culture is a struggle over cultural hegemony. This struggle is being waged at the sites of reception through various audience perspectives as well as through the production of politics at play when contending with the development of Black sitcoms. Understanding Hall's Black popular culture is vital to this book because it aids in understanding how television in general and Tandem Productions specifically aim to represent racial difference within the confines of racial hegemony. Of course, the influx of Black sitcoms in the 1970s offers an important shift from the televisual norm by offering various depictions of Black life being screened nationwide. However, control of the media was still in the hands of white men; it still worked to set these images of Blackness beneath whiteness in racial hegemony. This thirst for "the other" and the artistic difference that Black popular culture represents in America is still trapped beneath the confines of a favored national identity, one that represents what it means to be American.

Scratchin' and Survivin': Hustle Economics and the Black Sitcoms of Tandem Productions is a production history and study of Black labor in the Black sitcoms of Tandem Productions: *Sanford and Son* (1972–1977), *Good Times* (1974–1979), and *The Jeffersons* (1975–1985). These sitcoms challenged the subjective producer's control of 1970s television. Focusing on these Black sitcoms, *Scratchin' and Survivin'* engages the intersections of performance, production, politics, and reception to consider how this array of Black sitcoms intervened in both the history of television and in a rearticulation of Black identity in the early 1970s. With close attention to race, socioeconomics, gender, and politics, the sitcoms of Tandem had their distinct style in depicting Black American life on-screen. What is rarely discussed in the history of Tandem are the Black artists (creators, actors, writers, assistants, etc.) and the "hustle economics" they engaged in while becoming television auteurs within a space that wasn't built for them.

After my early viewing of *Sanford and Son*, I soon realized that as an immigrant from Trinidad and Tobago, my father had quickly grasped many elements of working-class Black American culture through the medium of television by watching Black sitcoms specifically. My father has always been a hustler. Yes, I know that term has largely been relegated to the criminal or the shyster, but as mentioned earlier, I use this book to repurpose that term from its limited, negative connotation. I see hustle/hustling as a mechanism, practice, and performance of survival by any means. That can't inherently be labeled as unscrupulous, can it? From working department store jobs during the holidays, working orderly duty at convalescent homes during the day, to dishwashing at restaurants at night, my father maneuvered and persuaded to make ends meet. Living in precarious economic conditions and with a lack of formal education, I saw so much of his hustle and negotiation to simply make due reflected in Black sitcom characters and hustlers of Tandem Productions. "Hustle economics" exists as a negotiation of Black labor in front of and behind the scenes. Indeed, the production of these sitcoms called for various forms of creative agency and labor resilience that transformed the television industry, and *Scratchin' and Survivin'* brings attention to the Black artists who were a part of these transformative acts. Foregrounding the agency of these Black artists and their hustle, the late scholar Richard Iton puts the matter simply: "In trying to map out the most effective strategies for emancipation, African Americans have had to try to understand the precise nature of the linkage between popular culture and this thing we call politics . . . in particular, the negotiation, representation, and reimagination of Black interests through cultural symbols has continued to be a major component in the making of Black politics."[14]

Established in 1970, the Financial Interest and Syndication Rules (or Fin/Syn) were a set of rules imposed by the Federal Communications Commission (FCC). To prevent the Big Three (ABC, NBC, and CBS) television networks from monopolizing the broadcast landscape, these rules limited network ownership of television programs produced for them and in subsequent syndication. Networks were now required to pay license fees to use the programs rather than paying for them outright. These rules quickly changed the power relationships between networks and television producers. Some scholars argue that the rules brought about a golden era of independent television production companies, such as Mary Tyler Moore and Grant Tinker's MTM Enterprises and Norman Lear and Bud Yorkin's Tandem Productions.[15] Through these rules, the independent producer rose to an unprecedented level of fame and prestige in television as they produced and sold programs to multiple networks and retained ownership of these productions. In the grander scheme, the industry truly became a "producer's medium," where the television producer, rather than a broadcast network, assumed almost complete control of a television show's vision.[16] Due to Fin/Syn, as an auteur, the producer garnered the agency to apply a highly centralized and subjective control to the many aspects of television's collaborative creative work.

One of the television auteurs who benefited from the control Fin/Syn provided was Norman Lear and his Tandem Productions. Although he partnered with Bud Yorkin, Tandem's creative power rested with Lear. As an independent film and television production company, Tandem's early years involved limited production success in television and in films, such as *Henry Fonda and the Family* (1966), *An Evening with Carol Channing* (1966), *Come Blow Your Horn* (1963), and *Divorce American Style* (1967). It was not until they focused their attention on situational comedy that the company reached the apex of its fame. Through the overwhelming success of his sitcoms *All in the Family* (1971–1979) and *Maude* (1972–1978), the Tandem name offered Lear a monopoly of television viewers and networks eager for his productions. Although it took the success of Lear's white sitcoms to get his Black sitcoms greenlit, it is the work of the Black artists that I focus on as collective authors, who contributed to 1970s Black sitcoms and their cultural importance. *Scratchin' and Survivin'* disrupts this myth of a single auteur within television and centers the work of Black artists practicing hustle economics and using industrial capital to visualize Blackness. By giving agency to Black artists and centering their struggles around representation amid precarious employment opportunities, I am firmly inserting Black artists into these moments largely written to satisfy white American history.

Scratchin' and Survivin' uncovers the contributions Tandem Productions and its Black artists made to Black cultural representation in situation comedies, the television industry, and society. These contributions have a central place in our understanding of the meaning of race in America because, as Herman Gray argues, television is "a dense site or a place of struggle over the symbolic meanings and uses of Blackness in the production of the nation that admittedly gives television a central role in cultural politics."[17] With such a central role in cultural politics and racial identity formation, it is important to address how television works to critically engage and communicate Black culture to mass audiences and the stakes of this engagement. I work to answer these questions by putting the production history of Tandem Productions into conversation with textual analyses of particular episodes of its Black sitcoms, not only to discuss specific intersections that addressed the state of Black Americans in the 1970s but to chronicle the agency and resilience of Tandem's Black artists. Through my analyses, I argue that we must read the representations of the Black communities in these sitcoms beyond the often-popular discussions of their stereotyping and "buffoonery." Rather, it is crucial to read them from the perspective of the intertextual narratives of the show's stars and creative talent who represented Black agency and resilience within an established racial and social order and to read them as a response to national politics and labor. *Scratchin' and Survivin'* draws attention to the artistic struggles of Black actors, writers, and creatives who challenged the production hegemony of Tandem's white executives in order to illuminate the complex history of an independent production company heralded for its advances in depicting Black American life through comedy. *Scratchin' and Survivin'* offers a theoretical space for discussions of meanings and questions regarding cultural, social, and political contexts; power; and implications of Black television imagery.

Through the personal papers of Bud Yorkin and Norman Lear; interviews, oral histories, production documents and budgets, original scripts, important events in national and Black politics; and popular magazine coverage of the shows, I trace a history that addresses Tandem Production's politics of representation while giving voice to the Black artists within. In order to address the production history (on- and off-screen) of Tandem in conversation with thematic analyses of particular episodes of its Black sitcoms, I also highlight the writers of particular episodes. Mainly, the Black writers who used their platform to respond to national, social, and political issues. The main intersection engaged throughout *Scratchin' and Survivin'* is "hustle economics"—the construction of the Black living spaces, the specific ways Black people engage with informal or sometimes illegal economies on/off-screen, coupled with negotiating Black identity and fair working wages. Hustle economics presents itself in two additional ways that I address throughout the book: the role of Black women—the historical and cultural traditions that construct the formation of Black women's visibility in the sitcom and the spaces that Black women occupy in the television industry—and dissent, creative disputes with television executives, engagement with topical political issues, and activism in the sitcom's writing and performance.

The representations of Black culture in Tandem's Black sitcoms are emblematic of economic and infrastructural shifts within the television industry in the 1970s. They are also responsive to 1970s national politics through narratives of Black agency and resilience within an established but increasingly contested and discriminatory racial and social order—both critical elements in the rise of Black cultural representation in network sitcoms. As indicated, along with select thematic analyses, I also address changes in the television industry throughout the 1970s. The scope of this project covers a particular period in U.S. history that is integral to understanding not only major changes to television but also racial and cultural representation throughout all forms of visual media. Engaging with this history tells us that Black artists were increasingly gaining agency and visibility in 1970s television production, and contemporary television was built from this labor.

Much more than a lyric from the hit sitcom *Good Times*, the phrase and title of this book, *Scratchin' and Survivin'*, represents Black struggle, fight, and scraping to gather resources by any means necessary in order to stay alive and leave a mark in an uncertain world. Whether through *Sanford and Son*, *Good Times*, or *The Jeffersons*, these shows chronicle Black characters who represent struggle (racial, societal, and economic), loss, and sometimes triumph from their persistent *scratchin'* to stay alive. The Black artists who embody these roles off-screen must also scratch their way through the white hegemony at Tandem and the television industry at large, in efforts to tear away at the status quo and build anew. These deliberate efforts to rework and restructure television were often met with the loss of employment, gender discrimination, blacklisting, or simply silencing. *Scratchin' and Survivin'* forefronts the hustle, scratches at the surface, and recenters these narratives of dissent, giving those who had the burden of representing their race the acknowledgment they deserve. Although they may not have had authoritative power in television production, the legacy of these Black artists has *survived* and altered the television industry, blazing a trail for the eras of Black television representation to follow.

While many shows of this early television era recycle varying situations, the Black sitcoms of Tandem Productions do in fact encounter situations that differ from the norm, situations that are inherently Black and stand as social satire with elements of seriality throughout. This book's focus on the sitcom genre is deliberate. The sitcom genre, because it is television's most basic format, has often been misread. Horace Newcomb finds the genre "limited in its capacity for ambiguity, developments and the ability to challenge our values."[18] However, I agree with Jane Feuer, in that certain authors can make the sitcom form into social satire and that the sitcom genre developed over time into the direction of the continuing serial.[19] The sitcom can be read to help lay bare the mores, images, ideals, prejudices, and ideologies in its topical moment. As Darrell Hamamoto expresses, "The study of the television situation comedy is an exercise in examining the relationship of popular art to its historically specific setting."[20] Surveying histories of television sitcoms in general offers a unique history of what is understood as national American humor. American humor in general, Black humor specifically, began as a "wrested freedom," the freedom to laugh at that which was unjust and cruel in order to create distance from what would otherwise obliterate a sense of self and community.[21] Sociologist Herman Gray categorizes Black sitcoms like *Sanford and Son*, *Good Times*, and *The Jeffersons* as being a part of a "separate but equal" or "pluralist" discourse.[22] In these sitcoms, predominantly Black casts demonstrate that Black families have the same basic problems as white families, "where Black characters live and work in hermetically sealed social milieus that are approximately equivalent to their white counterparts."[23] However, no matter their class status, the majority of sitcoms about white families (i.e., *All in the Family* and *Maude*) take place in favorable and safe living conditions, within single-family homes, and where race and socioeconomics are not the center of the narrative.

Much of the writing on pivotal Black sitcoms has largely focused on television's *The Cosby Show* (1984–1992). However, this series is the exception in scholarship and popular press rather than the rule.[24] Tandem paved the way for *The Cosby Show* in its address of the Black family sitcom, and I focus on Tandem's Black sitcoms as they show an interesting shift in viewing styles and influences during the 1970s. Through the situation comedy's early dependency on the three-camera structure and "one-room set" (the Sanford's home and business, the Evans' apartment, or the Jeffersons' high-rise), Tandem was able to enter the domiciles of Black families and offer to its viewers an inside look into the confines of Black life.[25] Tandem's Black sitcoms responded to their political moment through critical engagement with Black community issues, such as poverty, employment, health, education, and so on. As they are situation comedies, these shows dealt with the Black situation in America and the various ways in which Black families contend with these situations. Tandem Productions and its sitcom creations thus revolutionized both the subject matter and the business of network television. According to Christine Acham, "For cultural critics and members of the African American population to ignore television's potential as a forum of resistance is to misread levels of vernacular meaning inherent in many African American television texts."[26] Rejecting the reductive terms of "stereotypes" or "positive/negative images," I intend to reconstitute Black television as an intellectual tradition and as a present-day politics, which simultaneously reflects the topical moment in which the show was produced. In this instance, it is constructed, in large part, by the Black actors and writers of Tandem Productions. As such, the production histories of these specific series very much matter.

As the title of this book suggests, throughout I will be using the term "hustle economics" to define a particular practice and performance of labor,

Black women's embodiment, and dissent at Tandem Productions. These intersections are utilized strategically as they make it clear that there are specific ways Black-casted sitcoms are constructed as a counter to white-casted ones. Surveying the history of Black sitcoms and their content, I've found that these three intersections (hustle economics, Black women's embodiment, and dissent) are consistently negotiated within and outside the television production space.

I coined the term "hustle economics" to speak to the specific ways Black sitcom characters and artists engage with economics and labor, methods that are often the antithesis of their white counterparts. Hustle economics are the negotiated and racialized "under the table," "catch as catch can," and sometimes illegal methods working-class Blacks use to survive financially. Hustling is a rhythm of the working-class Black experience. I found the term "hustle" as a useful identifier from George Lipsitz's "The Meaning of Memory: Family, Class, and Ethnicity in Early Network Television Programs," where he labels the occupations of the characters Amos Jones, Andy Brown, and King-fish Stevens of The Amos 'n' Andy Show as cab driver and hustler.[27] However, when describing the characters in similar working-class white sitcoms, such as The Honeymooners (1955–1956), Ralph Kramden and Ed Norton's familiar dreams of overnight success and get-rich-quick schemes are simply cast as harmless fantasy. The strategies of getting by financially and surviving are cast differently, as felonious and informal, when Blackness is involved. Throughout this book, I address the spaces at Tandem and, in its Black-cast sitcoms, where economics is raced as a hustle. It is not just on-screen where hustle economics are present. I use the term to also describe the negotiations that take place in the production of Blackness in these shows. Combining research from recorded oral histories, interviews, and employment contracts, I make clear that Black artists struggled to negotiate higher salaries and more producer or writer credit in their scripts. The Black artists at Tandem had to hustle in these various ways to navigate through the company's racial hegemony, keep their jobs, and have a stake as auteurs in their representation. Hustle economics helps to understand the labor of Black artists specifically as they forcibly maneuvered through television and at Tandem.

Tracing Black women's embodiment in the Black sitcoms of Tandem, I discuss the historical and cultural traditions that construct the formation of Black women's visibility in the sitcom and the spaces that Black women occupy in the television industry through various methods of hustle economics. These spaces that Black women occupied were negotiated and hard-fought to reinvent how they existed in popular culture and society. In the

1970s, Black women played an important role in the cultural production of the television industry, specifically in Black sitcoms. Through her history in vaudeville and burlesque performance, to her blue comedy standup, to finally crossing over into mainstream network television on *Sanford and Son*, LaWanda Page complicated the preconceived identity formation of Black women in popular television. In addition, through their interviews and comments in mainstream trade and press magazines, Black actresses Esther Rolle of *Good Times*, as well as Isabel Sanford and Roxie Roker of *The Jeffersons*, participated in a culture of resistance by critiquing television's approach to race. Finally, throughout the book, I also discuss dissent as a critical strategy of hustle economics used by Black sitcom artists in their efforts to remain employed, employ other Black artists, and further complicate televised notions of Blackness. Whether through creative disputes with television executives, contract negotiations, or engagement with political issues and activism in sitcom writing/performance, the history of Black artists' dissent against white television executives has been integral to a changing industry landscape.

The following chapters of *Scratchin' and Survivin'* center analyses of Tandem's Black sitcoms and the intersections they address ("hustle economics," Black women, and dissent). I aim to interrogate the production model at Tandem Productions and how the Black artists involved with each show added to and complicated the company's production culture. All chapters will deal with the impact of Black artists, their labor, as well as their cultural and political contexts. The book is organized chronologically, yet the shows it discusses are inextricably linked. All of these shows and their Black artists are connected through what Jonathan Gray calls "paratext." The paratext considers the variety of materials that surround a text as part of it. Paratexts are not simply add-ons, spin-offs, and also-runs: they create texts, manage them, and fill them with many of the meanings that we associate with them.[28] Often taking tangible forms—such as posters, reviews, and merchandise—I am using paratext to piece together all aspects of Tandem Production's Black sitcoms to tell their story. Oral histories, interviews, employment contracts, trade press, and so on are all considered as part of the paratext that navigates across Tandem Productions. These paratexts help *Scratchin' and Survivin'* detail a developmental arc of Black racial formation and labor on network television.

Chapter 1, "Approaching Tandem Productions," addresses television history and American politics leading to the development of Tandem Productions. Founded in 1958 by television director Bud Yorkin and television writer Norman Lear, it was not until they focused their attention on sitcoms that Tandem reached the apex of its fame. The popularity of these sitcoms in television's "era of relevance," and the numerous themes discussed throughout, show a compelling shift in viewing styles and influences during the 1970s. With their prime-time hit *All in the Family*, as an independent production company, Tandem's grasp of American audiences gave them the power to produce across multiple networks. Interrogating the foundations of Tandem, their creative philosophy, and liberal politics, especially in the shows *All in the Family* and *Maude*, this network dominance led to them producing Black-cast sitcoms and engaging in even more controversial subjects. Chapters 2 through 4 will address how Tandem's Black artists contended with white executive power and how hustle economics took different forms in each of the Black sitcoms. Through these analyses, I chronicle the agency and resilience of Tandem's Black artists in their various efforts in complying with or resisting the authoritative power. This arc of racial formation is evident in the chronological production of these shows and their spin-offs.

Chapter 2 considers the prime-time influence and cultural impact of Tandem's *Sanford and Son* (1972–1977) by addressing "hustle economics," Black women, and dissent throughout its production history. *Sanford and Son*, the only non-spin-off discussed in this book, stars Redd Foxx as Fred Sanford, a widower, and operator of a junkyard in the Watts neighborhood of Los Angeles, California, Demond Wilson as his son Lamont Sanford, and LaWanda Page as Fred's sister-in-law, Aunt Esther. As an adaptation of the white British sitcom, *Steptoe and Son* (1962–1965, 1970–1974), *Sanford and Son* makes clear the industry's alignment of Blackness with the working-class poor. *Sanford and Son* became the first of Tandem's sitcoms to represent the Black domestic sphere, and at the same time (as discovered through textual analyses, scripts, contracts, and interviews), the Black actors and writers used the show to reframe how Black communities existed on television. I analyze *Sanford and Son*'s hustle economics by discussing (1) trickster narratives on-screen and lead actors (such as Redd Foxx) fighting for better wages; (2) the radical ambiguity of Black women's representation, specifically LaWanda Page; (3) and moments of dissent, which led to the introduction of Black television writers like Ilunga Adell, also the pivotal moment of Redd Foxx walking out of the show demanding change. These acts of hustle economics aid in the understanding of this sitcom as more than a show but as a redefining moment in television history as these artists set the tone for ways in which Black entertainers advocated for belonging in the television industry. This chapter also uses textual evidence to address the impact of

Sanford and Son's Black labor and imagery through analyses of episodes, such as but not limited to "The Dowry" (Sept. 29, 1972), "Lamont Goes African" (Jan. 19, 1973), and "Mama's Baby, Papa's Maybe" (Jan. 4, 1974)—episodes by Black writers that reflect working-class economics and shifts in production and reception once Black artists were given agency at Tandem.

Chapter 3 tracks television's first Black "nuclear family" on the prime-time sitcom *Good Times* (1974–1979). As a spin-off of Tandem's *Maude*, *Good Times* chronicles the lives of Florida (Esther Rolle) and James Evans (John Amos); their three children—James Jr., also known as J.J., Thelma, and Michael (Jimmie Walker, BernNadette Stanis, and Ralph Carter respectively)—and their neighbor Willona Woods (Ja'Net DuBois), living in a public housing project in inner-city Chicago. The chapter focuses on three areas of hustle economics in practice or performance: (1) space and place, specifically how hustle economics is practiced in housing projects as Chicago's North Side is used to foreground Black life; (2) actress and star Esther Rolle's ascension to prime time and her role as an agent of change in constructing what she calls a "complete Black family"; (3) and finally, costar John Amos's and cocreator Eric Monte's protests against the creative directions of Lear and Yorkin that eventually led to their departure from the series. Excavating *Good Times* episodes—such as but not limited to "Too Old Blues" (Feb. 8, 1974), "Getting Up the Rent" (Feb. 22, 1974), and "Florida's Protest" (Nov. 25, 1975)—makes clear the negotiations and hustle economics that took place at Tandem Productions for Black artists to redeem the imagery of the Black family through *Good Times*.

In chapter 4, with a deficit of existing scholarship on *The Jeffersons* (1975–1985), I use a great deal of this chapter to address its foundational history as a spin-off from *All in the Family*. The show focuses on George (Sherman Hemsley), Louise (Isabel Sanford), and their son, Lionel Jefferson (Mike Evans and Damon Evans), a former working-class Black family who have been able to move from Queens to Manhattan owing to the success of George's dry cleaning chain. Throughout this chapter, I discuss the cultural significance of *The Jeffersons* through (1) economic displacement while interrogating the show's theme of "movin' on up" that chronicles the financial ascension of Black characters from working class to nouveau riche and how this transition codes "hustling," and therefore hustle economics, in an alternative way. (2) I also make clear the impact of the actress Isabel Sanford, her hustle in the televisual space before *The Jeffersons*, and her stake in the narrative production. (3) Finally, concerning dissent, I focus on the show's themes of interracial conflict and marriage and how audiences responded to this new television phenomenon, much to the chagrin of many viewers nationwide and amid dangerous ramifications for the Black artists within. With the aid of episodic analyses of "George's Skeleton" (Feb. 22, 1975), "Louise Feels Useless" (Feb. 1, 1975), and "Like Father, like Son" (Apr. 5, 1975), I argue *The Jeffersons* and its cast's comedic portrayal of the American dream of Black financial ascension amid the reality of the confines of discrimination offered a new vision of Black hustle economics, distancing itself from the recycled image of the working-class poor. This chapter contributes to the overarching argument of this book as it traces the racial development of Black families in Tandem shows and how the Black artists of these shows had to practice resilience and learn how to hustle to infiltrate the television landscape and tell new Black stories.

In the concluding chapter, I investigate the impact of the last of Tandem's television productions, NBC's *Diff'rent Strokes* (1978–1986), and the Black authoritative power on this show. This show exists outside of my larger argument because *Diff'rent Strokes'* Black main characters are coupled with white costars, rather than Blackness being at the forefront. Here, I discuss the disbandment of Tandem Productions and *Diff'rent Strokes* as a product of Tandem that transitioned into a mixed-raced sitcom. Nevertheless, *Diff'rent Strokes* is an important intervention as it employed Tandem's first Black showrunner, Gerren Keith. Even with a Black showrunner, *Diff'rent Strokes* still fell to the white authoritative power structure at Tandem. I use the hustle that Keith was still forced to contend with as a showrunner without executive power as a case study to understand Tandem's concluding direction and how *Diff'rent Strokes* is placed within Tandem's arc of Black racial formation. With this show, Tandem actively moved away from the all-Black-casted sitcoms that addressed solely Black culture and politics to an image of seeming racial harmony, which abandoned the cultural specificity at the core of Tandem's Black sitcoms and moved toward a new trend in televisual Blackness, mixed-race casts, and Black stars on white shows.[29]

Through the intersections of how hustle economics was practiced and performed, these artists pushed the sitcom genre to look beyond the frivolous laughter they encouraged, and to look more intimately at the story and ascension of Black people in America. Although these artists made strides, the lack of authoritative power in the larger television industry to this day has left their stories largely untold and on the periphery in discussions of television histories. The lack of industrial acknowledgment forced artists like Redd Foxx to make his own Walk of Fame so that he and his compatriots could historicize themselves.

1

Approaching
Tandem Productions

I think it is necessary for us to realize that we have moved from the era of civil rights to the era of human rights. . . . When we see that there must be a radical redistribution of economic and political power, then we see that for the last twelve years, we have been in a reform movement. . . . That after Selma and the Voting Rights Bill, we moved into a new era, which must be an era of revolution. . . . In short, we have moved into an era where we are called upon to raise certain basic questions about the whole society.

—POOR PEOPLE'S CAMPAIGN OF 1968,
"Why a Poor People's Campaign?"[1]

Entering the 1960s, Black people in America were seeking a change in the political, cultural, and economic systems that have historically been against them. Efforts such as the Poor People's Campaign quoted above directly correlate with the Black sitcoms of Tandem Productions to come, as they discuss Black people and class status. Also, in conversation with the themes of Tandem's Black sitcoms, this period's fight for equality in jobs, housing, voting rights, education, and so on created what came to be known collectively as the civil rights movement. The civil rights movement refers to social movements in the United States guided by the goal of enforcing constitutional and legal rights for Black Americans. This movement brought about the prominence of many Black leaders, such as Dr. Martin Luther King Jr., Malcolm X, and Rosa Parks, to name a few. In the 1960 presidential election between Democratic candidate John F. Kennedy and Republican candidate Richard Nixon, Black people in America saw an ally in their struggle for civil rights in the young and charismatic Kennedy. At the time of this election, Black people in the Jim Crow South were barred from public facilities, subject to racist insults and violence, and denied the right to vote under various circumstances, which signaled a call for change in social and public policy across the United States. Viewed as a proponent of change and progress, Kennedy won the voting support of almost 70 percent of Black people across the nation.[2] The leadership of President Kennedy and others of that time worked to help Black people feel closer to something that they had never known: equality, liberty, and true American citizenship. Kennedy's first step in responding to civil rights pressures was appointing "unprecedented numbers of African Americans to high-level positions in the administration," in turn, strengthening the Commission on Civil Rights. Kennedy, along with his vice president, Lyndon Johnson (who ran the Equal Employment Opportunity Commission), spoke out in favor of school desegregation while praising a number of cities for integrating their schools.[3]

With attacks on Black people continuing across the Jim Crow South, activists argued that more action needed to be taken. In the spring of 1963, Birmingham, Alabama, became a site of mass protests, violence, and arrests. Dr. Martin Luther King Jr. and other Black leaders led the protests on the basis of civil disobedience and increased racial tension. To cease the protest, Alabama government officials called upon the Birmingham police force. Armed with batons, attack dogs, and water hoses, the Birmingham police forcibly restrained the protestors. After this mass catastrophe, which was broadcasted throughout the nation by various media sources, President Kennedy sped up the drafting of a comprehensive civil rights bill. In short, the bill can be described as such: "The divisions of this legislation included: (1) protecting African Americans against discrimination in voter qualification tests; (2) outlawing discrimination in hotels, motels, restaurants, theaters, and all other public accommodations engaged in interstate commerce; (3) authorizing the U.S. Attorney General's Office to file legal suits to enforce desegregation in public schools; (4) authorizing the withdrawal of federal funds from programs practicing discrimination; and (5) outlawing discrimination in employment in any business exceeding 25 people and creating an Equal Employment Opportunity Commission to review complaints."[4] Clearing several hurdles in its development, the Civil Rights Act won the endorsement of the House and Senate Republican leaders. However, before it was passed, President Kennedy was assassinated, depressing the hopes of many for a better America.

Upon the assassination of President Kennedy, Vice President Lyndon Johnson grabbed the reins of the U.S. presidency in 1963. Having served as a senator from Texas, Johnson was able to sway Southern politicians and pass the Civil Rights Act into law. In addition to the passing of this new act, Johnson constructed a political plan to tackle inequality and opportunity in America, the Great Society.[5] Figures from the 1960 census, Bureau of Labor Statistics, U.S. Department of Commerce, and the Federal Reserve estimated anywhere from forty to sixty million Americans—or 22 to 33 percent—lived below the poverty line. At the same time, the nature of poverty itself was changing as America's population increasingly lived in metropolitan cities.[6] A major part of the Great Society's plan to combat this came to be known as the "War on Poverty," which was part of President Johnson's attempt to expand the federal government's role in domestic policy. This called for those in poverty to receive federal aid for living expenses, obtaining jobs, medical care, and education. Arguably, the two most important initiatives for urban working-class Black people in the Great Society were the Economic Opportunity Act of 1964 and the Social Security Amendments of 1965.

These plans helped establish the Office of Economic Opportunity, another valuable asset to working-class Black people, as this office administered most of the War on Poverty's programs. Most of the jobs that Black people were able to obtain were unskilled labor and factory positions. With their pay still drastically low compared to their white counterparts, many Black people were forced to go on welfare and receive government aid for food and housing. In the years following the introduction of the War on Poverty in 1964, poverty in the United States dropped to its lowest level since comprehensive records began in 1958.[7] Data indicates that poverty was roughly 19 percent in the year the Economic Opportunity Act was implemented and decreased to 11.1 percent in 1973.[8] Yet poor Black people, particularly women, suffered from the racism and sexism that amplified the impact of poverty.

With a three-pronged approach—$30 billion annual appropriation for a real war on poverty, congressional passage of full employment and guaranteed income legislation (a guaranteed annual wage), and the construction of five hundred thousand low-cost housing units per year until slums were eliminated—Martin Luther King's Poor People's Campaign demanded economic and human rights for poor Americans of diverse backgrounds.[9] After presenting an organized set of demands to Congress and executive agencies, campaign activists set up a protest camp on the Washington Mall, where they stayed for six weeks in the spring of 1968.[10] The Poor People's Campaign was motivated by a desire for economic justice: the idea that all people should have what they need to live. King and the Southern Christian Leadership Conference shifted their focus to these issues after observing that gains in civil rights had not improved the material conditions of life for many Blacks. The campaign would help the poor by dramatizing their needs and uniting all races under the commonality of economic hardship. Unfortunately, the assassinations of Dr. King and Senator Robert Kennedy, a key proponent of the campaign and presidential candidate, only served to cripple the campaign and greatly limit its impact.

As the vocal group the Temptations' song "Ball of Confusion" indicated, these political tensions made their way into popular cultural discourse.

Fear in the air, tension everywhere
Unemployment rising fast,
The Beatles' new record's a gas
And the only safe place to live is
On an Indian reservation . . .[11]

The Temptations opened the 1970s with "their hit song 'Ball of Confusion,' an apt description of the current state of the world—particularly the ghetto."[12] The white middle-class critique of the War on Poverty, which claimed that they were footing the bill for services to the poor, led to diminished support for welfare state programs.

Some economists and right-winged politicians have criticized President Johnson's methods in fighting the War on Poverty; much of their discomfort came from the amount of money that was spent to fund welfare programs. Critics believed that Johnson's policies actually had a negative impact on the economy because of their interventionist nature. Those who believe this recommended that the best way to fight poverty was not through government spending but through economic growth. Along with the progressive figures of racial uplift, like Dr. King and Malcolm X, there were popular conservative figures halting the progress that these individuals sought to make. One of the most popular and vocal conservative critics of this welfare system was former U.S. senator Daniel Patrick Moynihan. As the assistant secretary of labor during the Kennedy administration, and during much of Johnson's, Moynihan was able to gather research on the future of America with the continuance of the War on Poverty programs. A trained sociologist, Moynihan published *The Negro Family: The Case for National Action* in 1965, now commonly referred to as the Moynihan Report.[13]

The Moynihan Report

Another major prefiguring force spurring Tandem's 1970s Black sitcoms was the Moynihan Report, which was originally released in 1965. Since the sitcom genre is largely about family, it is important to break down the relevance of Moynihan as these shows depict varying models of Black family life, while the Moynihan Report addressed limited notions of the Black family. The report argued that even though America had implemented new policies of government assistance, the gap between Black people and other groups in America was widening due to Black people's dependence on these systems of welfare. Moynihan attributed this to the "Negro" family structure. His evidence as to why the gap was widening was that the Negro family in these urban ghettos was crumbling.[14] Through qualitative and quantitative research methods, Moynihan's research aimed to provide evidence that America needed a new national goal: the establishment of a stable Negro family structure. He argued, "The Negro community has been forced into a matriarchal structure which, because it is so far out of line with the rest of American society, seriously retards the progress of the group as a whole, and imposes a crushing burden on the Negro male, in consequence, on a great many Negro women as well."[15] Without this collective goal of shifting the Negro family dynamic, according to Moynihan, the cycle of Black poverty and disadvantage in the United States would continue. His research demonstrated that even as fewer people were unemployed, more people were joining welfare rolls; to Moynihan, this meant that Black people were not self-sufficient. Moynihan categorized these recipients as families with children but only one parent, the mother in most cases. Moynihan cited a 1960 study of Aid to Dependent Children (ADC) recipients saying that "the 'typical' ADC mother in Cook County was married and had children by her husband, who deserted and left his whereabouts unknown . . . the woman is now left alone with illegitimate children to support."[16] Here, Moynihan attempts to define a "common" Black family structure in which the father is unknown, absent, or otherwise not providing economic support. With "one-fourth of Negro births being illegitimate," Moynihan believed that the Black family's dire need for welfare support was nothing more than a handout and that it was the responsibility of the nation to aid in the reconstructing of the Black family to a model similar to affluent whites.[17] The report contended that slavery had made Black people dependent on the dominant society and that this dependence still existed in America.[18]

As an outsider looking into the plight of Black families, he formulated a biased opinion to evaluate the inner workings of these families. Moynihan did not offer any data on specific family incomes, the number of children in the household, or job availability, making his data speculative. Moynihan stated, "It is the conclusion of this survey . . . that what is true of central Harlem, can be said to be true of the Negro American world in general."[19] Once the Black community is seen as static or fixed in this way, it becomes increasingly easy to cast all Black working-class people as "products of broken families, broken economies, and broken communities."[20] The Moynihan Report sparked critiques from Black people during the time of its release and more recently by scholars such as Hortense Spillers and Roderick Ferguson. However, its national impact played a large part in the negative portraits of Black communities and socioeconomics throughout mass media.[21] Moynihan's particular notion of Black familial life remains a popular work of discussion to comprehend the social and economic disintegration of the late twentieth-century Black urban life.

Constructing a Black Image

The uneven successes of the civil rights movement and the contradictions of the Moynihan Report are woven into the problem of constructing Black imagery in mass media and popular culture. Placing politics and social science research in discussion with how Black people were being written about, characterized, and ultimately projected on-screen through television is key to understanding the power of media production leading up to Tandem Productions' Black sitcoms. The Moynihan Report worked to place white and Black families in a web of binary meanings, one that renders Black bodies defenseless to challenge their representations in popular opinion, discourse, and in the case of this study, television. There is a very distinct way Black performance is portrayed in comparison with its white counterparts on the small screen.

From the 1950s to the 1980s, racial groups often faced defamation, where the Big Three networks (ABC, NBC, and CBS) were the only choices for television viewing. In this regard, another important aspect of this period is the broad industrial and cultural power of the television network. In an article titled "What Is U.S. Television Now?" Amanda Lotz discusses the early age of television beginning in the 1950s. During the "network era," between 1952 and the mid-1980s, the original Big Three networks controlled, produced, and distributed all American television.[22] This is particularly important because Tandem's future all-Black sitcoms had to contend with a highly regulated but competitive network schedule and competition from a variety of shows (mostly all white) for a finite viewership. Lotz contends that the network era provided the basic structure of television's industrial organization and social role. The three networks had complete control over the nation's viewing content and the images they saw on-screen. They "delivered content on a linear through-the-day schedule—shows were available only at appointed times."[23] Moreover, to appeal to the broadest demographic, they also relied heavily on "family viewing and the family audience."[24] An entire family sitting in front of a television with limited viewing options thus had a restricted power of choice. The networks in turn, with a finite roster of shows, sought images that featured broad and universal themes. As Lotz puts it, they were pushed toward "homogeneous content likely to be accepted by a heterogeneous audience."[25]

All-white casted family sitcoms of the 1950s onward—whether the perfect nuclear ones of *Father Knows Best* (1954–1960) and *Leave It to Beaver* (1957–1963) or the farcical family of *I Love Lucy* (1951–1957) and *The Honeymooners* (1955–1956)—told women that their domesticity was the highest form of female virtue. These shows were largely about the everyday experiences of white people raising a family and living in the large suburbs and cities of America. These shows rarely discussed social and economic issues, such as unemployment or battles with injustices. While in early network shows that did feature Black actors in starring roles like *Beulah* (1950–1952) and *Amos 'n' Andy* (1951–1953), Black people were portrayed as poverty-stricken and in comical or subservient terms. Yet Erik Barnouw's study of the evolution of American television makes clear that through civil rights figures like Malcolm X and Martin Luther King Jr., the shifting climate of the early 1960s put pressure on producers of television drama and commercials to change their largely "lily-white world."[26] Although the daytime serial remained almost untouched, progress was more noticeable in other areas. The inclusion of one or two Black people in crowd scenes became more standard, and some series, such as *The Defenders* (1961–1965), *Eastside/Westside* (1963–1964), and *Bonanza* (1959–1973), featured Black actors as lawyers, doctors, nurses, and so on.[27] Unfortunately, with this inclusion came resistance, ranging from sponsors like General Motors withdrawing commercials and many Southern-affiliate stations refusing to carry certain episodes.[28] The efforts of Black inclusion in the media seemed to consistently be met with pushback, mirroring the civil rights struggles still being fought across America.

In the late 1960s, amid numerous racial uprisings (mainly of the Black working class) in metropolitan cities nationwide, the local, state, and national governments were seeking answers to this unrest. At the national level, the government's response took the form of the National Advisory Commission on Civil Disorders. Known popularly as the Kerner Commission, this eleven-member presidential commission was established by President Lyndon B. Johnson and chaired by Governor Otto Kerner of Illinois. In an address to the nation, President Johnson calls for an attack on the social conditions that bred years of racial civil unrest: "The only, genuine, long-range solution for what has happened lies in an attack—mounted at every level—upon the conditions that breed despair and violence. All of us know what those conditions are: ignorance, discrimination, slums, poverty, disease, and not enough jobs. We should attack these conditions—not because we are fired by conscience. We should attack them because there is simply no other way to achieve a decent and orderly society in America."[29]

The Kerner Commission was created to investigate the causes of the 1967 racial uprisings in the United States and to provide recommendations for the future to end such social protests. The commission declared that "our nation is moving toward two societies, one Black, one White—separate and unequal," delivering an indictment of white racism for isolating and neglecting Black people and urging legislation to promote racial integration and enrich Black communities through the creation of jobs, job training programs, and decent housing.[30] The commission's report findings were that the uprisings resulted from Black frustration at the lack of economic opportunity as the commission berated federal and state governments for failed housing, education, and social service policies. The findings of the commission were not well received, and President Johnson refused their report.

In April 1968, rioting broke out in more than one hundred cities following the assassination of Dr. Martin Luther King Jr., which was one month after the release of the report. King had stated that the report was a "physician's warning of approaching death, with a prescription for life," and the findings had the potential to prevent racial civil unrest in America at large.[31] Notably, chapter 15 of the report aimed some of its sharpest criticism at the images in mainstream media, stating, "The press has too long basked in a White world looking out of it, if at all, with White men's eyes and a White perspective."[32] This section of the Kerner Commission report assessing media coverage recommended that the news media publish newspapers and produce programs that recognized the existence and activities of the Black community. The report states, "It would be a contribution of inestimable importance to race relations in the U.S. simply to treat ordinary news about Negroes as news of other groups is now treated."[33] This call to action made it clear that the news media of this moment was inherently biased toward the white community and that mass media images were distributed inequitably among the races. The Kerner Commission report also believed that "television should develop programming which integrates Negroes in all aspects of televised presentations. . . . Television is such a visible medium that constructive steps are easy and obvious. . . . Negro reporters should appear more frequently—and at primetime."[34]

Despite President Johnson's rejection of the Kerner Commission report, it was published and became a national bestseller. In response to its findings, 1968 sparked an influx of Black representations on the television screen and in television production. Network prime-time television produced situational comedies, dramas, and variety shows featuring Black lead actors such as *Julia* (1968–1971), *The Mod Squad* (1968–1973), *Room 222* (1969–1974), *The Flip Wilson Show* (1970–1974), and *Soul Train* (1971–2006). In 1968, two of these shows made the top thirty viewed shows in Nielsen ratings, with *Julia* at #7 and *The Mod Squad* at #28. As television sitcom content slowly began to become a place for more liberal discussion, 1960s television became increasingly more important to the national understanding of Black culture specifically.

The Kerner Commission report also addressed the need for public broadcast stations to create programs "whose subjects are rooted in the ghetto and its problems."[35] In a nationwide response, multiple public affairs broadcasting programs were created by and for Black people; these included *Soul!* (1968–1973), *Black Journal* (1968–1977), *Inside Bedford-Stuyvesant* (1968–1970, Brooklyn, NY), and *Say Brother* (1968–1982, Boston).[36] As Black people gained more control of the medium, they were able to produce local and national shows through public affairs broadcasting. For example, *Black*

Journal was one of the few nonfiction programs that focused on Black subject matter and "boasted a 75 percent Black technical crew and a 95 percent Black production crew, an unprecedented occurrence on a nationally televised program."[37] According to Christine Acham, "*Black Journal* was a site of Black cultural resistance because it was positioned within this mainstream forum yet still produced critical Black news coverage, which was seen by a cross-section of America."[38] *Black Journal* spawned many other local and national public affairs shows that worked to discuss issues, culture, and experiences of Black communities.[39] The import of these programs was linked to a growing sense of Black cultural identity in the wake of Dr. Martin Luther King's assassination in 1968. Devorah Heitner suggests that many of these community public affairs programs were broadcast to contain and domesticate Black people and alleviate them from an uprising in the wake of the said assassination.[40] Her assertions are corroborated when former television staffers for *Say Brother* claimed that "in exchange for giving African Americans their own television presence and a few jobs in the broadcasting industry, station executives and government officials hoped that African Americans would expose their discontent on the airwaves instead of engaging in street protests and uprisings."[41] Unfortunately, the progress of Black people who controlled their own images and created their own content was undermined by conservative political forces meant to stifle Black bodies. Since public access shows weren't competing for ratings and revenue, television executives didn't challenge these shows on their progressive tactics.

Although these shows were transformative in employing Black people behind the scenes, and in their representation of Black public affairs, many of these shows were still critiqued by scholars and popular press for being one-dimensional in their portrait of the American Black experience. With the risks being more calculated due to profitability, it was largely up to network television shows to promote Black social critique through fictional narratives. However, network shows of the 1960s also struggled in their use of Black imagery. Phillip Brian Harper's "Extra-Special Effects: Televisual Representation and the Claims of 'the Black Experience'" offers a productive intersection for this history.[42] While taking to task the complex politics of Black television representation during the 1960s, Harper offers an important distinction between the two conflicting demands by Black audiences and critics, representation and/or an authentic Black experience. Harper doesn't examine a specific show; instead, he explores commentary and criticisms through magazines and interviews on television to elucidate his claims. Discussing representation and the Black television experience, Harper puts into conversation simulacral versus mimetic realism. This distinction fuels Harper's reading of the anxieties produced by intraracial division that inform critical assessments of Black televisual performance in the 1960s. Simulacral realism is a representation that "would improve the objective conditions characterizing daily life for the mass of African Americans living within the scope of television's influence."[43] This term describes demands for a greater number of Blacks on television, regardless of their roles, to improve their social status. On the other hand, he identifies the contradictory demand for relevance or "mimetic realism . . . whereby television would 'reflect' the social reality on which it was implicitly modeled."[44] While problematizing each of these demands, Harper calls for the merging of the two. Televisual representations of Black people have long served as a focus of debate because they are seen as having effects that extend beyond the domain of signs and into the realm of Black people's material well-being—compromising the social relations through which Black people's status in this country is conditioned. If Black people were seen on television more frequently and in roles comparable to their white counterparts, Black people in the United States might achieve a better social status. However, Harper contends that the growing debate about Black visibility versus realism has placed Black people at odds in terms of identifying themselves and those around them. It is "precisely the intraracial distinctions of class that become particularly problematic in considerations of televisual representations of Black people, as both the medium and debate about it develop through the 1960s and early 1970s."[45]

In the 1960s—through shows like *Julia*, *I Spy*, and *Room 222*—Black life was exclusively "middle class."[46] These shows worked to negotiate intraracial social difference that was potentially disruptive to the political solidarity of the Black community. Harper ends his project by accounting that what is necessary for the future of Black television imagery is to reimagine this idea of a unitary Black experience and to embrace the diversity within the Black community. Doing so, Black characters on-screen will be less conflicted and fully embody an idea of Blackness that is universally accepted and will be met with less societal backlash. This escapist fictional fare that persisted throughout the 1960s prime time made little reference to what was being reported on the news and in the popular press about the realities of Black life. That changed in the late 1960s and early '70s, as some shows began to reflect the new cultural landscape. This new wave of redefined Black identities on-screen as a reflection of the political, social, and economic moment in the 1970s has been deemed the era of social relevance. This moment was produced largely by two white men, Bud Yorkin and Norman Lear, through their company, Tandem Productions. Aware that the Kerner report called on Americans to renew their promise of justice and opportunity for all, they possessed a keen knowledge of the temporal marketability of screening Black people and situations on television—a key factor to their company's future success.[47]

Tandem Productions

Norman Lear and his long-term colleague Bud Yorkin came together to form Tandem Productions in 1959. Having met and worked together in early variety shows, such as the *Colgate Comedy Hour* (1950–1955), Bud Yorkin stated that this partnership with Lear was developed as a package to write, produce, direct, and most importantly, own their own content.[48] It was called "Tandem" because at its inception, its creators Lear and Yorkin thought of themselves as "two guys on a tandem bicycle, pedaling uphill."[49] Coming from middle-class Jewish backgrounds, both men had means, extensive credits, and diverse interests when Tandem Productions emerged, and the company was designed to allow them to pursue those interests individually or together as they desired and was suitable for any given project.[50] Tandem was part of an innovative and expanding family of companies within the entertainment industry that focused on the development, production, and dissemination of television projects and theatrical motion pictures. Completing a string of films with varying success, notably *Come Blow Your Horn* (1963), *Divorce American Style* (1967), and *Cold Turkey* (1971), Tandem soon found their true calling in the medium of television, specifically the sitcom. After the directorial success of Tandem's film *Cold Turkey*, United Artists offered Lear a three-feature deal, an opportunity anyone would take. However, Lear refused the United Artists film deal when CBS offered a thirteen-episode television deal for what would come to be Tandem's best-known show, *All in the Family* (1971–1979).[51]

The timely financial success of Tandem Productions as an independent production company owes a great deal to the Financial Interest and Syndication Rules (or Fin/Syn). Fin/Syn was a set of rules imposed by the Federal Communications Commission (FCC) to prevent the Big Three networks from monopolizing the broadcast landscape. These rules limited network ownership of television programs produced for them and in subsequent syndication. Networks were now required to pay license fees to use the programs rather than paying for them outright. These rules quickly changed the power relationships between networks and television producers. To be clear, Tandem was not the only independent production company taking advantage of this moment of production ownership. For instance, Mary Tyler Moore's MTM Enterprises, like Tandem, used television to address social issues. However, MTM is an important counterpart and counterpoint to Tandem in their treatment of race. MTM received more prestige and became the emblem of quality television among critics, while Tandem was considered crass, stand-up adjacent, and not nearly as literate. But MTM also continued to marginalize Black people and to avoid putting forward hot-button racial issues through the voice and perspective of centralized Black protagonists. Tandem put Blackness front and center through all-Black cast sitcoms. Lear believed that through Tandem's work that "television and the American culture had been 'radicalized' overnight."[52]

Tandem's shift to television led to numerous acclaimed television shows that continued to challenge the social milieu and call to attention the private sphere in the typical American household through discussions of politics, race, and economics. Tandem's shows challenged society's social conventions and were necessary for America to fully understand the historical moment. Earlier television series employed a point of view that often ignored these issues head-on in order to hide harsh realities that privileged individuals were unwilling to confront race, gender, and class. As Lear himself noted in one of his autobiographies, television's silence on social issues was itself highly political because it tried to be apolitical. Before *All in the Family*, he writes, "For twenty years, TV comedy was telling us there was no hunger in America, no racial discrimination, no unemployment or inflation, no war, no drugs, and the citizenry was happy with whoever happened to be in the White House. Tell me that expressed no point of view!"[53] Describing the vast popularity of Tandem's productions, producer (and Tandem associate) Brad Lemack remarks that "national rating services statistics indicate that over half of the nation's population, as many as 120 million Americans, watch the television programs produced by the [Tandem] group each week."[54] With *All in the Family* securing the number one Nielsen rating throughout its run and *Sanford and Son*, *Good Times*, and *The Jeffersons* all securing the top five positions next to it, it's clear that Tandem possessed network dominance.[55]

To borrow a term from Darrell Hamamoto, this "nervous laughter," prompted by how sitcoms reflect, explain, legitimate, and challenge the society in which they are grounded, illuminates the power of laughter both to reaffirm and to question existing social structures.[56] The dominant liberal Democratic ideology expressed through Tandem's sitcoms was integral to their success. As explained by Lear, "Comedy with something in mind works as a kind of intravenous to the mind and spirit. After he winces and laughs, what the individual makes of the material depends on that individual, but he *has* been reached."[57] Critics like Michael Arlen, however, were not sold on Tandem's approach to comedy, categorizing them as "media dramas."[58] Arlen believed that the comedy in Lear's shows (except for the laugh track) was mainly angry. Although his shows address various topical issues, Arlen felt these political themes were delivered to the public through the "snarling anger" of his characters, interrupted periodically by stage-business jokes or sentiment.[59] I agree with Arlen's perspective that anger was often a means to address the social milieu. Tandem's later success with a mainstream audience for Black shows could not have been accomplished without the groundbreaking impact of Tandem's first sitcom and possibly its angriest protagonist, the fictional Archie Bunker in *All in the Family*. According to Lear, "*All in the Family* debuted, and the career that had been launched years before we [Lear and Yorkin] met now reached the stratosphere."[60]

According to Lear, the show came about when he read an article in *Variety* magazine on *Till Death Do Us Part* (original run 1966–1968; second run 1972–1975) and its success in the United Kingdom.[61] In 1971, television producers Lear and Yorkin, working with CBS, developed the television show *All in the Family*. The sitcom chronicled the life and times of Archie Bunker, a working-class bigot (played by Carroll O'Connor); his wife, Edith Bunker (played by Jean Stapleton); their daughter, Gloria Stivic (played by Sally Struthers); and their son-in-law, Michael Stivic (played by Rob Reiner). Archie was an outspoken, narrow-minded white man, seemingly prejudiced against anyone who was not a WASP. The two couples represent the real-life clash of values between the so-called Greatest Generation and the Baby Boomers. For much of the series, the Stivics (whose values are influenced and shaped by the counterculture of the 1960s) live in the Bunkers' home to save money, providing abundant opportunities for them to irritate each other. *All in the Family* is often rated as one of the greatest television shows of all time. It became the first television series to reach the milestone of having topped Nielsen ratings for five consecutive years.

To add to its production and artistic acclaim, in 2013, the Writers Guild of America ranked *All in the Family* the fourth-best-written television series ever, and *TV Guide* ranked it as the fourth-greatest show of all time.[62]

Although Archie and his on-screen persona were often critiqued, he was met with resounding praise by many viewers. In creating him, Lear believed "the point of the character was to show that if bigotry and intolerance didn't exist in the minds of good people, the average people, it would not be the endemic problem it is in our society."[63] Archie was meant to symbolize an ordinary man sharing prejudices probably felt by many behind closed doors. Speaking directly about these prejudices was integral to bringing social ills and beliefs into popular discussion.

Although *All in the Family* is not the focus of this book, it is integral in discussing the different ways that Tandem Productions created characters and settings in their future Black sitcoms and the company's broader approach to race, class, ethnicity, and difference. At Tandem Productions, Norman Lear and Bud Yorkin grew their media factory from the idea of the spin-off—exploiting success by transferring a character(s). As noted by Todd Gitlin, "If the single most important factor in series success is the appeal of its major characters, then it is logical to launch a show with characters whose appeal is pretested . . . when secondary characters are 'spun off' from current series to stand on their own, presumable they have already accumulated their followings on the road."[64] Spin-offs spring from the industry logic of putting capital to maximum use. Through the appeal of secondary characters, as well as the trusted name of Tandem attached to the product, after *All in the Family*, the spin-offs *Maude* and *The Jeffersons* were created, and to follow, *Maude* begat *Good Times*. All these shows are inextricably linked and detail a developmental arc of racial formation on network television. Before *All in the Family*, sitcoms were predominantly segregated and featured all-white casts. *All in the Family* slowly integrated race marginally through its inclusion of the Jefferson family as the Bunker's neighbors. *Sanford and Son* and *Good Times* represented a somewhat separate but [un]equal portrayal of a family as they featured all-Black casts, but their financial and social circumstances were unequal to their white counterparts. Finally, *The Jeffersons* represented an integrated-privileged model. Although Black characters were in leading roles, *The Jeffersons* featured a racially integrated cast, all possessing financial privilege. This arc of racial formation is evident in the chronological production of these shows and their spin-offs. In the following section, I will be giving background on the shows that will be discussed at length throughout this book: *Sanford and Son*, *The Jeffersons*, and *Good Times*. To start, the only popular Black sitcom created by Tandem Productions outside of the spin-off world of *All in the Family* was *Sanford and Son*.

Sanford and Son

The time is just about right for a series that shows the other side of the American dream. If the time isn't right now, it never will be. Sure, it's a side of life that television hasn't shown much, but don't forget there are people like Fred Sanford in the country at home watching television, then there are the folks you see on most other shows. These people can relate to the warmth of our show. To the small things that we're happy with.

—**REDD FOXX** on *Sanford and Son*[65]

In 1972, *Sanford and Son* drastically transformed the sitcom genre by introducing NBC's first all-Black-cast television sitcom. Based on the BBC Television program *Steptoe and Son* (1962–1974), in which Tandem paid for and licensed BBC intellectual property, *Sanford and Son* propelled an urban working-class Black family into the national spotlight. Similar to its Tandem Productions forebearer, *All in the Family*, *Sanford and Son* focused on the everyday trials of an elderly man, with one major difference: Fred Sanford (Redd Foxx) and his son Lamont (Demond Wilson) were Black—a separate but (un)equal racial arc that places Blackness at its center. *Sanford and Son* chronicles the challenges the Sanfords faced as poor businessmen running a junk and salvage yard in the Watts area of Los Angeles, California.

On the heels of Foxx's performance as a junkman in *Cotton Comes to Harlem* (1970), his crossover into prime time was inevitable. Following the success of *All in the Family* at CBS, Tandem pitched CBS the idea of *Sanford and Son*. After deliberation, CBS ultimately turned down the show. NBC saw the potential of *Sanford and Son*, and the show was in motion. With his focus primarily still on the success of *All in the Family*, Lear left much of the day-to-day production work on *Sanford and Son* to Yorkin. Much like Archie Bunker, Fred Sanford became renowned for his various racial epithets and prejudice directed at both Blacks and non-Blacks alike. Yet the show made clear that Sanford's bigotry was distinct from Bunker given the racial history in America and each man's own experiences. For Sanford, his experiences with American racism shaped his racial outlook. While Archie's racism is a tool of oppression, Fred's is a reaction to it. Through the series, the narrative highlights how his interactions with the government, law enforcement, and his inability to obtain health care, social security benefits, and countless more affronts contribute to his prejudices. Challenging those who imagined the inner cities to be overrun with welfare recipients, criminals, and those in poverty, *Sanford and Son* highlights a strong community made up of the working poor, which could be found throughout America.

With *Sanford and Son*, Foxx masterfully adjusted his comedic artistry to the confines, rules, and politics of national television.[66] Foxx brought aspects of the Black comedy performed in all-Black settings of the stand-up comedy circuit to this mainstream forum of network television and recruited many of his Chitlin' Circuit compatriots along with him as recurring and even special guests (namely, LaWanda Page, LeRoy, and Skillet).[67] His ability to bring to *Sanford and Son* artists and remnants of his own Black comedic tradition (ad-libbing, Black American dance forms, vernacular, etc.) points to the agency he was able to exercise in the production of the show. Through the use of this vernacular Black comedy, *Sanford and Son* specifically addressed a Black audience familiar with the tropes of Black comedy while crossing over to a wider mainstream white audience.[68] *Sanford and Son* remained NBC's most popular show from 1972–1973 through 1975–1976. The popularity of the show arguably spawned other Black sitcoms, including *Roll Out* (1973–1974), *That's My Mama* (1974–1975), and *What's Happening!!* (1976–1979).[69] However, except for *Good Times* and *The Jeffersons*, none would equal *Sanford and Son* in longevity or popularity. This crossover ability proved profitable for Tandem and their Black sitcoms to follow.

Good Times

My view is that we made comedy safe for reality. That reality included Black people.

—NORMAN LEAR on *Good Times*[70]

Just two years later in 1974, with the increasing demand for shows on the Black experience due to the success of *Sanford and Son*, Lear and Yorkin created another television show that discusses the everyday woes of the Black poor, a transition I cover more thoroughly in chapter 3. *Good Times* is a development from *Sanford and Son* as it further worked to integrate Blackness into the mainstream but through a nuclear family. Also featuring an all-Black cast, *Good Times* premiered in February 1974; high ratings led CBS to renew the program for the 1974–1975 season, as it was the seventeenth-highest-rated program that year.[71] A spin-off from Tandem's popular sitcom *Maude, Good Times* features a poor Black family living in a housing project in Chicago, Illinois, the Evans family. Endowed with a great sense of humor, there are many laughs that accompany their harsh journeys struggling with poverty, joblessness, and inner-city crime all the while trying to keep their head above water. Florida Evans (Esther Rolle), the family's matriarch, is the show's central character as the episodes revolve around her daily life. Florida spends her days taking care of the home and her children as her husband works. Florida is the symbol of hope in the family, known for being spiritually in tune with the Lord and praying for His aid in their times of great struggle. To make ends meet, the patriarch James (John Amos) worked odd jobs at all hours of the day and night, always overworked and underpaid. J.J. (Jimmie Walker) is the Evans' oldest child, blessed with supreme artistic skill; he uses his art pieces for get-rich-quick schemes and extra cash to take girls on dates. Thelma (BernNadette Stanis), the Evans' only daughter, represents America's Black teenage girls and the social pressures they face in the inner city. Michael (Ralph Carter), the youngest of the children, is a boy who is trapped in the spirit of 1960s civil rights and militancy. With aspirations of becoming a lawyer, he is constantly looked upon as the smartest member of the family. Last but not least, the supporting character of the show, Willona Woods (Ja'Net DuBois), is the Evans' next-door neighbor and Florida's best friend. Beaming with beauty and energy, Willona's quick-witted humor acts as a powerful supporter of the Evans family.

Sporting natural Afros and speaking 1970s slang, *Good Times* offers an additionally powerful Afrocentric flavor to its predecessor, *Sanford and Son*. Although they struggled with poverty, the idea of a Black nuclear family on television was a new direction in how visual culture depicted Black life. This image of the strong Black family worked to counter Moynihan's research on "The Negro Family in America," which, as mentioned prior, described Black American families as those who lived off the matriarch after the patriarch has walked out, divorced his wife, or was otherwise missing. Lear addressed his additional motive to portray such a strong family as a means to keep the Black cast members and writers that the show employed on the payroll. Lear makes clear, "I could be confessing to a bit of inverse racism here when I admit that it even pleased me to see them credited and paid. That would not have happened, at least not gratuitously, if they were white."[72] Through this quote, I believe Lear is addressing that this new wave of Black creatives being given the chance to be credited in television was a feat in it itself. As white creatives have always been the dominant faces in the industry, these new mainstream Black artists were hustling to rewrite how they fit in the television industry at large. A key part of this rearticulation of Blackness in prime-time television came in Tandem's next Black sitcom, *The Jeffersons*.

The Jeffersons

Continuing the arc of racial development throughout Tandem's shows, *The Jeffersons* moved toward an integrated-privileged representation of Blackness as it featured a wealthy Black family at its center and their daily interactions within their largely white community. Although produced through TAT Communications, *The Jeffersons* (1975–1985) was the last show focusing on a majority Black cast before Lear and Yorkin ended their Tandem Productions partnership in 1975.[73] It was also a spin-off of Lear and Yorkin's first television creation, *All in the Family*. This last installment of Tandem (specifically Lear and Yorkin's partnership) took a drastically different form by portraying a Black family with money. The premise of *The Jeffersons* demonstrates a unique approach to the Black situation in comparison to other Black sitcoms of Tandem.

The arrogant patriarch, George Jefferson (Sherman Hemsley); his wife, Louise "Weezy" Jefferson (Isabel Sanford); and their son, Lionel Jefferson (*Good Times* cocreator Mike Evans [seasons 1, 6–11]), and Damon Evans (seasons 2–4) were the first Black two-parent family on television that wasn't impoverished. Mainly through the perspective of George, this show's comedy lies in the "fish out of water" narrative of a financially well-to-do Black family "movin' on up" to live in an Upper East Side Manhattan highrise amid an established rich and white space. A critical success in its first season, *The Jeffersons* challenged the idea of Black ascension and upward mobility by continuously reminding the Jefferson family that although they have moved on up financially, their Blackness keeps them out of the culture of old money.[74] The show centers on the Jefferson family who have been able to move from Queens (next door to the Bunkers of *All in the Family*) to the wealthy Upper East Side of Manhattan owing to the success of George's dry cleaner chain.[75] As strangers in an already established setting, *The Jeffersons* not only put forth discussion of race and class but also tackled issues such as alcoholism, racism, suicide, gun control, being transgender, and adult illiteracy. Other supporting characters were George's mother, lovingly named Mother Jefferson (Zara Cully); their back talking and lovable maid,

Florence (Marla Gibbs); and their ever-amusing British neighbor, Harry Bentley (Paul Benedict). What also made this show so transformative to the Black image was that it was the first to prominently feature a married interracial couple Helen Willis and Tom Willis (played by Roxie Roker and Franklin Cover, respectively). George frequently attempted to insert himself into the culture of the bourgeoisie by wearing three-piece suits tailored to fit, buying large musical instruments as furniture, having brunch, and tipping $20 bills to his doorman. However, his roots as a struggling Black man from Harlem are inescapable. Whether a humbling act or one meant to keep a Black man down even when he attains wealth, it's clear that money can't buy one's way fully into a society that wasn't built for them.

Bud Yorkin and Norman Lear are credited with the creations of *Sanford and Son*, *Good Times*, and *The Jeffersons*. These shows marked a new approach to the representation of Black people and Blackness. Robin Means Coleman writes, "In Black-centered worlds and through Black-oriented circumstances, a never seen before consciousness was added to the comedic discourse in which race, racism, class, and cultural differences were explored."[76] The Black sitcoms and the Black artists of Tandem Productions were integral to this consciousness building as they complicated popular understandings of the Black situation in America. I craft this work as a reconstitution of Black television, cementing it in an intellectual tradition and present-day politics. Black humor in this case and Black sitcoms specifically have been and continue to be both a bountiful source of creativity and pleasure and an energetic mode of social and political critique.[77] If television history is meant to help open up a way forward, it will need to encompass the multiple varieties of Black television aesthetics and images, past and present. Looking at the 1970s and Tandem Productions particularly, it is important to analyze the historical conditions of Black America and how those in power interpreted these conditions.

Scratchin' and Survivin' is intended to give voice to the Black creators, actors, and writers who contributed on-screen and behind the scenes at Tandem Productions. Black actors and writers were forced to contend with racism and ill-treatment at the hands of Hollywood executives and often put themselves and their careers on the line in order to contribute to the imagination of Blackness on television. The acts of hustle economics are what make these Black artists the true auteurs of these sitcom creations. However, these individuals fade into the periphery in discussions of television history because of their lack of authority in an industry that privileges whiteness. Whether through a junkyard tale of a father and son struggling to make it, a loving family stricken with the ills of poverty in the projects, or a nouveau riche family fighting to balance the new lifestyle that wealth has afforded them, these Black sitcoms of Tandem are all about the situation of race and class. They are intertextually connected with the complex political backdrop of television during the 1970s; therefore, these Black artists, who hustled to be a part of this compelling vision, deserve recognition.

2

Sanford and Son

The new Black visibility can be noticeably traced to the unsophisticated world of situation comedy. Three comedy series built around Black characters are among the most popular programs currently on TV, and all three come out of the phenomenal Norman Lear factory.

—JOHN J. O'CONNOR, "TV View:
Good Times for the Black Image,"
New York Times.[1]

As the *New York Times* suggests, Tandem Productions worked as a "factory," building Black imagery to break through to the mainstream.[2] However, to call this world of situational comedy and Black visibility "unsophisticated" was to misread levels of vernacular meaning that made such visibility important and popular. Black humor has the potential power as an unabashed tool for social change, for the unfiltered venting of cultural and political anger, and for the annunciation of Blackness.[3] Yet those in control of mainstream Black humor lived outside of the Black experience. With none of the close to nine hundred commercial and educational television stations being owned or operated by Black people, Norman Lear and Bud Yorkin's Tandem Productions was where Black was made visible.[4]

Producing shows that played off, spun off, or were linked to one another, Tandem Productions put into play a particular politics of representation that was repeatedly produced and sold on-screen and behind the scenes. With Tandem being founded and run by two white Jewish men, alongside a majority white staff, it is important to question what is at stake in this production of Black communities. As a factory, Tandem Productions constructed multiple shows that served to depict life and the social milieus of the 1970s. Whether through *All in the Family* (1971–1979), *Maude* (1972–1978), or *Sanford and Son* (1972–1977), there are distinct styles and formats through which the Tandem factory chose to (or didn't) portray identities on-screen and behind the scenes.

This chapter will consider the prime-time influence and cultural impact of Tandem Production's *Sanford and Son* (1972–1977) and how its Black artists hustled to make television a forum for Black creativity and identity formation, acting as auteurs to this successful series. Throughout this chapter, my argument takes three paths to analyze *Sanford and Son's* hustle economics: (1) trickster narratives on-screen and lead actors (such as Redd Foxx) fighting for better wages; (2) the radical ambiguity of Black women's representation, specifically LaWanda Page; (3) and moments of dissent, with the introduction of Black television writers like Ilunga Adell and Redd Foxx walking out of the show demanding change. *Sanford and Son* was the first of Tandem's sitcoms to represent the Black domestic sphere, and its Black actors and writers used the show to reframe how Black communities existed on television. Analyzing *Sanford and Son's* cultural impact in terms of hustle economics, how it works to envision Black women, and how it functions in various moments of production dissent will better aid in the understanding of this sitcom as more than a show but a redefining moment in television history.

The combined efforts of the Kerner Commission's call to action and Black people being featured more prominently throughout public affairs television and prime time in the late 1960s begat *Sanford and Son* in 1972 as the first all-Black-casted sitcom since *Amos 'n' Andy* in 1953. Although *Sanford and Son* did indeed bring more Black faces to television, Robin Means Coleman views *Sanford and Son* and other Tandem Black sitcoms as possibly the Kerner Commission's greatest nightmare.[5] Particularly, Means Coleman asserts that since Tandem's Black sitcoms deployed images of Blacks operating in separate and unequal worlds from whites, they are exactly what

FIG. 2.1 Demond Wilson and Redd Foxx as Lamont and Fred Sanford.

the commission warned against.[6] Although the imagery in Tandem's Black sitcoms represented a segregated world from white people, the existence of these sitcoms as a look into Black life and culture that were formerly non-existent on television is in fact in line with the commission's call for greater representation of the Black experience. The ways Black characters were written in comparison to their white sitcom counterparts is exactly why these images are so critically important.

The Greatest Show in Watts

Sanford and Son's setting in Watts, a poverty-stricken suburb in Los Angeles, California, is deliberate in its placing of the working-class Black poor. In 1965, the CBS Reports documentary *Watts: Riot or Revolt?* was a crucial moment in national television programming as it called attention to the cause, effect, and ramifications of the Watts Rebellion.[7] Although popular in its reception, the documentary displayed many shortcomings due to its racial biases. The Watts Rebellion, or uprising, ignited on August 11, 1965, when Marquette Frye, a Black motorist, was pulled over for reckless driving in Watts, a predominantly Black working-class neighborhood in South Los Angeles. A minor roadside argument broke out, which then escalated into a fight with the police. Community members reported that the police had hurt a pregnant Black woman during the altercation, and six days of civil unrest followed. Watts in 1965 represented a people, a race, fighting for itself. With a history of police harassment toward the larger Black community in a radically underfunded and underserved Watts neighborhood, this represented a moment of Black rebellion. Unfortunately, through the mainstream media coverage in *Watts: Riot or Revolt?*, the Black community members of Watts were only given a small portion of interview coverage to explain their unrest. This CBS white mainstream television documentary took a heavy-handed and biased approach to the cause and effect of the uprisings by mainly interviewing white correspondents and police. Just three years after the Watts Rebellion, through her public affairs television series, *Blacks, Blues, Black!*, renowned poet and writer Maya Angelou tours Watts with "riot expert" and educator Mary Jane Hewitt, looking for evidence of gains and positive development since the 1965 uprising and to celebrate the breakthroughs the community has made since.[8] While touring the Watts community festival, Angelou speaks vehemently on the self-determination and pride of Watts' Black community and their efforts to rebuild and grow after the uprising triggered by the unjust authority of the police. With the opening of the Watts Cultural Center, skills center for job placement, doctor's offices, and social service buildings, many new spaces for community welfare and social development were now local to Watts citizens. The rise of these new spaces were direct responses to the spatial and racial segregation that caused members of the community to rebel in the first place. Watts was *seemingly* becoming a community that was finally benefiting from county funding, support, and attention.

Arguably the most important moment of her time in Watts is when Angelou interviews members of the community on camera and allows them to speak for themselves freely, openly, and without reservation, self-expression largely absent from CBS's coverage. Though this episode of *Blacks, Blues, Black!* showed a Watts piecing itself back together, it also made clear the frustration and rage of the Black community that was still present. This Black rage is comedically articulated by Redd Foxx (as Fred Sanford) as he uses his star role in *Sanford and Son* to attract mainstream (white) audiences while attempting to articulate the rage of his Black kinfolk. The choice of setting for *Sanford and Son*—Watts, Los Angeles, California—was deliberate in situating the story line amid the experiences of everyday Black life and culture. As Christine Acham proclaims, "Watts had come to represent a space of Black uprising and was intimately connected to the ideas of contemporary Black protest because of the urban revolt within the community."[9]

Surviving in the world of the Sanfords required creativity. Whether through selling apples on the street corner, having a rent party, or "selling their own blood," the characters in *Sanford and Son* bring forth a myriad of strategies they have devised to make ends meet throughout the series. To be clear, the fictionalized Fred Sanford of *Sanford and Son* is a business owner and entrepreneur who lived in his junkyard. It is important to note that although he is an entrepreneur and business owner, Fred Sanford was consistently in a quandary with regard to his insufficient finances and keeping his business afloat, often leading him to engage with hustle economics (i.e., scheming, negotiating, gambling, blackmail). This reliance on hustle economics worked to show that although a Black family may run a legitimate business and are contributing members of society, formal economies (the part of an economy of which the government is fully aware and that is regulated by government authorities, particularly in the areas of contract and company law, taxation and labor law) often do not favor or work to the advantage of Black communities in the same way they may for their white counterparts, on or off the screen.

Throughout this chapter, I discuss the various methods and modalities in which Black artists who work on *Sanford and Son* must engage in what I deem as hustling—or more specifically, "hustle economics"—in efforts to get by, stay afloat, and initiate change in the larger television industry, on and off the screen. Hustle economics are racialized informal economies that include, but are not limited to, under-the-table deals, negotiating, scheming, gambling, blackmail, contractual disagreements, and favors.[10] My use of hustle economics is an effort to rearticulate the negative connotation of hustle, to be understood as survival and transcending the societal odds that are often against Black people. In conversation with LaShawn Harris's use of the underground or informal economy, hustle economics serve "as a catalyst in working-class Black women's creation of employment opportunities, occupational identities, and survival strategies that provided financial stability and a sense of labor autonomy and mobility."[11] Hustle economics speaks specifically to the histories of economic negotiations and practices of Black television artists fighting to remain visible in a precarious work environment. The word "hustle" or "hustler" is in line with the ways that Black men specifically have historically been identified in sitcoms, even before *Sanford and Son*. For instance, in George Lipsitz's "The Meaning of Memory," he describes the main characters of *Amos 'n' Andy*'s occupations as "Cab Driver/Hustler."[12] As the characters often fell short in their participation in many "get-rich-quick schemes," their hustles were almost never actualized for long-term financial gain. A "hustler" is a go-getter who often makes their money outside of solely formal occupations, mainly because their formal occupation income isn't lucrative enough to serve as a living wage. This casting of a Black man as a "hustler" is translated over time in *Sanford and Son*. Within the 1970s televisual context, these various modes of economics are unique to Black communities and are integral to making ends meet, serving as critical counterparts to the modes of economic stability that white communities and families generally have access to on American television and in the industry. Representing Black people on-screen resorting to and practicing these hustle economics faces the potential problem of reinforcing fixed representations of Black life. However, through a rereading of these actions, I believe that racialized informal economies at Tandem are represented, although comedically, as a matter of survival and a demonstration of resilience. Even when these modes of economic security or advancement fail, Black characters demonstrate the capacity to recover quickly from these difficulties, a steadfastness and resilience necessary for them to keep their heads above water and try again.

I also use the terms "hustle" or "hustle economics" to describe the negotiations that take place in the production of Blackness specifically and in the production of the Black sitcoms of Tandem generally. Combining recorded oral histories, interviews, and employment contracts, it is clear that Black artists struggled to negotiate higher salaries and more production credits in the writers' room. The Black artists at Tandem had to hustle in various ways to navigate through the company's racial hegemony, keep their jobs, and have a stake as auteurs in their own representation. Hustle economics helps us understand the labor of Black artists specifically as they maneuvered through Tandem and the television industry as a whole.

There was no one better to play the "wheelin' and dealin'" Fred Sanford than Redd Foxx, a multitalented Black artist who, throughout his career, was forced to hustle. Born John Elroy Sanford, Foxx was raised in a poor midwestern family throughout St. Louis and Chicago, and finding ways to make money was essential to his survival. Redd's own father, an electrician, earned extra cash from his other sidelight as a hustler in the local pool halls, which was barely enough to keep his family from a life of abject poverty.[13] As a teenager, Foxx himself would rummage through trash cans for newspapers and half-rotten apples to sell on the street corner, hustling to make a buck here and there, trying to survive through his wits and street smarts.[14] As a young struggling musician, Foxx's hustle economy of petty theft led to various stints in jail. Working as a busboy or wheeling dresses around New York's garment district was just enough to still be sleeping on rooftops in Harlem. Whether stealing milk, running out on restaurant checks, or being caught with marijuana he had intended to barter, Foxx's rap sheet read criminal but stood as a testament to hustling to survive.[15]

From performing with a three-man washboard band on street corners and in talent shows, to working as a dishwasher with a young Malcolm Little (Malcolm X), to practicing his comedy routines in local Harlem clubs and at the Apollo Theater, to later becoming the King of Party Records, it's clear that Foxx's trajectory to *Sanford and Son* (at the age of forty-nine) was all but linear and was fueled through hustling.[16] Working the Chitlin' Circuit through song, dance, and comedy routines in partnership with fellow comedian Slappy White, Foxx grew a name for himself, particularly in communal Black venues. Simply put by Christine Acham, "His comedy was specifically created for Black audiences and was not easily extricated from that context."[17] With his uncensored comedic style harkening to Black comedic traditions and culturally specific material, on the stand-up circuit, young Foxx was never able to cross over and break into white settings. Relegated to a mainly Black audience, Foxx's voice, swagger, and pull-no-punches attitude helped pioneer, according to Terrence T. Tucker, "the fusion of humor and rage by introducing the figure of the Comic Bad Nigger into the fabric of African American folk/street culture."[18]

"The Bad Nigger," or "angry Black man" persona was first depicted in 1920s urban Black folklore. The Bad Nigger was more aggressive than the trickster and more openly confronted white society. The Bad Nigger in general (and Foxx specifically) was therefore to be feared by mainstream America.[19] Through his unmistakably Black voice and relentlessly aggressive stage image, Foxx's act ran counter to the impulse of other Black comics in the 1960s who were attempting to appeal to white audiences.[20] Foxx's pride, belligerence, and bluntness closely resembled the more militant factions of the Black community. Foxx's militant stand-up persona and unwillingness to conform to a mainstream Black imagination are seen clearly in this following joke: "I ain't gonna do no marching nonviolently. Ain't no way I'm gonna let a cracker go upside my head with a stick and do nothin' but hum 'We Shall Overcome.' I'm going to cut him. I'm from St. Louis, and we wake up buck-naked with our knife on."[21] Here, Foxx not only makes clear his rage toward state-sanctioned violence at the hands of white officials but also offers his perspective on nonviolent protest movements, using humor to point out what he sees as the absurdity of nonviolent protest, much like his old dishwashing buddy Malcolm X. If threatened with violence, Foxx's comedic persona is choosing to meet it with violence, counter to the mainstream white acceptance and support of nonviolent strategies popularized by Martin Luther King Jr. One's comedic performance is an act of hustle economics. Comedic performance is an act, a persona that is negotiated for a particular impact that can have economic ramifications. Assuming this identity comedically, Foxx's material negotiated and confronted issues of race while often bringing into question the incongruities of American life. His negotiation worked well within Black spaces but often barred him from the white audiences he was speaking about. According to Terrence T. Tucker, "If [Moms] Mabley took on the persona of a mammy figure in order to subvert popular thinking about African American women and sexuality, Foxx became the Bad Nigger to lend authenticity to his comic claims and boasts."[22] The fearlessness of the Comic Bad Nigger persona became a recognizable part of Foxx's act that audiences began to rely on, requiring Foxx to consistently negotiate this persona within his stand-up in order to keep the hustle going with his established fan base.

Foxx's fame as a comedic powerhouse in the Black community led to him later being cast as Uncle Budd, a junkman in Ossie Davis's Black action-comedy thriller *Cotton Comes to Harlem* (1970), a role that would catapult Foxx's career to the mainstream. From this role, Lear and Yorkin of Tandem Productions decided to cast Foxx in the lead role of the American remake of the British sitcom *Steptoe and Son* (1962–1974), as the junk-dealing Fred Sanford of *Sanford and Son*. These moves from Black comedy venues and Black film to prime-time television took a renegotiating of his identity, a new hustle for economic means. Transitioning from Redd Foxx to Fred Sanford, the Comic Bad Nigger to the more universally acceptable on-screen trickster, Foxx used mainstream network television and the format of the situation comedy to bring traditional African American folklore (like signi-fyin' and toasts) and the comedy of Black communal spaces aboveground.[23]

Black visual culture consistently mines its historical roots through vari-ous art forms. Of those recycled and reimagined narrative traditions is the tale of the trickster. The trickster is linked to an economy of hustle, and Fred Sanford embodies many elements of this trickster tradition. The history of the "trickster" follows folklore dating back to African diasporic traditions that predated American slavery.[24] The tradition started in West Africa in the form of a tricky spider named Anansi. This West African god frequently takes the form of a spider and holds the knowledge of all of the folktales and stories; he is cunning and tricky and uses his cunning guile to try to get what he wants. The stories made up an exclusively oral tradition, and indeed Anansi himself was synonymous with skill and wisdom in speech. These tales crossed to the Caribbean and other parts of the New World with cap-tives via the Atlantic slave trade.[25] Anansi is often celebrated as a symbol of slave resistance and survival. As historian Lawrence Levine argues in *Black Culture and Consciousness*, enslaved Africans in the New World devoted "the structure and message of their tales to the compulsions and needs of their present situation."[26] Tricksters are often disadvantaged characters who create and adhere to moral codes that are not traditionally accepted. These codes require them to use their wit to outsmart their more advantaged opponents.[27] In essence, Brer Rabbit and similar stories about tricksters were meant to instill faith and pride in characters who used their wits or trickery in order for these historically disadvantaged figures to get over on those who historically displayed hegemonic power over them.

During slavery, trickster tales with human characters reflected the actual behavior of the people telling/hearing stories about slaves who challenged the dominant order. Lawrence Levine notes, "A significant number of slaves lied, cheated, stole, feigned illness, loafed, pretended to misunder-stand the orders they were given, put rocks in the bottom of their cotton baskets in order to meet their quota."[28] These tales during slavery and for decades after, with their subtlety and indirection, were—and are—necessary because Black people could not risk a direct attack on white people that might result in pain, punishment, or death. Tricksters are self-consciously aware of their manipulation, and they recognize, as they are reminded every day, of the differences between them and their victims. They engage in trick-ery to overcome social inequality. While frequently humorous, trickster tales often convey social critiques and serve as serious commentary on ineq-uities that exist in a country where the promises of democracy have been denied to many.[29] The tales, in fact, represent persistence or resilience, with the oppressed subject using whatever they may possess in order to live.

The trickster also falls short along its paths of trickery. As these tales were historically told in secret to other slaves or historically disadvantaged peoples, they represent narratives that reinforce community moral codes of unity. It is integral to point out that within this mythology, when the disadvantaged use their trickery on another disadvantaged person, their trickery will often be reversed on them. In order to survive or stay afloat, and often in comical ways, Black people may be forced to lie, cheat, deceive, or trick. In this way, the trickster tradition has evolved over time from West African traditions, to U.S. chattel slavery, to a mode of performance in popular art forms such as television.

As Mel Watkins claims, around the 1950s, "Black comedians turned to their own folk roots to add another dimension to their stage humor. They clearly began their acts with motifs derived from the trickster tales that dominated slave humor."[30] The Black comic sensibility of the trickster was fully unleashed in the stage routines of comedians such as Moms Mabley, Dick Gregory, Flip Wilson, and of course, Redd Foxx.[31] These examples of the trickster in these stand-up comedy routines became a point of reference for the writers and creators at Tandem to construct narratives about their Black characters—specifically Redd Foxx in his portrayal of Fred Sanford. To be clear, main characters often scheme and plot to get ahead, and the trickster, as well as their engagement in informal economies, also exists in sitcoms starring white characters. For example, Ralph Kramden in almost every episode of *The Honeymooners* (1955–1956). However, the trickster in Black sitcoms is often made to engage in informal economies and trickery specifically because of their race and economic disenfranchisement, resulting in hustle economics.

In "The Great Sanford Siege" episode of *Sanford and Son*, Fred's failure to pay his bills brings a collection agency to his home and business that threatens to turn off his utilities and repossess his furniture.[32] The episode begins with Lamont walking into the house with a handful of mail, complaining that it's obviously the first of the month due to all of the bills. The collection of bills is impressive, including gas, electric, telephone, and credit that they have accrued at the local drugstore and the grocery store. Also, within these bills is the demand for payment from the "Luau Layaway Furniture Company," an establishment from which the Sanfords rent every piece of their furniture. Frustrated with the multiple "final notice" stamps, Lamont asks his father, "Why haven't you paid the bills? Aren't they coming on time?"

A sarcastic Fred responds, "Yeah the bills come on time, but there's been a slight delay in the money." Fred's response here leads to an uproar of laughter from the studio audience; however, the humor in this quick one-liner is much more layered than it appears. The line is funny to some because of Foxx's (as Fred) timing, his serious tone, and the deadpan he's able to maintain.

Admittedly, that is what I believe first caused me to laugh at *Sanford and Son*—namely, Fred's often deadpan or blunt humor that is always met with Lamont's chagrin. More importantly, this exchange produces a feeling of discomfort as it is particularly relatable to working-class Black communities with similar financial hardships. Speaking subtly about Black economics in ways like this is very particular to the Black sitcom model of Tandem that is not translated the same way in white sitcoms. For instance, Archie Bunker in *All in the Family* would not face a collection agency repossessing his belongings; his whiteness allows him a certain social capital to own the furniture in his home. Although "working class" like Fred, Archie's job as a unionized loading dock foreman offers him a level of financial stability and steady income; in contrast, Fred is a capitalist who owns his own small business, but he is barely surviving. These contradictions complicate the shared class status of the two men and bring attention to the white character's race adding to his social capital. Laughing at Fred's predicament here, for many Black audience members, is what Glenda Carpio calls a "'wrested freedom,' the freedom to laugh at that which was unjust and cruel in order to create distance from what would otherwise obliterate a sense of self and community."[33] For many, there's a pain in the laughter that comes here, the pain of a struggling economic reality that ironically the laughter will (we hope) help ease. The performance here is striking as it's able to call attention to temporal injustices, in such a quick-witted way that without pause for reflection, many will fail to grasp.

Having no way of being able to pay the bills, Fred suggests putting the bills back into the mailbox so it seems as if they never received them. Upon Lamont's evident frustration, Fred reaches into his obviously empty pocket and states, "Son, our budget is in serious trouble." Meanwhile, a white process server with a court order to repossess all their furniture approaches their door. Unwilling to let him inside, Lamont and Fred must wait him out, hoping that he leaves. With the phone, gas, and electricity now being off, the Sanfords are cornered inside their home. Returning to the Sanford home with two sheriffs, the process server again demands that they open the door. Finally letting them enter the house, while Lamont discusses the possibility of a payment plan, Fred attempts to reason with the Black sheriff via racial identification, saying, "You a brotha', why you gonna take our stuff? . . . Why don't you get a respectable job?" Stated in a comedic tone, Fred uses the term "respectable" to hint at a complicated history of Black men working in law enforcement. A job that often requires them to be seen as the enemy or less than respectable to their poor Black counterparts, as Black police officers are often forced to arrest other Blacks, gun them down, or in this case, repossess their belongings. After failing to reason with the sheriff, Fred and Lamont whisper to each other as the audience sees that Fred purposefully tumbled down the stairs and then accuses the process server of pushing him. Not seeing the altercation take place, the sheriffs warn the process server that Fred may have a strong case of "attempted murder," and if he doesn't want to go to court, he should attempt to make a deal with the Sanfords. Begging that they don't take him to court, the process server relieves the Sanfords of their debt and gives them an extra $200 for "hospital expenses." Exaggerating the fake injury that he experienced, Fred loudly moans and groans in pain, combining the verbal with the physical in his exertion of the trickster. After the process server apologizes and leaves, the Sanfords rejoice, having successfully manipulated the system and sticking it to the man.

Across the show's five-year series run, one can see the themes that Norman Lear and Bud Yorkin constantly recreate throughout the series in their depiction of poor urban Blacks. One of the most prominent themes is the lack of financial security and the inability to pay bills. At the end of each episode, keeping up with traditional sitcom form and returning to stasis, somehow the Sanfords remain in their cycle of poverty, hoping that luck and a bit of hustlin' will somehow again work in their favor. Like the trickster Brer Rabbit, there is no true end to the quotidian situations that require Fred to muster up his creativity and hustle out of hardship, as his survival depends on it. This example however is a story of trickery written by a white Tandem producer (Aaron Ruben). As a rewrite from the British show that spawned *Sanford and Son*, *Steptoe and Son* (1962–1974), the episode "The Great Sanford Siege" is actually based on the *Steptoe and Son* episode "The Siege of Steptoe Street."[34]

Although the plot follows the same basic narrative of a father and son facing a collection agency and resorting to trickery to stay afloat, how this trickery is established with the white characters in *Steptoe and Son* is different from how it is performed in *Sanford and Son*. In "The Siege of Steptoe Street," amid bill collectors repossessing their furniture, the son (Harold) doesn't attempt to reason with them and willingly lets them price the furniture. With the camera focused on Harold, the audience hears screaming and the father (Albert) falling down the stairs off-screen. Harold actually thinks that Albert has hurt himself, and it isn't until they are paid off that Harold (and the audience) realizes that Albert was faking it. Although trickery isn't particularly a racial act, when Black characters practice it, the audience is involved in the collective hustle that the Black characters are initiating on scene. While white tricksters performing tricks are kept out of sight and more subtle—even the way they trick is somewhat more acceptable, as it's hidden from plain view. With this episode being rewritten by a white writer to frame Black hustle/trickery in *Sanford and Son*, small changes such as these make it seem that Black trickery is more common-place and expected. This begs curiosity to the ways in which Black writers visualized tropes of comedic Blackness and forms of hustle economics once they entered the mainstream.

As *Sanford and Son* became more entrenched in the NBC schedule, Lear and Yorkin hired more Black writers and script editors, giving them opportunities to play more active roles in the production of this show and others at Tandem. Though the show had two white producers, scripts created and edited by Black writers, coupled with Foxx's incorporation of Chitlin' Circuit actors, brought about considerable modification in the show's overall direction and tone. From communal issues of everyday racism, problems with the police, and a lack of job opportunities, inner-city communities were given a more intimate voice in the scripts of *Sanford and Son* once Black writers entered the writing room. Notable comedians such as Richard Pryor and Paul Mooney were among the new collective of Black writers hustling to code a political agenda for network television viewers to witness. This agenda is set forth in many ways; one important way is the use of the words *nigger* and *honkey* brought to mainstream television. The terms were shifted from being taboo or derogatory to communicating a resonance of the language used in all Black spaces/settings. I see these instances at times as a nod from Black writers communicating directly to Black audiences, albeit through the antics of Fred Sanford. The use of the trickster and his performance of practicing hustle economics is also seen in a different way at the hands of Black writers.

For example, in "The Dowry," Richard Pryor and Paul Mooney write a script that fully embraces the spirit of a tricky hustler setting up a plot for financial gain.[35] When Fred's cousin Grady comes to visit, Fred and Grady scheme a plan for Lamont and Grady's new stepdaughter (Betty Jean) to wed. This idea is created once Fred realizes that whoever weds Judy stands to receive a $10,000 dowry on their wedding day, and of course, Fred wants a piece of that small fortune. When Grady and his new family visit, Fred and Lamont joke and laugh at Judy's weight and general appearance. However, once Grady informs Fred of the dowry, Fred's tune changes, and he begins to use deception in order to urge Lamont to consider marrying her. Fred's con begins the very next morning by making Lamont his favorite breakfast in order to distract him.

> FRED: You might think I'm crazy for saying this, but I wouldn't mind having Betty Jean for a daughter-in-law. (*The camera zooms in on Lamont midchew as he pauses in confusion.*)
>
> LAMONT: Have you been in the Applejack this morning?
>
> FRED: You can learn to love her. Love conquers all, even fat.

In this brief exchange, Fred attempts to coax Lamont with lies for his own future financial gain. Lamont assumes Fred has been drinking early in the morning as that is the only way he could make such claims. At the conclusion of the episode, Lamont and Betty Jean figure out the deception of their fathers and fake their own engagement as payback. When a sinister Fred and Grady think that their plan has come to fruition, they rejoice until Lamont mentions that the two newlyweds would move to St. Louis. Once the trickster (Fred) is tricked, he becomes a victim of his own scheme, and he ruins the idea of the two marrying.

Later in the series, another Black writer, Odie Hawkins, focused his episode on hustle economics as the Sanfords are in a financial bind and try to raise money by throwing a rent party in "The Big Party" (season 2, episode 15). This episode highlights the Black cultural tradition of the "rent party," which emerged during the first half of the twentieth century in urban communities, reminiscent of popular southern working-class Black afterhours amusements. According to LaShawn Harris, these spaces of fellowship and hustle were "organized in response to overpriced apartment rentals and race discrimination within urban housing markets, rent parties, also commonly known in New York as 'whist parties,' were hosted by money-strapped Blacks or 'whoever might feel the urge during a poverty-stricken interlude to pay exorbitant rent prices.'"[36] These parties played a major role in community engagement, financial support, and socialization. Facing the first of the month, Lamont bemoans, "Pop, we ain't gonna make it. . . . We got thirty bucks between us, and we got bills here that total over two hundred dollars." Fred reluctantly agrees, "We ain't gonna make it." As they deliberate on options to pay rent, Lamont even mentions them possibly going on welfare, in which Fred proudly responds, "Watch your mouth! Fred Sanford on relief? Never!" His pride here doesn't allow Fred to use formal government resources for financial aid, resources he considers to be a handout. This tells us something crucial about the show's approach to poverty, as it seems to denigrate the idea of being on welfare. Though poverty can be shown, the resources that Lyndon Johnson's "Great Society" provided are not something a "proud" Black man should indulge in according to the show's ideological position, which is also seen with John Amos's character in *Good Times* (see chapter 3). Even when Lamont explains that welfare is meant for people like them, Fred fights against it.

> LAMONT: What do you think we pay taxes for? We would just be taking advantage of something that is set up for people like us.
> FRED: What's that mean? People like us?
> LAMONT: Well, you know, poor people, the have-nots.
> FRED: Have-nots? Well, say the haves gave the have-nots half of what they have, then the haves will still be the haves, and the have-nots will be the have-somethings.

Although set up through a comedic delivery, Odie Hawkins uses this exchange to comment on a larger socioeconomic issue regarding the concentration of finances with the rich and how it might trickle down to the poor. Hawkins uses this joke to state a critique of class and the distribution of wealth, giving a solution that the rich who have the financial means can grant opportunity to those who don't by giving a portion of their money to the poor. This redistribution of wealth would (in theory) eliminate the need for welfare programs and government assistance and rid the category of "have-nots." The comedy here lightens the delivery; however, the message still rings clear.

After considering going to such lengths as selling apples on the street corner or even selling blood, Fred comes up with the idea to use their last thirty dollars to buy food and drinks and sell it to patrons at a house party, as Fred says, "Ya know, like them old Harlem rent parties." Rather than pursuing more formal means (such as welfare or payment extensions), the informal economy of the rent party is their chosen route of hustle. Although they make the required funds, gangsters show up and force them to make their home into an endless party that Fred manages. In the conclusion of the episode, Fred calls on his sister-in-law nemesis, Aunt Esther, to bring her church friends through the home and raid the gangsters out.

Hustle economics often work for Fred and Lamont, but the show's success is predicated on the characters' economic failure and, to true sitcom form, returning to stasis. This suggests that the trickster must be tricked in order for the show to go on. The instances of hustle economics in *Sanford and Son* are largely important because whether written by a Black *or* white writer, Black characters are predestined to fail for the sake of comedy. Although Fred and Lamont are dedicated members of the workforce and own their own business, profitability or business success are rarely narrative foci. Involvement in the formal economies of capitalism seems to not be enough or be in favor of Black communities, so they must often break from the formalities. It seems the Sanford's business is often what pulls them further into financial ruin. Their inability to earn a profit by selling junk forces them into an economic model that only works for the short term—earning just enough to get by until the next bill is due. As the first show to feature an all-Black cast in over twenty years, the consistent focus on the financial woes of the Sanford family set a precedent that even the working-class Black citizens who attempt to "pull themselves up by their bootstraps" do not have the capacity to do so without resorting to the hustle to get by. The overwhelming majority of these instances of trickery and hustle economics are seen through the actions of Black men on the show. As a sitcom that primarily chronicles the life and occurrences of two Black men, the masculinity in the show often overshadows the representation of Black women on *Sanford and Son* who were also made to hustle and negotiate on and off the screen in order to occupy space in a changing television industry.

Black Women Hustle Too:
LaWanda Page and *Sanford and Son*

When it comes to women's on-screen depictions in Tandem's television series, each show makes clear a particular politics in its representation. Yet at this moment in history, Black television in general, and Tandem's shows specifically, offered even less diverse acting roles to Black women than they did to Black men and close to zero credits behind the scenes in production. My particular concern here is to include in the history of television programming, the negotiated visibility, and production of Black women's embodiment on *Sanford and Son*.

Scholarly discussion has scantly focused on Black women's representation, labor, and hustle in *Sanford and Son*. I consider these actions from

Black women to be labor because this Tandem factory, so evidently controlled by men, is unable to succeed without the input of every worker; Black women as workers were on the margins. These Black women's bodies of work and the working of their bodies (how they were visually constructed), in and outside of the televisual space, speak to historical constructions of negotiated and hustled imagery of Black womanhood that must be addressed.[37] Of course, I would be remiss to not mention the scholars that have centered Black women's representation on television. In *Shaded Lives: African-American Women and Television*, Beretta Smith-Shomade charts the characterization of Black women on television in various genres from the 1980s to the new millennium—largely after this book's particular focus on the 1970s and the sitcom.[38] In Christine Acham's *Revolution Televised: Prime Time and the Struggle for Black Power*, Acham does center on Black television from the late 1960s through the '70s, charting the ways Black bodies occupied television production. However, Acham's focus on the Black women in this space is primarily centered on the actresses Diahann Carroll and Esther Rolle.[39] The space that Black women occupy on *Sanford and Son* is largely underanalyzed.

In this popular cultural context on-screen, being a woman often meant adhering to social norms of femininity, such as being nurturing, caring, social, emotional, vulnerable, and concerned with appearance, with the pretense of assuming "appropriate" roles.[40] On the front lines, this cultural backdrop also saw a rise in various women's movements for social equality. Television producers were soon moved to respond to this changing social climate. The beginning of this process happened in 1970, a watershed year in American second-wave feminism and in American prime-time television.[41] The debut of *The Mary Tyler Moore Show* (1970–1977, MTM Enterprises) and a "wave of media attention to women's liberation in 1970 marked a qualitative shift in the public consciousness of the presence of an organized feminist movement."[42] Prior to this, prime-time television's preferred mode of representing women was as contented housewives.[43] With its focus on the intelligent and competent single working woman on-screen and with a woman at its helm of production, Bonnie Dow contends that "*Mary Tyler Moore*'s [the show] greater longevity, the greater maturity and autonomy of its lead character, and its timing in relation to the women's liberation movement made it, then and now, television's breakthrough feminist representation."[44] However, this "breakthrough feminist representation" was solely white and middle class. As seen within MTM Enterprises, women did in fact exist on the production side of television with a large influence but, similarly, at Tandem Productions, those women were white. For instance, women such as Jane Murray (casting director for 135 *Sanford and Son* episodes), Rita Riggs (costume designer for 84 *Sanford and Son* episodes), and Joni Rhodes (script supervisor for 65 *Sanford and Son* episodes) played integral roles in the production of *Sanford and Son* at Tandem Productions. With the lack of Black people in general and the lack of Black women as a whole on the production side of Tandem, their narratives of Black womanhood were precarious from the start.

With no authority in *Sanford and Son*'s production, Black women not only had to perform the characters written for them but also had to attend to societal concerns of portraying a redeeming image—on and off the screen. Black women's presence on *Sanford and Son* shows a progression of how the show grew to rely on their labor, specifically through the characters: Elizabeth, Donna (played by Lynn Hamilton), and climactically through the hustle and ambiguity of Aunt Esther (played by LaWanda Page). The dialogue coupled with these performances is crucial to understanding just how much race and gender have influenced imagery and production through television history and the roots at which these changes came to fruition.

History has shown that sitcoms in general and Black sitcoms, in particular, are occupied by men. These overtly male spaces address Lynne Joyrich's contention that television possesses a tension of "culturally constituted notions of the feminine and the masculine."[45] As television addresses the male viewers, it simultaneously elevates the "infantile [which offers and then denies] the feminine conventionally associated with television. . . . A common strategy is thus to construct a violent hypermasculinity—an excess of 'maleness' that acts as a shield."[46] As a show that focuses on the daily trials and tribulations of Fred and Lamont Sanford, much of the scholarship on *Sanford and Son* addresses Black men and negotiated masculinity. The Black women in this show have often been treated as nonexistent; however, their presence—and absence—play a large part in the show's tone, direction, and characterization of the main male characters, especially when speaking in terms of the hustle economics that took place to create said roles. With *Sanford and Son* scarcely discussed in Norman Lear's personal papers, and the lack of an archive regarding the Black women who were a part of the series, I am working around archival absences and filling the gaps, often via intertext and paratext when available (textual analysis of episodes, fan mail, comedy albums, magazine articles, etc.), to create a narrative about the Black women and their roles hustling on-screen and in production of *Sanford and Son*. Tales of tricksters and hustlers are historically gendered as men's work. However, like the men in this show, Black women had to hustle in various ways to navigate through television's racial (and gender) hegemony to have a stake in their own representation. These spaces that Black women occupied were negotiated in order to reinvent how they existed in popular culture and society.

The selling of the American dream has been at the center of the prime-time television enterprise. However, I question, How are Black women placed within this dream? Until the late 1960s, this dream popularly portrayed Black women and their labor on television as domestic workers in docile and compliant roles, such as those in the radio program and later sitcom *Beulah* (1950–1952). While it is unhelpful to characterize these roles through the binary "positive" or "negative"—in fact, these roles broke barriers and allowed important access—they offered no fluidity in the visualization of Black women on television. It is crucial here to take a step back before *Sanford and Son* to analyze the modes in which Black women were imagined and performed. I would be remiss here to not address Diahann Carroll's role as Julia Baker in *Julia* (1968–1971, Hancarr Productions and Savannah Productions) as it stands as the paramount image of Black women and Black femininity in this televisual temporal moment. Television in the 1960s, *Julia* especially, is often frowned upon for retreating from the real-life conflicts taking place in the United States regarding civil unrest and struggles of Black life in general.[47] When asked to reflect on her role in *Julia*, Carroll herself addresses that her role in *Julia* was an "acceptable" image to break down barriers so that Black people could move on from there. Further, while working on *Julia*, Carroll exclaimed to the show's producers, "At the moment we are presenting the White Negro, and he has very little Negro-ness."[48] Just as Black women took on the roles of domestics in order to infiltrate Hollywood, Carroll saw her role in *Julia*, as a respectable embodiment of Black womanhood imagined by white producers, as a necessary building block to Black women's possibilities of televisual humanity and the fluidity of their identification. Although groundbreaking in representation, Carroll's role as Julia was crafted as the universally respectable image of Black women. Aniko Bodroghkozy makes clear how Hal Kanter cemented this static image by analyzing an early episode of *Julia*. While searching for a housekeeper and nanny for her son Corey, Julia interviews four women. Three of the four "characters play to the limited repertoire of representations of Black women, marking 'Blackness' as inadequate and unpleasant. All are little more than familiar stereotypes."[49] The "mammy," the "church lady," and the "militant" are all interviewed, yet the final, and successful, applicant comes with no markers of Blackness.[50] This assemblage of one-dimensional Black women characters suggests a real crisis in representation. What Carroll was unable to produce within the television image, she counteracted loudly within other media contexts, such as print media—opening up the concept of the television text beyond what was on the screen.[51] Carroll utilized her interviews with *JET* and *Ebony* magazines to speak about her politics in support of the civil rights and Black Power movements during a time of civil unrest where her character on-screen, Julia, was silent to them.

With the employment of only a handful of women at Tandem, the company likely, at least quantitatively, attempts to do its due diligence on gender diversity at the production level. In addition, they attempt this with shows like *Maude*, where Tandem gave liberal white women a voice (through Beatrice Arthur's character, Maude Findlay) by comically addressing the issues women were facing in a male-dominated world. Further pushed into silence were the voices of Black women. Made even more evident through *Sanford and Son*, the majority of white male writers and producers wrote the dialogue and therefore often controlled the Black woman's voice and actions on-screen. With much of the archival material and trade journal coverage addressing the turmoil suffered by the Black male actors on Tandem's shows, at times it is unclear whether the Black women on these shows ever had the opportunity to speak for themselves. In fact, the disproportionate attention given to the Black men in Tandem's shows begs the question of whether the Black women of Tandem faced issues similar to those that the men raised regarding sufficient pay, wanting a stake in writing credits, and better working facilities.[52] Through hustle with network executives (protest, walkouts, contract withholding, and negotiation), the male actors of *Sanford and Son* (Redd Foxx in particular) were granted agency to address their production concerns—concerns that were soon validated and acceded to.[53] Where, however, is the voice of Black women on this show? A key factor in the frequent silencing of Black women to define themselves and their own politics is that they are in a daily battle of multiple oppressions. Not having the racial or gendered privilege to rely on, there is minimal access to resources and platforms to fight these multiple oppressions. These restrictive factors in the livelihood, television production, and on-screen performance of Black women required them to hustle, to practice unarchived, uncredited, and exhaustive emotional and material labor in representing not only their race but also their gender.

Reviewing the 1974 television season, the National Black Feminist Organization had this to say on the matter:

1. Black shows are slanted toward the ridiculous with no redeeming counter images;
2. Third World peoples are consistently cast in extremes;
3. When Blacks are cast as professional people, the characters they portray generally lack professionalism and give the impression that Black people are incapable and inferior in such positions;
4. When older persons are featured, Black people are usually cast as shiftless derelicts or non-productive individuals.[54]

With this review from an organization whose focus is on Black women, it begs the question of what is the image or representation of Black women, or the Black feminine subject, in shows such as *Sanford and Son*? In Tandem's *Sanford and Son*, the junk-dealing widower Fred Sanford and his son Lamont are undoubtedly at the show's center. From the construction of their home to their varying discussions about the woes of life, the show is poignantly Black male-centric. When analyzing the portrayal, role, and representation of Black women, *Sanford and Son* leaves the audience with mainly three reoccurring characters: the spiritual presence of Elizabeth Sanford, the bodily representation of Donna Harris (played by Lynn Hamilton), and the complete embodiment and ambiguous on- and off-screen persona of Aunt Esther (played by LaWanda Page). Although each of these characters represents a progression of Black women's labor and hustling to be seen on prime-time television, this section will focus solely on Page. LaWanda Page's hustle from the all-Black stand-up comedy scene to prime-time television represents the full embodiment of Black women's hustle economics, negotiation, and labor on and off the screen. LaWanda Page is the first Black woman stand-up performer to have reoccurring television sitcom success. Equally as important, she is a Black female comedian who practices hustle economics by negotiating different articulations of Black femininity within alternative *and* mainstream spaces. I use the term "negotiation" throughout this chapter (and book) because as Christine Gledhill writes, "Meaning is neither imposed, nor passively imbibed, but arises out of a struggle or negotiation between competing frames of reference, motivation, and experience."[55] The concept of negotiation helps us understand how and why LaWanda Page was able to successfully balance her stand-up identity with her role on *Sanford and Son*, all working to complicate the cultural perception of Black women.

The Radical Ambiguity of LaWanda Page

FIG. 2.2 LaWanda Page as Aunt Esther.

From fire dancing, to burlesque shows, to waiting tables, to stand-up comedy, to taking a guest character spot and creating it into a permanent recurring role on mainstream television, Page hustled, scratched, and survived as a mainstay in television memory. Like LaShawn Harris's discussion of the "underground economy," LaWanda Page's hustle economics and negotiation of varying odd jobs "served as a catalyst in working-class Black women's creation of employment opportunities, occupational identities, and survival strategies that provided financial stability and a sense of labor autonomy and mobility."[56] In casting supporting characters on the show, Redd Foxx recommended relatively unknown performers that he'd met in the days of segregated public entertainment, such as the Chitlin' Circuit and popular Black nightclubs. One of these unknown performers was LaWanda Page. Following in the tradition of Redd Foxx and coming from blue comedy stand-up, Page, like Foxx, worked to shift the traditional format of sitcom humor.[57] The affluence and stardom that Foxx achieved never interfered with his decision to remember and hire his "Black brothers and sisters."[58] In an interview with *Sanford and Son* executive producer and writer, Saul Turteltaub, he revealed just how mindful of his community Redd Foxx was.[59] Turteltaub stated that many of the extras that audiences see throughout the series were friends of Foxx. When it came to a day of shooting, Turteltaub reminisces that Foxx would say in his raspy voice, "Hey, Turtle, can you put them somewhere in the episode?" With Tandem paying these Black artists and extras $500 for a spot in an episode, Foxx worked to keep his community employed and used his star power to hustle Black dollars within Tandem, steadily raising his own production power and making the sitcom as Black as can be. Of the individuals recommended for employment, the only woman that became a permanent character was LaWanda Page as Aunt Esther.

An old friend of Foxx through their adolescent years in St. Louis, Page was introduced as a one-time extra and gained a recurring role that until this day is heralded in sitcom history as Fred's sister-in-law (sister of the late Elizabeth), Aunt Esther—the most prolific regular apart from Fred and Lamont.[60] Through her ascension to prime time, LaWanda Page is the definition of a hustler, working her way through various entertainment venues in order to make ends meet. Known earlier for her stripteasing act that was later incorporated with fire-swallowing, earning her the title the "Bronze Goddess of Fire,"[61] Page's artistry had always been eclectic. Through stand-up comedy, she came to be heralded as the "Queen of Comedy" to Black audiences and the "Black Queen of Comedy" to the mainstream.[62] Having to transition her raunchy stand-up persona to the small screen (similar to Foxx), Page premiered in season two's "The Big Party," playing Aunt Esther, a combative overtly Christian "Holy Roller" and arch nemesis of Fred Sanford.[63]

As part of Page's characterization of Aunt Esther, she is married, she shouts from scripture, consistently calls upon the Holy Spirit, dresses conservatively in skirts to her ankles, and always holds a Bible while screaming "Oh, Glory!" Similar to Flip Wilson's lampooning of the Black church with his reoccurring character Reverend Leroy on *The Flip Wilson Show* (1970–1974), Aunt Esther is meant to represent contention in the historic relationship between African Americans and forced institutionalized religion in a comedic form.[64] While Esther is used as a character to question and represent the Black church, she is positioned in opposition to Fred, "a secular Black character who does not accept the incongruities of the church."[65]

"The Big Party" features Page as Aunt Esther pleading to use Fred's home for Bible study. Upon walking into the Sanford home and seeing a raunchy rent party, Aunt Esther and her crew of "holy raiders" beat everyone out of the home using their Bibles. Page and Foxx's on-screen partnership added a newfound energy to the scripts, and their chemistry was arguably unmatched by anything on television at the time. As with the general sitcom structure, where the main protagonist barely changes from one episode to the next, Fred Sanford remains the stubborn and grumpy trickster who is the source of much of the show's comedic one-liners and situations. In every episode, the situation ends largely as it began; hence, if Fred feels distaste for another character, it continues in all subsequent episodes. With the introduction of Aunt Esther, the comic structure of the show shifts in season two, making Aunt Esther an equal source of comedy in many of her exchanges with Fred, and the two forever have a relationship as enemies. With Fred often calling attention to her physical appearance and Aunt Esther responding to him with jabs about his age and his heathenism, the exchange between the two is always one that garners the most laughter from the studio audiences. In the first appearance of Esther on-screen, we see an example of this exchange that the two became known for.

> ESTHER: Down and out again, huh, Fred? You were a deadbeat the day my sister married you, and you still a deadbeat today.
>
> FRED: Listen, Esther, you know good and well the day I married your sister, I was loaded.
>
> ESTHER: Yeah, you was loaded all right. You was so drunk you fell on the preacher.
>
> FRED: Well, I had to get drunk to look at your ugly family.[66]

Through this exchange, Esther produces the initial comedic jab, thereby reversing the typical role that Fred takes as the show's star and comedic center. Written by a Black writer (Odie Hawkins), this episode marks the first instance in the show in which a Black woman initiates the source of comedy. Through her dialogue, Esther is given a level of power and voice here that complicated the traditional structure of *Sanford and Son*. Calling attention to Fred's shortcomings and defending herself against his comebacks marks a shift in the narrative as there is now a character present that challenges the leading man to be at his defenses. While her relationship with Fred was usually confrontational in their comedic riffs with each other, Esther also portrays a matriarchal side when it came to her husband, Woodrow, and her nephew Lamont, showing that her ability to speak up against an oppressive voice can be and is coupled by a maternal spirit. Very seldom are Black women in television at this moment shown to have the ability to perform these multiple personalities.

Satisfied with this new direction, executive producer Aaron Ruben gave credit to Foxx rather than the labor of Page for embodying such a character. Ruben believed that with Page's addition, Foxx had "opened up a whole new reservoir of rich talent to use . . . and that's what helps give the show its authentic flavor."[67] Although Page became a hit on the show, her hustle was often underappreciated, and the initial reaction to her from Tandem producers was unfavorable. Although she was offered the role, prior to taping, the producers became concerned when Page, whose experience was limited primarily to nightclub stages, seemed to have difficulty working in a sitcom format and was unable to memorize her lines.[68] Since "Black comedy, in its literal and literary construction, has always overtly *and* covertly explored the trials, tribulations, and triumphs of African American communities," the act of Page crossing over from her communal all-Black space of stand-up comedy and blue material to a mainstream white liberal industry had its share of difficulties yet indicates her radical ambiguity.[69]

Eventually, one of the *Sanford and Son* producers informed Foxx that Page would need to be fired and that another actor would need to be cast before the show could begin taping. Foxx responded by insisting that Page keep the part, even threatening to walk away from the show if Page were fired. By working with Page on her lines, and Foxx telling her to simply "stop acting and start acting like yourself," the producers eventually relented.[70] Yet another early example of the influence Foxx wielded at Tandem in support of a crucial character on the show, as well as the lack of authoritative power Black women were able to possess in production.

Through *Sanford and Son,* Page as Aunt Esther was able to add complexity to the images and representations of Black women *on-screen* in the early 1970s. However, in terms of off-screen or behind-the-scenes influences of Black women defining themselves and redefining the racial gender politics at play in the television industry as a whole, Tandem fell short with regard to *Sanford and Son.* A significant indicator of this failure is the lack of voice that Black actresses of the show were able to wield in the writing of episodes and in interviews via trade and popular culture magazines. It seems, in fact, that the most outspoken of the Black women on *Sanford and Son*, LaWanda Page, spoke her personal politics not on-screen or in magazines but in the nightclub and blue comedy scene. This radical ambiguity proves that in order to reach stardom and remain financially stable, Black women's hustle and negotiations in 1970s television often required that they distance themselves from the network television space. Viewers of Tandem sitcoms would often write letters to discuss how much they enjoyed (or didn't) certain characters. While the letters written in reference to the character Fred Sanford were a mixture of positive and negative responses, fan mail to Tandem Productions consistently pleaded for "more Aunt Esther," with comments like "The show wouldn't be a hit without her. . . . Her and Fred play off of one another perfectly. . . . She's hysterical."[71] With such appreciation, it was often encouraged for Page to go off script and improvise from time to time in order to make the character her own, yet because she was not given her due in terms of the actual writing or production at Tandem, she made sure to always remain relevant in the stand-up comedy circuit. Her Black comic personae, like the Black condition in the United States, was diffused and often distorted in the mainstream televisual popular consciousness.[72] A dedicated fan's truest vision of LaWanda Page was through her stand-up comedy.

What Page was able to do with her successes as a Black woman in stand-up during the late 1960s and throughout the 1970s is a feat to which very little scholarly attention has been given. Attention to this fact is important because Black women in the blue comedy scene were scarce, and those able to transition (or crossover) in and out of mainstream television should be historicized for their ability to alter their comedic performance and often their politics on-screen.[73] Indeed, Bambi Haggins's *Laughing Mad* offers many parallels to this focus as it critically examines the comic televisual and cinematic personae of multiple stand-up comedians to analyze the transition from Black comedy for Black audiences to Black comics becoming progressively more mainstream.[74] However, other than a primary focus on Moms Mabley and Whoopi Goldberg, *Laughing Mad* centers on multiple Black men and how they have navigated their comic transitions.

LaWanda Page stands apart from those individuals focused on in other scholarship because she never *fully* crosses over to the mainstream. Similar to how Jennifer Fuller makes clear that Nell Carter's television character Nell in *Gimme a Break!* (1981–1987) "was a negotiation between the maid, the mammy, and the 'modern Black women,'"[75] performing her blue stand-up comedy as "LaWanda: The Queen of Comedy" while acting as Aunt Esther on *Sanford and Son*, Page negotiates multiple personae that are filtered from one medium to the next. Her stand-up didn't allow for retakes, reviews of scripts, and practice; her performance was live and catered to playing off an all-Black audience. As "LaWanda: The Queen of Comedy," she wasn't bound to network politics. She unabashedly used curse words, spoke openly about her body and sexuality, and wrote, improvised, and spoke for herself. While on television, Page's

Aunt Esther is an ironic commentary on her stand-up persona as she is a devout churchgoer and tough-as-nails realist, unafraid to state whatever was on her mind so long as it followed the "Good Book." On the sound stage, Page was restricted to the words written for her. And although both (television and stand-up) are versions of a Black female embodiment, Aunt Esther and LaWanda are one body that works to show the complexity of Black female performance, one way that Tandem deemed acceptable and another that Page was given supreme agency. For the same Black woman to have a space to speak to a national audience preaching to Fred Sanford that his home is "reeking with sin—a den of iniquity" and to be able to also tell a primarily Black nightclub audience that she's "as nervous as a whore in church" offers an important contrast to where certain performances, identities, and Black women's voices are restricted (figures 3 and 4).

FIG. 2.3 LaWanda: Queen of Comedy, *Preach On Sister, Preach On!*, album cover (1973).

FIG. 2.4 LaWanda: Queen of Comedy, *Watch It, Sucker!*, album cover (1977).

As stated earlier in the chapter, according to Terrence T. Tucker, "If [Moms] Mabley took on the persona of a mammy figure in order to subvert popular thinking about African American women and sexuality, Foxx became the Bad Nigger to lend authenticity to his comic claims and boasts."[76] I would add to this and say that LaWanda Page adopted the persona of the "Holy Roller," the Black Christian woman, to complicate popular understanding of Black women and their sexuality. This persona, used on *Sanford and Son* and in her stand-up routines, is her hustle economics as she uses her agency to gain notoriety and negotiate the ambiguity of the Black woman. On television, Page's words, scripted for her, contrast with the words and persona she crafted for herself in the stand-up scene. The two different but interrelated spaces not only are ironic but clearly suggest the ambiguity of LaWanda Page as a Black woman mining these two arenas and more generally the performative control of white male-dominated television productions.

Before her fame as the religiously conservative Aunt Esther, Page garnered fame and honed her feisty demeanor through her solo comedy albums and as a member of the comedy group Skillet, Leroy, and Co.[77] Along with Ernest "Skillet" Mayhand and Wilbert "LeRoy" Daniel, Page performed stand-up acts and made numerous ribald party records for the Los Angeles–based Laff Records.[78] With few Black women comedians gaining praise at this moment, much of their popularity was relegated to male-dominated sexually explicit and socially irreverent blue material. Black women have been forced to utilize the stand-up (especially blue material) space to annihilate heteronormative prescriptions of racialized and gendered sexuality.[79] Page was arguably the bluest of all female comics. As comedy challenges social and cultural mores, Page utilized stand-up comedy to challenge the symbols rampant in popular culture that ignored Black women's sexuality and desire by distributing those symbols head-on, deconstructing societal norms of Black women. Although Page held her own on *Sanford and Son* as Aunt Esther when it came to bouts between her and Fred, it was ultimately Redd Foxx's show. As the "Queen of Comedy," the stand-up space was where Page excelled on her own. Although Page produced two solo albums before her time on *Sanford and Son*, the albums after her Sanford fame were where she was able to lean into the stardom of this new audience base and where she saw her audience grow from a Black in-group community to the mainstream, yet her authentic Black voice remained.

In 1973, just months following Page's premiere on *Sanford and Son*, she released her third solo comedy album, *Preach On Sister, Preach On!* This album marks a moment in which LaWanda Page's ambiguity is in full form as her multiple performed identities collide, seen not just in the album's artwork that states "Featured as Aunt Esther on *Sanford and Son*" but in the album's actual subject material and Page's persona (figure 3). Leaning on the acclaim that Page was beginning to receive while performing as the Baptist holier-than-thou Aunt Esther on *Sanford and Son*, she uses the space of stand-up in *Preach On Sister, Preach On!* to counter that televisual identity and perform as a Baptist preacher who is anything but holy. Here, Page masterfully complicates the space and culture of Black religion by redefining how it may look in two separate venues, television and the stand-up stage. The physicality of her personae matched her content. Through her covered body on television, her sexuality is instructed to be unobtrusive, while her stand-up attire and content were quite the opposite.

With her introduction by the emcee as the "Queen of Comedy, LaWanda," LaWanda begins her performance of scripture with a story of Adam and Eve and their sexual conquests. With audience members shouting and passing scotch around in place of an offering plate while LaWanda promotes call-and-response actions, riffs and rhymes, curses, and calls churchgoers "niggas," LaWanda employs Black religious vernacular and culture in her performance to represent and convey her desires, something Aunt Esther is unable to do. It is clear that although performed through the same body, LaWanda and Aunt Esther are meant to antithesize Black spaces and work to offer a fluidity of Black women's expression and representation. Through stand-up, Page effectively plays with and against the cultural politics of sexuality, desire, gender, and race. She "sings natural desires of her body, as opposed to basking in the quiet dignity of her womanhood," challenging the essence of a singular often desexualized Black female subject that existed on television.[80]

Following the success of *Preach On Sister, Preach On!* in 1977, Page released her fourth and most acclaimed comedy album, *Watch It, Sucker!*[81] This was the first album where a group of musicians accompanied her, creating more of the "party album" atmosphere. Given the name of the album, one can speculate that it was certified gold largely due to the comic's now firmly established national success as Aunt Esther on *Sanford and Son*.[82] This album was largely catered to an audience that is equally entertained by the Bible-toting Aunt Esther *and* the no-holds-barred "Queen of Comedy." Strikingly different from fans of Foxx who were cited as "appalled" by Foxx's stand-up performance. Specifically, Foxx's fans in Trinidad that were expecting the much beloved Fred G. Sanford on stage were not prepared for the comedian's stand-up blue material.[83] With Page's *Preach On Sister, Preach On!* and the *Watch It, Sucker!* album being certified gold, the hustle of her performances is clear—in fact, I believe it intrigued universal audiences because it blatantly countered the traditional tropes of Black women's performance across various art forms.

The Holy Roller identity that Page embodied on *Sanford and Son* actually makes the otherwise "dangerous" blue comedy LaWanda "safe" for prime-time audiences. The ability of Page to transition her styles of comedy from raw, uncensored, indecent, and profane to a mixture of religious, stern, and conservative added depth to how audiences were able to view Black women in popular culture—challenging the popular forms in which Black women's performances were restricted. These roles were often relegated to insipid or monolithic portrayals of Black womanhood in which the multifaceted identity and voices of Black women seemed nonexistent.

For instance, *Watch It, Sucker!* includes skits about pastors masturbating and sex workers in the church. In the first track entitled "The Whores in Church," LaWanda tells the story of sex workers or "whores" who could no longer find money on the streets so they decide to join the church.[84] In fact, LaWanda identifies with these workers when she talks to the audience, saying that her being onstage has her as "nervous as a whore in church." Through the analysis of Page using stand-up performances as "trickster tropes," L. H. Stallings suggests that "Page's 'Whores in Church' is an act filled with profanity, sexually explicit references, and a critical assessment of Christian devised representations of women—sacred ribaldry. Her voice never falters or hesitates over intertwining the sacred, secular, and so-called lewd."[85] With this performance, like *Preach On Sister, Preach On!*, Page subverts her Aunt Esther identity and uses vernacular of the Black church transgressively—violating the acceptable boundaries of religion, gender, and Black women's sexual subjectivity.

Although her characterization of Aunt Esther stayed relatively the same in the early seasons of the sitcom, Tandem's hiring of more Black television writers brought noticeable changes to the sitcom. This change in the show's production is quite possibly the cause of the show's highest viewed season (season three), as the sitcom more effectively reflected the language of Black communities through the jokes written, the comedic timing, the jargon, messages within each episode, and the vaudevillian-style acting it encouraged.[86] Among these Black writers was the first ever Black associate story editor on network television, Ilunga Adell.[87] For Tandem, Adell was the answer to critics who suggested the popular series could hardly be an authentic portrayal of Black life since it was produced and mostly written by white writers. Adell played a large part in the range of the show's moral lessons and character depth, including Aunt Esther's character development, language, and screen presence. I see Adell occupying a space within the writer's room at Tandem a clear example of hustle economics. Not only does his exceptional writing make way for Black artists to have a creative and economic stake in television production, but Adell also used his agency to negotiate Black visibility on-screen. As the writer for eight of the twenty-four scripts in season three, including the "best show of the season, 'Mama's Baby, Papa's Maybe,'" Adell claims that he had a great influence on the series and its direction.[88] This particular episode, "Mama's Baby, Papa's Maybe," featured Page in one of her most important performances on *Sanford and Son*, perfectly negotiating her radical ambiguity.[89] In this episode, Fred's feathers get ruffled when an old friend named "Big Money Grip" from St. Louis comes to town claiming to be Lamont's real father, stating that he and Elizabeth had an affair during his weekend pass in the army.

The phrase itself, "Mama's Baby, Papa's Maybe," is used as a title drop from Fred's friend Grady in the episode. The phrase is a term colloquially familiar to Black communities. Prior to the days of DNA testing, it was basically impossible to verify a child's paternity. The only evidence besides the word of the mother was the child's physical attributes. In Hortense Spillers's article of the same name, "Mama's Baby, Papa's Maybe: An American Grammar Book," she describes Black women as "marked" by this country and individuals whose existence describes a locus of confounded identities.[90] Black women have largely been the victims of these markings by their position in the system of patriarchy and race. This historical pain delivered to Black women's bodies (violent physical, emotional, and visual abuse) is often regarded as staid matters in society.[91] Black women have largely been unable to define themselves and speak for themselves, and in this case of Black motherhood, specifically in this *Sanford and Son* episode, the paternity of their children and even the presence of a father are often given much more attention or importance. Page, off-screen, exists as a breaker of these confounded identities, while on-screen as Aunt Esther, although her character retracts from the norm of Black women's representation, she still finds difficulty in defining and speaking for herself at the mercy of a male-centric space (and writer's room).

Although Elizabeth had passed away many years prior, Fred argues against her accusations of an affair. Thus, the female, matriarch, and maternal line are left defenseless and faulted by the show's men. Throughout the episode, as the men argue over Lamont's paternity, Fred succumbs to his fears and doubts. As a man who has played sole parent to Lamont for so long, he becomes fearful of losing him. Looking at baby pictures of Lamont while Fred's friend Grady comments, "Wow he looks just like you, Grip!" and seeing the present resemblance of Lamont and Grip (both darker skinned with full heads of hair, while Fred is lighter skinned and balding), Fred slowly loses faith that Lamont is, in fact, his son. These actions lead him to question Elizabeth, his beloved wife, whose name and body are now sites of attack, yelling to the sky questioning her character and her virtue. Even in her death, her bodily actions are up to scrutiny by men, and she has no opportunity to defend herself. Questioning the virtue and fidelity of his dead wife, Fred calls upon his often nemesis, Aunt Esther, in his search for the truth amid these allegations that Lamont might not be his son. As the only woman in the episode, Aunt Esther is the only person to defend Elizabeth. Once questioned by Fred, Aunt Esther takes extreme offense to the claim and is ready to battle in her sister's honor.

ESTHER: Fred Sanford, you gotta be ashamed to even let something like that come out of your heathenous mouth. My baby sister was as pure as the driven snow!

FRED: Yeah, but who was doing the driving? (*Crowd roars in laughter.*)

ESTHER: Elizabeth was faithful to you, until the day she died! Only someone with a foul mouth and a foul mind could come up with such a foul idea! Fred Sanford, you're foul!

This exchange between the two marks Aunt Esther as the only line of defense of not only her sister but to the virtue of Black womanhood. With Fred trying to lighten the situation with jokes, Aunt Esther responds assertively and confidently, talking down to Fred and the claims he is making. Casting shame on Fred for making such claims against his own wife, Aunt Esther takes control of the scene and changes the narrative of the men shaming Elizabeth. Only after Aunt Esther's rant is Fred's faith restored in his deceased wife's fidelity. When Grip enters the room, he remembers Aunt Esther from their adolescence, so they begin to talk and reminisce until Fred tells him to tell Aunt Esther of the claim he is making. As Grip confidently states "Lamont Sanford is my son," Aunt Esther comes out of her Holy Roller persona and into her stand-up identity of LaWanda, stands to strike, and yells, "What did you say, Nigga?!" The only time in the series where Aunt Esther has such an intense reaction and uses the n-word, the live off-screen audience is in an uproar of claps and laughter as Aunt Esther asks Fred to join her in "beating the Hell out of him."

With Grip still believing that Lamont is his son, he confronts Lamont and tells him to make a choice. In a heartfelt moment, Lamont declares to Fred that he's the only father that he ever knew, and that's how it's forever going to be. This short moment of emotion (which caused tears from Fred and Aunt Esther) is quickly taken back to comedy when Lamont says, "Now, Grip, if you are my father, that was between you and my mother. I ain't got nothing to do with that!" In the conclusion of the episode, Aunt Esther's morally upright image is deflated when it is revealed that in her youth, Grip had sneaked into *her* room and had sex with her, mistaking her for Elizabeth in the dark. A grossly embarrassed Aunt Esther storms off the scene, praying, "He who is without sin among you, let him cast the first stone!" Evident here, the show signals the radical ambiguity of LaWanda Page.

This episode works to show not only the powerful force of Aunt Esther's presence in the show but also the necessity of her character in defense of Black women, physically and spiritually. Aunt Esther puts her body on the line in defense of her sister while her own bodily actions end up being called into question. The introduction of Black writers invested in these stories—but more importantly, the embodiment of Elizabeth's spirit, the physical presence of Lynn Hamilton as Donna, and the radical ambiguity of the "Queen of Comedy" LaWanda Page as Aunt Esther—solidified ground for the ways in which Black women had to hustle in efforts to be employed and stay relevant in popular culture and the television industry. The radical ambiguity of these representations makes it clear how racial and gender politics must be negotiated outside of the televisual space. Page's work on *Sanford and Son* lasted past the show's tenure as she was able to revive her role as Aunt Esther in the show's spin-off *The Sanford Arms* (Sept. 16–Oct. 14, 1977) as a recurring character. Although the show was short-lived, it marks an instance in which Black women's labor was acknowledged and they were given their due, paving a way for future Black leading women in television comedy. Unfortunately, often as the result of sacrifices other Black artists had to endure.

Given Their Due: Dissent and Protests on *Sanford and Son*

In a post–civil rights era so heavily influenced by electoral politics, community building, activism, and self-determination, it is important to address how dissent and protest, as forms of hustle economics, surfaced within the production of television. Through audience pressure and the hiring of new writers, Tandem eventually utilized *Sanford and Son* episodes to focus on many popular Black issues, ranging from housing policies to critiques of local political elections. These episodes emphasize local issues significant to urban Black communities. While political and social critiques existed as forms of protest on-screen, Black artists' dissent toward white executives can be seen through Redd Foxx's public opposition and protest with Tandem and challenging NBC at large. These protests are forms of resistance that seek to bring about social change by influencing the knowledge, attitudes, and behaviors of the public or the policies of an organization or institution. Whether through critiquing local housing policy on-screen or actors expressing their discontent off-screen, *Sanford and Son* was often a site of controversial dialogue and resistance. As the show's star, Redd Foxx used his agency to resist the Tandem executives in efforts to hustle for a more equitable salary and working conditions to his white counterparts and to redeem/negotiate the Black image on television. To reiterate, hustle economics are racialized informal economies that include, but are not limited to, under-the-table deals, scheming, gambling, blackmail, contractual disagreements, negotiations, favors, and so on. Here, for instance, Foxx had to use creative negotiation strategies in his battle for a higher salary, writer's credit, and a production stake in *Sanford and Son*. In direct opposition to Tandem executives and NBC, Redd Foxx risked his star role to fight for Black people's rights of self-expression through acting and writing, and for his own advancement.

"Niggas Don't Say That!"

Before risking his star role, Foxx helped bring *Sanford and Son* to the number two spot in the Nielsen ratings following the show's second season. This led Foxx to reaffirm how important Black writers are on the show in his discussions with showrunner and executive producer Aaron Ruben. "Aaron," Foxx said, "we got so high up there in the ratings because you finally cuttin' them Caucasian lines outta the scripts. Can't blame you though, after all, you only been a nigger for six months."[92] Here, it is evident that Foxx felt that merely revising scripts from *Steptoe and Son* (*Sanford and Son*'s British predecessor), as Ruben did for the entire first season, was preventing the show from grappling with its cultural and racial specificity. *New York Times* writer Eugenia Collier supports this claim when she states, "To begin with, the show [*Sanford and Son*] is not based upon Black realities but upon a British TV series, *Steptoe and Son*. Now, you simply cannot substitute Black characters for white, sprinkle around a little Black English, and think you have a Black show. For in spite of Redd Foxx's jokes and Demond Wilson's Black beauty, *Sanford and Son* remains white to the core."[93] In an interview with former showrunner (seasons 3–6) and coexecutive producer of *Sanford and Son*, Saul Turteltaub, he explains some of the struggles he was forced to contend with upon taking this position after Aaron Ruben was fired. He recalls with great clarity a conversation that he had with *Sanford and Son* costars, actors Redd Foxx and Demond Wilson, while at a table read for an upcoming episode:

FOXX TO TURTELTAUB: "Hey, Turtle, what's this line right here? Niggas wouldn't say that!"

WILSON TO FOXX: "I would say this."

FOXX: "Well, you not a real Nigga."[94]

This negotiation with scriptwriting was frequent with not only the actors but also much of the audience of the show. With only white writers in the early seasons of *Sanford and Son*, the episodes lacked a Black cultural perspective relating to its characters. Tandem addressed these concerns with the hiring of many Black male writers, such as comedians Paul Mooney and Richard Pryor and former theater writer Ilunga Adell (sometimes credited as Adell Stevenson). As media scholar Christine Acham notes, with the hiring of Black writers, "the language of the scripts began to reflect a contemporary understanding of urban Black America. There were everyday references to the concerns of living in inner-city communities, such as problems with the police, lack of job opportunities, and racism."[95] These new hires led to episodes strikingly different in tone and language when Black writers were credited. These episodes served as examples of the writers using their agency to negotiate narratives of Black protest. Whether through Ilunga Adell's "Lamont Goes African," where Lamont educates himself in Afrocentric thought, garb, and even casts away his "slave name," or through Paul Mooney's "Fred Sanford, Legal Eagle," where Fred and his Black contemporaries must contend with the judicial system, the introduction of more Black writers helped imagine new Black television possibility.[96] This new way Black writers used *Sanford and Son* to address the temporal social and political climate kept the ratings high and was soon witnessed through multiple episodes, which were written by Black and white writers alike. Episodes like "Fred the Activist" clearly address this new direction of *Sanford and Son* writers. Angered by the age discrimination policy of a local electronics store, Fred rallies a troop of "Gray Foxes" and leads the charge to change the policy.[97] With a clear nod to the revolutionary practices of the Black Panther Party, this put front and center the activist fights against ageism in business, effectively putting large-scale social issues on-screen via the sitcom.

Although we as the audience may see the characters on *Sanford and Son* in various protests and negotiations on-screen, the same can't be said for all the actors off-screen in their dealings with Tandem. For instance, off-screen, costar Demond Wilson, who often portrays Lamont Sanford as an agent for social and political change in multiple episodes, chose to distance himself from rocking the boat at the production level. Saul Turteltaub even commented that "no one on set really got along with Demond other than in a business sense—which is all he cared for."[98] In a one-on-one interview with Wilson, a writer for *TV Guide* determined that Wilson is a great guy, works well with others, and keeps his "nose clean" of situations he is not a part of.[99] Wilson sees his involvement with *Sanford and Son* as first and foremost a business and playing the role that is written for him. Although he often chose to distance himself from production conflict, that in itself is a practice of hustle economics as he did what he felt was best to remain employed. In Wilson's view, it isn't his role as a professional to take sides in such disputes. On the matter, Wilson commented, "I don't take any action in terms of rebelling until the right moment. Like when it's time to renegotiate contracts."[100] Wilson's sentiments later ring true when Redd Foxx departs NBC (and *Sanford and Son*) after the show's sixth season, leaving Wilson to no longer be second banana in the series. Set to appear as the sole lead in the spin-off *Sanford Arms* (1977), Wilson ultimately departs when NBC refuses to meet his salary demands.[101] In contrast, throughout the tenure of *Sanford and Son*, Foxx continuously practiced various modes of hustle economics, putting his own career at stake to battle the executives at Tandem and NBC head-on.

"Trouble in Paradise"

Toward the end of the third season, *Sanford and Son* was still enjoying its success, maintaining the number three spot in the Nielsen ratings between 1973 and 1974.[102] When it came time to reevaluate contract specifics, Foxx walked out on the show midseason in protest. Written immediately after the third season, Bill Davidson's "Trouble in Paradise" was *TV Guide*'s feature article that focused specifically on the issues that Norman Lear and Bud Yorkin faced with the stars of their three major Tandem shows—Foxx of *Sanford and Son*, Carroll O'Connor of *All in the Family*, and Bill Macy of *Maude*, which explains the guide's cover art featuring caricatures of the stars defacing a portrait of Norman Lear into the devil.[103] The article paints Lear as a tyrant over Tandem and hints at the possible end to his thirty-five-year partnership with Yorkin. As the chief executive producer over *Sanford and Son*, Yorkin was asked to comment on Foxx and the recent debacle around him leaving the show. Yorkin states, "Redd Foxx's people came in and said Redd couldn't work in our NBC rehearsal hall anymore. It has no windows and Redd, they said, is claustrophobic. I said that's ridiculous, none of the NBC rehearsal halls have windows."[104] After negotiating with Foxx and his agents, Tandem offered him a hotel with floor-to-ceiling windows to look through, and after a week there, Foxx could no longer stand all the people looking at him through the windows, so he conceded back to the windowless halls of NBC.[105]

Leaving the series for these seemingly fickle reasons, the show was forced to find a way to end the third season without its star. From season 3 episode 19 ("Lamont Goes Karate") to the finale (episode 24, "Hello Cousin Emma, Goodbye Cousin Emma"), Whitman Mayo, a recurring cast member who played Fred's best friend Grady, took Foxx's place and moved into the junkyard with Lamont. Mayo showed tremendous grace under the pressure of being thrown into the top spot. When asked about this predicament, Mayo stated that "nobody could ever replace Redd ... but I'm doing this best I can under the circumstances."[106] Putting this article in conversation with the actual show, writers were frantically revising scripts, writing Foxx out of the action on the pretense that Fred Sanford had gone to St. Louis for a relative's funeral.

Various newspaper articles and archival materials reveal that Foxx's pretense of walking out of the show in disagreement was much deeper than a rehearsal hall change. Foxx's walkout from his hit show was initially attributed to various health concerns, yet according to a writer of the *Chicago Tribune*, Foxx's complaints of being too ill to work were a lie. In addition, another journalist suggested that although he was drawing around $25,000 per episode of *Sanford and Son*, Foxx frankly admitted that he wanted $1 more than any NBC star has ever been paid.[107] With Foxx at the helm of the most profitable NBC show of this period and the second most of Tandem Productions (the first being *All in the Family* on CBS), his ask for a salary that reflects this is not farfetched. However, Bud Yorkin received many letters from viewers that felt otherwise. In fact, in Tandem Productions' interoffice correspondence, Yorkin even comments, "Mail is running in favor of us forgetting about Foxx 8 to 1," in essence ignoring Foxx's demands and writing him out of *Sanford and Son* completely.[108] These conflicting accounts seem to draw a conclusion that although Foxx's walkout was initially under false pretenses, once his true goals were made public, Yorkin and Tandem attempted to save face by writing *Sanford and Son* successfully without Foxx's presence.

Fan mail sent to Tandem after Foxx's strike was marked by Tandem office assistants as "pro-Grady" (the character portrayed by Whitman Mayo) or "pro–Redd Foxx," given the content of whether the letter was against or in support of Foxx's strike.[109] The letters listed "pro-Grady" speak largely to the success of Whitman Mayo and his newfound stardom as the show's lead in Foxx's absence. These letters make comments like "*Sanford and Son* is better than ever with Mayo;" "Foxx is too raunchy, Foxx is a dirty old man;" "we plan to boycott the show if Foxx returns;" and that Mayo's humor is much cleaner and respectable. A writer even commented, "Foxx is holding Yorkin up for an egotistical salary increase. I'm really boiled to think that this foul-mouthed egotistical jerk may ever be seen on TV again!"[110] These letters that are "pro-Grady" are in fact anti-Foxx in their writing, tone, and content. Each "pro-Grady" letter seems to mention Grady's respectability—how tame he is, his calm, safety, and his overall less aggressive humor—in essence, he is a more manageable Black man and actor. As *Sanford and Son* exists as a Black sitcom through its language and cultural specificity, its popularity, like most sitcoms during the network era, undoubtedly rests on its pure comedy (or pure sitcom) appeal to a universal (or white) audience.[111] The safeness that this universal white audience picked up on in Mayo's comedy as Grady, in contrast to the relentlessly aggressive Black voice of Foxx, is useful in understanding whom prime-time television is created for, no matter the cast's racial makeup. This assurance of Mayo's comedic tone ultimately leads to his own spin-off, *Grady* (1975–1976), which proves to be unsuccessful due to its pure comedic form without the cultural depth that exists in *Sanford and Son*. One specific letter from a disgruntled viewer addressed to Norman Lear suggests that Lear has too many Black people in his programs. This letter deserves to be quoted at length here: "Redd Foxx, you took from out of the gutter with his foul mouth, what does he do like all of them, thinks he deserves more money, he never had it so good as now. Don't give in to him, he is not that good, you always can find a new one. Please no more Blacks, the more you do for them, the more they want."[112]

Although this letter is blatantly prejudiced, it points to an existing viewership's perspective on Black actors fighting for what they deserve. The letters repeatedly attack Foxx's character and identity outside of the show but seem to leave the matter of his impact on television at large and his demonstrated reasons for his salary increase ignored. This letter further highlights the need for Black people to serve in production as well as acting roles in this age of television in order to debunk the idea that white executives are doing favors for their Black artists and that the Black artists must silently abide by whatever conditions they are dealt. The Black actors and writers work to visualize a Black authenticity on-screen, yet they are scarcely given their due.

Foxx himself, in an interview on the *Mike Douglas Show*, later denied the reports of illnesses as well as walking out for monetary gain.[113] Foxx's disappearance from his TV series, he claimed, was a protest on behalf of all Black entertainers.[114] Although his needs for a less physically demanding distance from his dressing room to rehearsal facilities are true, Foxx admitted that money was not the issue in his walkout but instead the dignity of Blacks in the series. In order to code his true intentions for walking off the show, Foxx resorted to misinformation and negotiation as a method of hustling for the greater good of Black artists in television at large.

In his protest, Foxx's list of demands included more control over the *Sanford and Son* scripts. Foxx comments in the interview that although he occasionally changes dialogue, puts things into the show, and takes things out, he wants more to say in future shows if he is to return to the series in its fourth season. He admits above all that "[*Sanford and Son*] could not honestly be reflective of Black community life because everything takes place in a junkyard," and his greater role in the writing and development process can work to be more reflective of the reality of Black life he seeks to see.[115]

Upon the knowledge of Foxx's true intentions in his strike against NBC and Tandem, many letters received were labeled "pro–Redd Foxx." These letters supported Foxx in asking for more money, mentioned Black mistreatment at every level in America, demanded that Foxx deserved more respect, and even lamented that *Sanford and Son* is failing because it has lost its backbone—Redd Foxx.[116] The majority of these letters of support seem, given the diction and message, to be from members of Black communities standing in solidarity with Foxx. One particular fan, "pro–Redd Foxx," exclaims in her letter that Redd has loads of support in his corner and that "he is too much of a man to allow such a caricature of his Blackness and his manhood to stream all over this country!! Do your thing, Redd!! Try to get yourself together NBC!"[117] Although such expressions of support were few and far between, it is important to see here that members of Black communities can identify with Foxx's distaste for the show's direction and respect him for what he risks, so they join him in calling Tandem and NBC to task. Redd Foxx's true mission of his strike inspired collective activism among his fans and supporters. In a letter addressed to Bud Yorkin, a community organization called the "Friends of Fred Sanford" expressed that they were actively campaigning for the return of Redd Foxx to *Sanford and Son* and were contacting the show's national sponsors in order to get the network's attention. To quote further, "The producer and writers used white perspectives to write a Black show.... Lamont and Grady are doing irreparable damage to the strong Black character of Redd Foxx (Fred Sanford) in the past as well as demonstrating 'Uncle Tom' behavior in that they have chosen to continue to perform instead of supporting Mr. Foxx and halting all filming until a satisfactory arrangement was reached."[118]

At the end of the letter, the "Friends of Fred Sanford" solicited support from other Black media individuals and groups such as Tony Brown of the

Black public affairs program *Black Journal* (1968–1970), Black Efforts for Soul in TV (BEST), Black newspapers, and magazines asking them to also send letters in support of Foxx.[119] Although initiated for numerous reasons, Foxx's strike against NBC and Tandem was above all to take a stand and advocate for his voice to be heard not only on-screen as Fred Sanford but as Redd Foxx behind the scenes. This strike is yet another example of hustle economics as Foxx had to resort to informal methods, misinformation, and walking out and risking economic precarity in order to bring relevancy, authenticity, and a more robust depiction of Black life to television's imagination. Albeit met with strife and backlash, Foxx's actions inspired a movement of Black artists standing up for themselves and the agency they have earned through their stardom.

Amid his fight with Tandem and NBC, in a conversation with *JET Magazine*, Foxx calls on Black support to win this battle.[120] In the article, Foxx makes clear that in addition to more money per episode, he wants a true economic stake in the show so that he can make money from it long after it goes off the air. Foxx states in length,

> I want some money now because I deserve it now. And when I'm gone, I want my family to have 25 percent of something rather than 100 percent of nothing. I just want one-fourth of myself to own. If I can't have one-fourth of me, then why am I living. . . . I'm a man and my manhood demands that I own a piece of myself and not let them own all of me. . . . If the script ain't right for Blacks, if the wardrobe ain't right for Blacks, if the money ain't right for Blacks, then I don't want no parts of the show. If there are any Blacks who read *JET* and think I'm right, I want *JET* to send me the letters so I can forward them to NBC.[121]

In his address to *JET*, it is clear that above all, Foxx's hustle economics has multiple goals in mind: he is fighting for his own humanity and what he believes best serves all Black people as audiences and artists. As an auteur whose talents are responsible for the show's success, he firmly believes that he deserves a contractual ownership in the show's creation and should be credited as such. A source close to Foxx claimed that after the departure of Flip Wilson from television and other Black-oriented shows, "Redd represents the only leverage left for Blacks to force some real economic gains."[122] Through the contention with Tandem and NBC, Foxx sought a 25 percent ownership stake in the series, and Tandem Productions fought back with a $10 million lawsuit. The dispute was resolved in June of 1974, with Foxx receiving $25,000 per episode, plus 25 percent of the producers' net profits.[123]

Upon the start of the fourth season, Foxx came back to *Sanford and Son*, bringing the show from a number three position in the Nielsen ratings to a number two in the 1974–1975 year.[124] Foxx's strike led to the firing of previous executive producer and showrunner Aaron Ruben and the promotion of Saul Turteltaub and Bernie Orenstein as the coexecutive producers and showrunners. Turteltaub and Orenstein understood that there was no show without Redd and that his presence was integral to its success and worked to always support him in whatever gripes he had moving forward.[125] Later in Foxx's *JET Magazine* address, he comments that "I also want some credit for the writing which I've been doing. I've had to change the script many times to make Black folks talk like Black folks and not like niggers in slavery. I want the screen credits to give credit to the producer but add 'in association with Redd Foxx, Inc.'"[126] In response to the demand, the strike also led to Foxx's future credits as a story consultant on the show as well as the credited writer for two episodes, "The Masquerade Party" and "Sergeant Gork."[127] Equally important, Foxx's dissent had effects on his costars. Demond Wilson acknowledged that it is "Redd's show," and as his partner on the show, he supports the decisions that drew Redd to step away.[128] Wilson saw tremendous value in the show that without Redd wouldn't be what it is. He saw *Sanford and Son* as a real image of Blacks countering images seen in things such as blaxploitation films. Wilson believed that these films glamorized crime to Black and Chicano kids who are stuck without any real future and that crime is their only way out.[129] Wilson saw the value in Foxx's protest but at arm's length.

Finally, through Foxx's dissent, Whitman Mayo became a star in his own right. Having to step into the star role won Mayo national attention, leading to NBC producing an unsuccessful spin-off of *Sanford and Son*, *Grady* (1975–1976). Through a *JET Magazine* interview with Mayo regarding his new series, it's clear that although Mayo stepped into the starring role upon Foxx's strike, there was no bad blood between them and that the two remained friends and supported each other. The *JET* interview states, "One of the biggest fans of the new show is Redd Foxx, who not only shares screen credit as its creator but owns a reported 25 percent of the series."[130] With fan letters that were "pro-Grady" and "pro–Redd Foxx," audiences inherently pitted the two Black men against each other when in reality, the fight was between the forces of actor/artist and executive—Black and white. Through these actions of unrest at the site of *Sanford and Son*, Foxx engaged with hustle economics and put his career on the line to negotiate a salary and working space equitable to his contributions at Tandem. Lear and Yorkin's freshman entry into the Black sitcom category faced many challenges and successes throughout its run. *Sanford and Son* put front and center the economic disadvantages of Black communities in America through the hiring of Black writers, and the show also witnessed the slow entry of Black women comedians into the mainstream. All these transformative acts in the television industry were buttressed by the hustle economics of Redd Foxx as the leading man in advocating for change. His actions not only drew national attention to Black actors sacrificing themselves for the larger struggle of identification in television but also created other avenues of Black performance and activism at the Tandem factory of television production.

3

Good Times

"Keeping Your Head above Water"

In this chapter, I discuss television's first Black "nuclear family" on the prime-time sitcom, *Good Times* (1974–1979). This program consistently displays the various, often comical and dysfunctional but always relevant, modes of resilience utilized by the Black working class. These varying practices of hustle economics used by the characters to "keep their head above water" are a reflection of the tireless off-screen negotiations, agency, hustle, and resilience of *Good Times*' Black artists. This chapter focuses on three areas of hustle economics: (1) space and place and specifically how hustle economics is practiced in housing projects, as Chicago's North Side is used on this show to foreground Black life; (2) actress and star Esther Rolle's ascension to prime time and her role as an agent of change in negotiating what she calls a "complete Black family"; (3) and finally, costar John Amos's and cocreator Eric Monte's protests against the creative directions of Lear and Yorkin that eventually led to their departure from the series and blacklisting. Analyses of particular episodes, production documents, trade press, contract negotiations, and protests make clear the hustle economics that took place at

Tandem Productions in order for Black artists to redeem the imagery of the Black family through *Good Times*.

The theme song of each *Good Times* production rehearsed for viewers the plights that would be covered in episode plotlines. Each line in the upbeat theme song describes the intricacies of working-class public housing or "project" life that many Black families in urban areas encountered in the 1970s.

Not gettin' hassled, not gettin' hustled
Keepin' your head above water
Making a way when you can
Temporary layoffs
Good Times . . .[1]

"Keepin' your head above water" (i.e., staying afloat during tough times, especially financial ones) is in line with the culture of hustle economics that the Evans family practiced on-screen. From the *Good Times* setting and attire, to how they dealt with financial crises on-screen, Tandem narrated various modes of the Evans' "keeping their heads above water," some relatable and some damaging (due to Tandem's problematic depiction of them) to the reality of Black life in the ghettos of project housing. Hustle economics is not simply the way in which Black people must resort to informal networks and economies to make ends meet but also the space and place that these economies are lived.

Space and Place

There is a rich power in the concept of space and place. However, as urban landscape theorist Dolores Hayden notes, "Social scientists have frequently avoided 'place' as a concept, and thus have sidetracked the sensory, aesthetic, and environmental components of the urbanized world in favor of more quantifiable research with fewer epistemological problems."[2] But I believe that the process that transforms and creates a place demands more analysis because a place is a source of identification and memory. According to Courtney R. Baker, "Visual culture of the 1970s offered various images of the home as a crucial location for Black self-knowledge that was nevertheless frequently under threat and in need of protection."[3] *Good Times* is fictionally set at the Cabrini-Green Homes, a former Chicago Housing Authority public housing project on the Near North Side of Chicago, Illinois. Across various popular culture platforms, Cabrini-Green has sustained an identity and memory as an enclave for the Black poor hustling to survive. Whether through the coming-of-age drama *Cooley High* (Michael Schultz, 1975) or the horrors of *Candyman* (Bernard Rose 1992, Nia DaCosta 2021), Cabrini-Green has been used in media productions as an ever-evolving character and as a space/place that is central to Black urban survival. As Hayden suggests, "If place does provide an overload of possible meanings for the researcher, it is place's very same assault on all ways of knowing (sight, sound, smell, touch, and taste) that makes it powerful as a source of memory."[4] Whether through the built environment of the *Good Times* set or through the actual Cabrini-Green Homes that it is based on, space and place create a culture and identity in an urban landscape that is subject to viewer identification.

According to Norman Lear, *Good Times* producers invited Black audiences more frequently to tapings: at their maximum, they made up 60–80 percent of the audience.[5] With *Good Times*, Lear claims that "Black audiences gave to the show the way that they give to preachers, as they fully embraced their emotions in the live tapings."[6] To Lear, that was the greatest experience in working on *Good Times*—seeing a Black audience give full voice to seeing themselves on set.[7] But how exactly are they seeing themselves? What is rarely discussed is actually how Lear, Yorkin, and Tandem Productions handled the production of this Black space in the housing projects and how they utilized *Good Times* as the symbol of life in this space and place. The choice of setting for *Good Times* is integral to understanding the show's approach to Black urban and working-class communities in the 1970s. Housing projects, of course, are government-owned properties largely rented to the poor and underserved, such as the Evans family in *Good Times*.

Despite the critical acclaim from television reviewers, critics, and audiences, *Good Times* had the potential to vitiate its art if it failed to remain sensitive to housing projects' political history and its community members' socioeconomic realities. As Soyini Madison puts it, "Entering a public sphere enlivens scrutiny, enlarges responsibility, and cracks open into plain sight hidden wrongs."[8] When using a public space for the sake of art, it is important to have a knowledge of the history and culture of that space and place so as to not reflect the space counter to its reality. Television writer, producer, and scholar Felicia Henderson notes that in the 1990s, producers of the FOX Black-cast sitcom *South Central* went to South Central Los Angeles to organize an ethnographic study of the community and its inhabitants to research material for scripts on single mothers and their children.[9]

Although twenty years earlier, the CBS network did send crews to the Cabrini-Green Homes in Chicago for the authenticity of the show, the task of connecting with poor Black communities was largely left to the show's stars.[10] CBS's parachute authenticity of simply dropping in and then leaving makes space for misinterpretation of project housing living conditions, different from FOX's producers doing ethnographic studies of their focused space and place twenty years later.

Instead of relying on the production hierarchy to embody the lived experience of public housing, the stars of *Good Times*, Esther Rolle and John Amos, circumvented the network's actions and took it upon themselves to initiate additional trips to housing projects to connect with the community they portrayed on-screen. In an *Ebony Magazine* article covering the stars' visits to Cabrini-Green, Esther Rolle comments that she wants *Good Times* to be "a show of quality, rather than doing a pure comedy."[11] Here, I believe Rolle is saying that a quality show depends on realism, so visiting the space and place in which their show is framed around is essential to that realism. This statement was coupled with a picture of Rolle in Chicago, where she visited Cabrini-Green, talked to its residents, and engaged with the neighborhood children.[12] In addition, in a letter from the Atlanta, Georgia, City-Wide Advisory Council on Public Housing, Inc., Chairperson Lilla Capers thanks CBS's vice president of programming (Perry Lafferty) for John Amos's presence in Atlanta.[13] As their guest of honor on Public Housing Day, July 26, 1975, Amos was presented with awards declaring him head of the household of public housing's First Family, an honorary citizen of the City of Atlanta, and an honorary tenant of public housing. With this letter, it is clear that some public housing representatives across the nation valued and appreciated the representation of low-income housing and families as seen on *Good Times*. This program allowed Lilla Capers and her community to see themselves on-screen.

After the breakout success of Tandem's crown jewel, *All in the Family*, the company worked their CBS television shows through the production offices in the upper levels of Hollywood's Television City. It is critical to note the circumstances and space in which these sitcoms were produced. Citing media scholar Lynn Spigel and her analysis on the rise of network television, it is understood that "television is not just programs, but also trademarks, advertisements, credit sequences, and station graphics."[14] The Television City soundstages became sites in which (through fantasy and staging) a production places its viewers in worlds outside of Hollywood. For example, *Good Times*, televised live in Hollywood, imagines its audience in the Evans'

FIG. 3.1 Opening shot, *Good Times*.

home in the projects on the North Side of Chicago, Illinois. Like almost all of the Tandem sitcoms, the opening credits consist of a flyover opening to establish the city in which the show takes place.

The opening credits of *Good Times* begin with long shots of Chicago at large, then to the North Side of Chicago with children playing in the street, to the outside of the Cabrini-Green Homes where the Evans family lives, and finally, the opening credits end by zooming in through the window into the domestic space of the Evans' apartment. The Black poor have a deeply rooted history with housing projects such as these across major urban cities in the United States, such as New York, Los Angeles, and Chicago. These projects pack individuals tightly together and represent spaces of immobility.

Ironically, the spaces in which Tandem's Black sitcoms took place are also reflective of the 1960s uprisings by Black communities in major cities (e.g., New York City, Los Angeles, and Chicago).[15] These were highlighted as areas of national concern by President Lyndon B. Johnson in his establishment of the National Advisory Commission on Civil Disorders, also known as the Kerner Commission (1967). This commission sought to find strategies to end the racial uprisings in these various locations across the United States.

The commission suggested that one of the main causes of urban violence and racial uprisings was white racism and that white America bore much of the responsibility for Black rioting and rebellion. In response, the commission's report called for the creation of new jobs and, more importantly here, the construction of new housing to put a stop to de facto segregation and to wipe out the destructive ghetto environment.[16] The report goes further to recommend that government programs provide needed services, including the help of more diverse and sensitive police forces and, most notably, investing billions in housing programs aimed at breaking up residential segregation.[17] Further suggestions included,

- Unless there are sharp changes in the factors influencing Negro settlement patterns within metropolitan areas, there is little doubt that the trend toward Negro majorities will continue.
- Providing employment for the swelling Negro ghetto population will require . . . opening suburban residential areas to Negroes and encouraging them to move closer to industrial centers.
- Cities will have Negro majorities by 1985 and the suburbs ringing them will remain largely all-white unless there are major changes in Negro fertility rates, in migration settlement patterns or public policy.
- We believe that the emphasis of the program should be changed from traditional publicly built slum based high rise projects to smaller units on scattered sites.[18]

Through these points of action, the Kerner Commission called for major shifts in residential areas in the major metropolises throughout the United States. They believed that these changes in desegregating housing would offer access to more industrial jobs and comfortable living spaces, which would, in turn, decrease political angst of the Black working class so often forced to hustle to make ends meet. Moving from the slum-based high-rises to smaller scattered sites would help Black people become engrained in major cities rather than literally stacked on top of one another. Breaking up residential segregation had the potential for transformative societal and socioeconomic change. This report was created as a call to action in shifting racial unrest just seven years before the premiere of *Good Times*, which may suggest that Lear and Yorkin of Tandem Productions considered policy research or residential segregation in their production choices.

In a Massachusetts Institute of Technology newsletter focused on the goals of the Chicago Housing Authority, MIT professor of urban planning

Lawrence Vale explains a major reason why housing projects were so attractive to the working class. Until the mid-twentieth century in Chicago and across the nation, public housing was often "a kind of reward" for steadily employed working-class families who soon left for private housing.[19] While the first decades of projects were built with higher construction standards, a broader range of incomes, and the same white applicants, over time, project housing increasingly became the housing of last resort in many cities. Furthermore, housing projects have also been seen to greatly increase concentrated poverty in a community, leading to several negative externalities.[20] Trends showing an increase in geographic concentration of poverty became evident by the 1970s as upper- and middle-class residents vacated the projects in major U.S. cities.[21] Those in city governments, political organizations, and suburban communities resisted the creation of project housing units in middle- and working-class neighborhoods, leading to the construction of such units around ghetto neighborhoods, which already exhibited signs of poverty.[22] Thus by the 1970s, the urban poor had become concentrated in these high-rises.

Specifically, the notorious Cabrini-Green Homes in Chicago hold a long national symbol of urban blight. According to the *New York Times*, "At its peak, Cabrini-Green was home to 15,000 people, living in mid- and high-rise apartment buildings totaling over 3,607 units."[23] Over the years, crime, gang violence, and neglect created deplorable living conditions for the residents, and the "Cabrini-Green" name became synonymous with the problems associated with public housing in the United States.[24] For Tandem and CBS to frame America's first Black television family in such a space/place speaks to a popular raced-based understanding of a homogeneous Black working-class livelihood.

Sociologist and media scholar Herman Gray categorizes Black sitcoms like *Good Times* as being a part of a "separate but equal" or "pluralist" discourse.[25] In these sitcoms, predominantly Black casts demonstrate that Black families have the same basic problems as white families. However, no matter their class status, the majority of sitcoms about white families (i.e., *All in the Family* and *Maude*) take place in more favorable and safe living conditions within single-family homes. White families also lived in the projects; however, a study of project housing found that project housing has differing effects on the concentration of Black poverty versus white poverty.[26] Project housing's effect on concentrated poverty is doubled for Blacks as compared to whites.[27] *Good Times*, and many other Black sitcoms of this era (such as *Sanford and Son*), recycles the image of the inner-city ghetto. Yet when the Black cocreator and writer of *Good Times* Eric Monte (who in fact based the original plot on his own life growing up in Cabrini-Green) was asked how *Good Times* differed from its Tandem predecessor, Monte made an important point. Speaking on *Sanford and Son*, Monte stated, "Why ol' man Sanford owns his own home, his own business; he's got a credit rating. He's practically middle class. These people own nothing."[28] Together, these two shows (*Sanford and Son* and *Good Times*) made poverty a staple of Black televisual representation in the 1970s. Hence this reproduced image of Black families struggling in the inner city begs the question of historical accuracy. In his article "Racial Order of Suburban Communities: Past, Present, and Future," Bruce Haynes discusses postwar American communities and the shift of suburban lifestyles and inhabitants. He finds that post–World War II America is characterized by the steady growth of the suburban Black middle class. However, looking at media and housing policy, "this growth has been overshadowed by the mischaracterization of the suburbs as conformist and racially homogeneous."[29]

Featuring the Evans in *Good Times* as the Black American family living in the ghetto has the potential to create a fixed image of all Black people stuck in urban ghettos in the postwar United States. Through recycled images similar to *Good Times*, Blacks have become synonymous with inner-city ghettos while whites have been the symbol of home ownership and the suburbs. When television shows do not represent the heterogeneity of Black communities, it has the potential to cast Black folks as invariable or lacking distinction.

Screening Hustle Economics

To develop a greater understanding of the racial space and place of *Good Times*, it is important to look beyond the North Side of Chicago and the Cabrini-Green Homes to the specific built image of the Evans' fictional apartment home. Hustle economics has a particular look that represents Blackness that differs from the visual casting of white counterparts in television production. Throughout the show's run, the audience witnessed the daily lives of the Evans family taking place in the private sphere of their home. Through set design and artistic direction two thousand miles away in Television City, CBS and Tandem created the space of a low-income Chicago project. Therefore, it is crucial to consider the role of production design in *Good Times* as integral to our understanding of the racial framing of the show at large. The mise-en-scène, or "placing on stage," is a catchall term for everything that contributes to the visual presentation and overall look of a production. The mise-en-scène is essential to production as it creates a sense of place for the audience whether they realize it or not. The actors, location, lighting, set design, and so on are all critical mise-en-scène components of setting a sense of place on *Good Times*.

A key figure in the creation of the Evans' space is the sitcom's art director and production designer, Edward Stephenson. A long-term partner of Tandem, Stephenson worked to design the sets for almost all of Lear and Yorkin's productions. In this role, Stephenson was responsible for the entire look of the program. Writing on the practice of production design on television, Terry Byrne believes that "to work successfully the production designer must be capable of originating a style which will identify a particular program in the public mind, from the look of the lighting sets, and costumes to the typefaces used in the opening graphics and closing credits."[30] Watching an episode of *Good Times* in conversation with *All in the Family*, for example, it is clear that the set designs of a working-class family are raced (i.e., inherent differences exist in the construction of a Black vs. a white home setting). The Evans family fits a family of five in a small two-bedroom apartment stacked upon a series of other apartments. Their furniture is minimal, secondhand, and worn; the paint on the walls is bland; and the chipped furniture ranging from browns, yellows, oranges, and the occasional green make their living space rather bleak, even as their clothing brought vibrancy and flavor. Space is cramped in the Evans' home with James and Florida sleeping in the master bedroom, while the two sons, Michael and J.J., share the couch pullout bed. Only the sole daughter, Thelma, has her own room. This setting suggested that the Black working class bears little resemblance to the white working class.

Stephenson's role shaped the visual space of the Black family. His papers and set design sketches for the entire first season of *Good Times* tell a deeper narrative of the racial politics of the show's development and its difficulties in establishing continuity. The first sketch layout of the Evans home describes the drawing as the "Esther Rolle Series, Basic Setting."[31] Notably, Stephenson describes the sketch as the "Interior of the *Black* Apartment"—not yet knowing that they were to be named the Evans family.[32] Although a small detail, this description begs the question of whether the family surname was "Black," or if, in fact, Stephenson's visualization of this home is representative of all "Black" families. Either way, calling the family "Black" indicates the show's racial politics at play in constructing this setting. Along with the

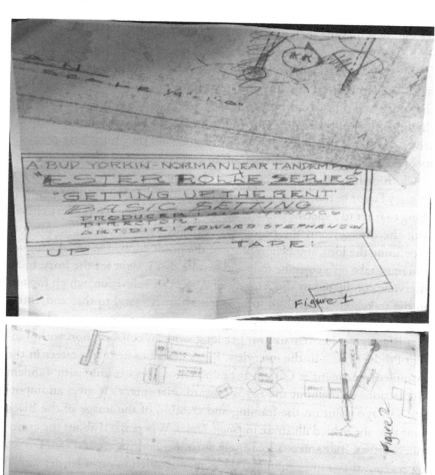

Figure 1

A BUD YORKIN - NORMAN LEAR TANDEM
"ESTER ROLLE SERIES"
"GETTING UP THE RENT"
BASIC SETTING
PRODUCER
DIRECTOR
ART DIR: EDWARD STEPHANSON

Figure 2

LIVING ROOM   DINING AREA   KITCHEN   INT. DEPT

INT. BLACK APT.

FIGS. 3.2 AND 3.3   "Esther Rolle Series" and "The Black Apartment."

setting, building the image of the Black family required particular artistry in the character's acting, line delivery, and especially the costuming. In *Hollywood, USA: From Script to Screen*, Alice Evans Field claims that "clothes must be harmonized to the mood, be it comedy, tragedy, or romance; they must add subtly to the grace of the wearer; and they must enhance the rhythmic flow of the story. Never must they call undue attention to themselves, unless for sharp definition of character, and they must have originality of detail within the certain bounds of good tastes."[33]

Clothing helps define the character of a given person on camera and is a primary factor in the visual process by which the audience decides how it is going to react to a specific person.[34] The costume designer works very closely with the director and the production designer, taking an important role in defining the look and believability of the production. The entire production must take on a costume style and texture that is right for the story. In an interview conducted by the Archive of American Television, which focuses on the stakeholders involved in broadcast history—and to that end, interviews TV legends in all professions—the award-winning costume designer Rita Riggs gives her remarks on her long work in collaboration with Tandem Productions.[35] In the interview, Riggs describes her early career in the costume department at CBS in 1954 and chronicles working with Tandem Productions throughout the 1970s onward. Her interview gives an important vantage point on the framing and creation of the image of the Black poor that she helped illustrate in *Good Times*. When asked about the atmosphere on set, Riggs takes a seemingly uncomfortable pause and states, "Not always fun; they came around to the comedy sometimes in a harder way."[36] Coming around to the comedy in *Good Times* was often difficult for certain stars of the show as the comedy that was written for them did not reflect the ways in which they intended to use their characters in portraying Black life in the projects. This discontent often led to the set being "not always fun" as it consistently drew disputes between actors, writers, and even producers. Whether from issues with narrative content to costuming, where everyone wanted to look their best, the development of this environment was at times met with controversy.

At the beginning of the interview, in comparison to *Sanford and Son*, Riggs describes her costuming experience with *Good Times* as "the best, because everything had to be in an economic range, you wanted it to look real, and washed down, and lived in."[37] In this opening line of the interview, it is established that what is real and believable to audiences of poor Black families are the worn clothes and the story they help illuminate. Riggs essentially styled the imagination of the 1970s Black poor. Describing the palette of the show, Riggs states, "I tried to keep it poor . . . asking myself what can be stylish and fashionable on very little money,"[38] much in line with the previously mentioned sets that Edward Stephenson constructed. Costume detail "often stood, again and again, for the same thing and could be counted on to provide the most basic information about a character for the spectator, that is, it typified."[39] Riggs often chose to dress the lead character Florida (Esther Rolle) in apricots and orange colors to accentuate the warmth and maternal air of her character. Riggs hints that even the sewing machine prop on the set was a part of Florida's costume.[40] The sewing machine helped create the illusion of Florida's hands as never idle. Whether cooking, cleaning, or sewing the children's clothes, the women's work was never done. The patriarch, James Evans Sr., constantly expressed his manhood and control over the household. To make ends meet, James worked odd jobs throughout the day and night, always overworked, underpaid, and stressed. John Amos, who played older than he actually was for the role of James Evans, was often clothed in tattered and worn apparel to appear as being overworked. However, his costume was uniquely used at times to push the narrative story line in often exaggerated ways for the sake of comedy. For instance, in "Too Old Blues," when James is on his way to an important job interview, he rids himself of his usual plaid Pendleton shirt, khakis, and boots and throws on an olive-green suit. Wearing what Florida calls his "going to a funeral shirt," to the comedic pleasure of the audience, James laughs and responds, "Why not?! Today I'm burying poverty!"[41] Here, it is apparent that the clothing choice works to advance the narrative of a poverty-stricken man attempting to "look the part" in order to gain employment. Unfortunately, James doesn't receive the job, so the next day, his plaid and khakis are put back into the daily rotation, a fixed identity that the audience is accustomed to.

J.J., the Evans' oldest child, was often written as the comic relief and the constant running gag of the show. Riggs claims, "The most outrageous clothes that I have ever done were for J.J., as he was a walking sight gag."[42] J.J. was often draped in long turtlenecks that defined his lengthy figure, and he often was adorned with a floppy cap atop his head to symbolize his clownish personality. Thelma, the Evans' only daughter, was understated every day in her role as the person who assists her mother with household duties while trying to keep up with her image as a beautiful young woman. Michael, the youngest of the children, was trapped in the spirit of the 1960s militancy of the civil rights movements. Riggs believed Michael's character to be a symbol of "hope of the next generation for Black viewers watching the show, the generation that was going to march."[43] As his character reflected militancy and Black Power, Riggs costumed Michael with clothing from army surplus stores, further adding to the hand-me-down look and feel of the hustle economy that the show illustrates. For example, in the episode "Getting Up the Rent," Michael storms into the Evans' home after playing a game of "Cops vs. Militants" outside.[44] He is angry that his friend kept making Michael the cop when, in actuality, Michael is dressed in a green fatigued army jacket adorned with Black Power pins and Africa patches. Embodying the militaristic spirit of Michael, the costuming here is fitted to the character like a second skin—and relays information to the viewer about a "person" and their "personality" that exists throughout the series.[45]

Last but not least, beaming with beauty and energy, Willona's quick-witted humor acts as a powerful supporter of the Evans family. Described by Riggs as the most difficult character to dress, Riggs sees Willona as the "fashion plate for the ghetto. I don't care what color you are, she had style and we tried to make it look as though it didn't cost very much."[46] Willona personified hustle economics by making the most of what you have to define your self-image because "style doesn't always cost a lot."[47] The costuming helped set the scene and developed the characters in a way that solely their dialogue was unable to do. In framing a poor Black family on television, these production choices were integral in building and popularizing how Black communities in the projects are ever resilient to keep their heads above water. Along with the styling of the stage and the character's attire, the narrative content of *Good Times* episodes worked to further illustrate hustle economics on-screen.

"Getting Up the Rent"

Again, hustle economics are methodical practices utilized by Black people who must resort to informal networks and economies (under-the-table deals, negotiating, scheming, blackmail, favors) to make ends meet, counter to the economic measures that many white people are able to rely on (family networks, union jobs, etc.). Resorting to and practicing these informal economies exist in real life for Black artists working in Hollywood as well as on-screen in the sitcoms they create. These acts of hustle should be read not with a negative connotation but as modes of survival within the confines of racial hegemony. In *Good Times* "Getting Up the Rent," written by the Black writer and cocreator of the show, Eric Monte, the Evans are forced to rush

FIG. 3.4 Costuming on *Good Times*.

and gather rent money, or else they will be evicted at the end of the day. This rush resorts to them considering multiple forms of hustle economics. After coming home from a long night of work, James comes home with only six dollars of payment. James explains that he was paid a lot more, but after they took out "federal withholding taxes, state withholding taxes, unemployment compensation, and state disability insurance," that was all he was left with. James chuckles to himself and says, "If I worked for them a few more hours, I'd end up owing them ten bucks." It is later discovered that James is hired on a case-by-case basis by a good friend of his who informs him about various odd jobs. His unstable employment contributes to his lack of financial stability.

This particular *Good Times* episode considers the culture of Black men in the blue-collar sector. Deidre Royster's research on the disparities between Black and white blue-collar workers in *Race and the Invisible Hand: How White Networks Exclude Black Men from Blue-Collar Jobs* is in conversation with *Good Times* and compels us to think about how television sitcoms highlight these racial disparities regarding socioeconomic status.[48] Royster carries out her own study after observing the apparent predicament of many Black men she had grown up with who have experienced racism and negative life outcomes. Many of these Black men, having a limited education, must train for various types of skilled labor in order to obtain a place in the blue-collar job market. She finds that although they have received adequate training, the ability to obtain and maintain employment is consequently more difficult for Black men than white, blue-collar workers. Royster then focuses her study to discuss the problem of *embeddedness* with regard to job networks. This idea of embeddedness suggests that "personal and institutional contacts may be extremely valuable in connecting workers to employment opportunities, and a lack of useful contacts may hinder many individuals . . . from finding out opportunities and being considered for available positions."[49] Surveying a history of segregated job networks, it is clear how the idea of embeddedness works to create greater racial disparities in the blue-collar job market.

The history of Blacks in America has left them in a position in which they have historically never been "affiliated with well-placed institutions or enmeshed with powerful informal networks."[50] The greater one's network, the greater their opportunity to hear about job openings and promotional opportunities, if that network is reliable and useful. Although the triumphs of the civil rights movement included a greater sense of equal opportunity among Black people, the numbers of employed Black men in blue-collar fields were still unequal to their white counterparts when discussing population percentages of Blacks and whites. These interpersonal and institutional networks that white people are accustomed to have remained before and after civil rights. *Good Times* conforms to this image as the audience sees that James is often led astray by his fellow project dwellers when he is in need of employment or advice. As *Good Times* received critique regarding its portrayal of a Black father struggling to find employment, journalist Carl T. Rowan came to the defense of the show. Rowan believes that what the critics don't seem to know is that in this society, one able-bodied Black out of nine can't even get a job, let alone hold one, and that means a million Black people out of work.[51] *Good Times'* father is tragically "typical" of what the Black male worker faces in America.[52]

Looking further into "Getting Up the Rent," the laborious tasks of a Black blue-collar father and his family being forced to engage with hustle economics in multiple ways are evident. In the episode, when repossession men come to remove the contents of the Evans' home, Michael plays the race card. In an effort of cultural engagement and pity from the repossession men, Michael calls the man a "jive Brotha" and scolds him for putting other brothas out on the street. Here, we see Tandem recycling stories of Black property struggles as this resistance of the repossession men connects to the resistance of Fred Sanford in *Sanford and Son* (chapter 2) when his furniture is being taken. James, realizing that he is left with no other choice, pleads with the repossession men for an extension. They oblige and give him until the end of the day to gather the funds for rent. When granted the extension, the family quickly gathers to discuss methods of getting the money. Here is where various hustle economics come into play. First, J.J. constructs an elaborate department store hustle idea, in which his siblings would faint in the middle of the store to gain sympathy and financial assistance from passersby. Florida admonishes J.J.'s method of "finding money" in this illegal manner. Thus, although relying on hustle economics, *Good Times* supports a specific type of *legal* hustle economics where the children aren't subject to questionable methods. Too prideful and unwilling to take a "handout," James refuses Willona's idea of receiving an emergency loan from the welfare office, so he resorts to his past days as a gambler and heads to the pool hall to hustle money through a couple of rounds of billiards. Still believing that there is a chance, Willona takes Florida to the welfare office where they are denied welfare assistance. Claiming that because James made $100 too much the previous year in his annual income, the welfare system falls short in its design meant for assistance. To her surprise, Florida says, "I didn't know $4,200 was the limit for a family with three kids."

The plot of this *Good Times* episode deals with the family doing whatever they can so that they do not sink deeper into poverty, "making a way when they can" as the theme song suggests. Three instances of hustle economics are illustrated here: first, the reliance on racial oneness to receive a rent extension; second, the plan to lie and scheme at a department store; third, and finally, the act of James heading to the pool hall to hustle the money through a string of pool games. In contrast, Florida and Willona attempt to resort to the formal economy of seeking government assistance through welfare; however, their attempts of gathering funds in legal and formal matters are blocked—forcing them to accept money from the informal routes. Ever resilient, these working-class Black people in the projects may scheme, succumb to desperation, and break the law as a means to attain money and stay afloat, even if just for another day.

Wielding his cue stick in hand, James goes to the pool hall and hustles other pool players for the rent money. This hustle economy of underground gambling speaks to the lengths that the Black working class must go to scratch and survive. Through numerous instances such as these, the Evans family is put to the test throughout the duration of the series. Their agency, resilience, and strength as a family is continuously tested through their woes of living in the projects, feeding themselves, clothing themselves, and getting up the rent. These scenes of engagement with hustle economics, along with those on *Sanford and Son*, add to a developing history of economic instability in Black sitcoms. However, through this instability, Black families are forced to contend with whatever means possible in order to remain in their perpetual state of poverty—just barely making it by. At the helm of all these tests is the matriarch Florida Evans, played by Esther Rolle. The tests of agency and resilience that Rolle had to endure consistently took place while hustling to make a name for herself on-screen with *Good Times* and off the screen with Tandem and CBS.

"Remember, I've Been Black the Longest": Esther Rolle's Hustle at Tandem Productions

In the 1970s, Black women played an important role in publicizing the concerns of Black artists within the television industry—specifically in Black sitcoms. Through interviews and comments in mainstream magazines, Black actresses participated in a culture of resistance by critiquing television's images and the industry's approach to race. Invested in tactics of hustle economics, Black women were forced to negotiate from the bottom up in order to remain employed and have a vested interest in depicting Black people in prime time. This section focuses on Esther Rolle as a force of revolution in television through her role as the supporting character Florida Evans on *Maude* (1972–1978) to the lead on *Good Times* and in her acts of resistance at Tandem Productions in efforts to define herself as a Black woman and defend the image of Black communities. It is important to state here that many of the interviews cited are from *Ebony Magazine*, a monthly magazine written by and for the African American market. To be clear, this source may often have a bias that is written by and for a Black audience, but I believe this source is of serious importance in discussing the woes of Black artists and serves as a space where they can speak freely and with depth. As archival sources reveal little about Black women at Tandem, this section relies heavily on interviews, news coverage, magazines, and textual analyses of particular episodes to create an important narrative that encapsulates Esther Rolle's impact at Tandem Productions and television at large. As an agent of change in 1970s television production, Esther Rolle used her characters in Tandem sitcoms to not only add nuance to the identity of Black womanhood on television but also advocate for more broad perspectives of Black communities.

An *Ebony Magazine* cover story from September 1975 makes clear that a great majority of the *Good Times* cast fought for change in its writing and production.[53] In summary of the article, *Ebony* writer Louie Robinson concluded that the cast wanted changes, including expansion and deepening of the program's characters and plot. Not all of the cast felt this duty to redeem Black images on-screen. For instance, Jimmie Walker (who played J.J.) disassociated himself from talk of significant representations, alienating himself from his television family and quite possibly many Black actors in general. Playing the series' most central comedic role as the quirky teen artist with the signature catchphrase "Dy-no-mite!" Walker understood the stardom this role bestowed upon him and did not see his role as anything but that, a *role*. When inquired about his role as J.J., Walker is quoted in the article stating, "I play it the way I see it for the humor of it. I don't think anybody 20 years from now is going to remember what I said. I am not trying to have my lines etched in some archives or on a wall in some place. . . . I don't think any TV show can put out an image to save people. . . . My advice is, do not follow me. I don't want to be a follower or a leader, just a *doer*."[54]

Yet almost fifty years later, his words are a crucial counter to understanding the labor and hustle that Black actors at Tandem were forced to contend with. Although one image is not going to save an entire people, images are often a reflection of their political and social moment and one must reflect on what that image means, whom it is coming from, and what its ramifications are. Walker's position on Black TV images differs from his costars and their push for better characterizations, particularly Esther Rolle. In direct response to the claims of Walker, Rolle "resents the imagery that says to Black kids that you can make it by standing on a corner saying 'Dynomite!'"[55] The crux of the *Ebony* article covers the continuing battle among the cast members to keep the comedic flavor of the program from becoming so outlandish as to be embarrassing to Black communities. Rolle did not want Walker's humor and "funny little ways cut out," but she thought they had the potential to be real, a happy medium.[56] Ja'Net DuBois, who plays Willona—the witty, eccentric, and loyal friend of the Evans family—pleads for humanity in the cast's representation of this family and community. She loved *Good Times* because it "pays the rent;" however, she challenged producers of the program, claiming that "we [the Black cast] should have a little more to say about what we do because *we* only know how *we* feel."[57] With a white executive producer and majority white male writing staff, DuBois articulated how difficult it was to play the roles that were written for her and her cast. Asking the poignant question, "How can you tell a Black woman how to portray a Black woman when she's been one all her life?"[58] Even as a teenager, BernNadette Stanis (who plays the Evans' only daughter, Thelma) understood the implications of her television role. Since her role was the only teenage Black girl consistently shown on television, Stanis felt certain responsibilities. She claimed, "A lot of young people look up to me. . . . I'm very conscious of that. I want to do the best I can for them."[59] Acknowledging the importance of their representations, these Black actresses are among the first to address how Black women should actually be written.

Although *Good Times'* Black actresses as a whole demonstrated agency in speaking for their own representations, Esther Rolle's efforts in this fight were central. *Good Times* was conceived—even by the show's white producers—as Esther Rolle's show, and her fellow cast members consistently commented that she was not only a phenomenal actor but also the head of the series and the leader of their fight for better representation with production heads. DuBois boldly states, "She [Rolle] fights every week for the characters," and she always put herself up against Lear and other Tandem executives, advocating for a depiction of a Black family that exudes pride.[60] Through Rolle's work, she not only changed the image of Black women on television but also exhibited that Black actors must not simply settle for the roles that are written for them. While she concedes that every Black actor must make their own decisions, she continued to show that she is "more dedicated to doing a show of worth than to doing a funny show," and that every role she takes will have an impact on her community.[61] Rolle had the foresight that each image involuntarily held the burden of representing the race. In an *Ebony* interview, Rolle affirms, "I've always been selective about my roles . . . still am. . . . First of all, I have to like me, and I couldn't like me if I depicted crap that made a Black child hang its head. I feel an obligation to do something that will make him stick his little chest out and say, 'Did you see *that*?!' My goal is to give Black women dignity."[62] With the dual role of actress and advocate, Esther Rolle made clear that she used her platform in a transformative manner. Tired of seeing the oversaturation of Black women as grinning domestics, Rolle utilized her agency in the creation of *Good Times* to bring a new visualization of Black womanhood to the mainstream. Through *Good Times*, Rolle made it her duty to address popular understandings of the matriarchal

Black family and help diversify the televisual image of Black women to one that is deserving of honor and respect.

Until the late 1960s, with *Julia* (1968–1971), the popular characterization of Black women was as domestic workers in often docile and compliant roles, such as those in the radio show and sitcom *Beulah* (1950–1952). These roles as domestics mark a history of what Victoria Sturtevant calls "dissemblance."[63] This term describes the double consciousness and performance of twoness that Black women were forced to take on and put away as necessary for survival and employment, as 80 percent of Black women worked as domestics in the 1930s.[64] Dissemblance, like hustle economics, was a consciously adopted strategy by Black women to play a compliant and docile role in a white household that could effectively protect their true selves from scrutiny.[65] As was true of Hattie McDaniel's acclaimed role as "Mammy" in *Gone with the Wind* (1939), dissemblance as performance was necessary for many Black women to receive a shot in show business. On set, Black women were forced to be compliant, as the role required that they were only able to be their true selves off-screen.

Shortly before Rolle starred as Florida on *Good Times*, the sole image of the Black woman star on television was through Diahann Carroll as Julia in the sitcom *Julia*. Rolle felt as though *Julia* was a step above the grinning domestic and that Black communities were so tired of being inundated with that imagery that they accepted *Julia* as a breath of fresh air amid its drawbacks on Black realism.[66] Carroll herself believed that her role in *Julia* was an "acceptable" image to break down barriers so that Black people could move on from there.[67] This statement is supported by media scholar Aniko Bodroghkozy when she states that throughout the show's run, popular press articles "castigated *Julia* for being extraordinarily out of touch with and silent to the realities of Negro life in the late 1960s."[68] Although *Julia* often functioned as a site of social tension, Diahann Carroll attempted to use the power of her fame to voice her activism on the realities of Black life in America. Christine Acham addresses this power that Black women were able to wield in their images on television (Diahann Carroll in *Julia* and Esther Rolle in *Good Times*) through their engagement with "hidden transcripts," spaces where they voiced their activism off-screen in popular magazines and journals.[69] These various transcripts, in magazines like *Ebony* and *JET*, concluded that Rolle believed it was her responsibility to place a corrective lens over the representation of the Black family, not only for the Black audience but for the large white television audience also. What is important to add here is how this power is translated on-screen and where contentions may have led to certain production decisions on set. Particularly what I'd like to add to the conversation is Rolle's introduction into the mainstream as a domestic like no other.

Through her acting and interviews, Esther Rolle participates in a culture of resistance by critiquing television's images and the industry's approach to race, specifically here, the Black domestic in the sitcom *Maude*. Much of the existing literature on Rolle involves her work as Florida Evans on *Good Times*, but along with that, I also want to bring into the discussion the show where that character came to fruition. Eager to leave her own mark in this system of reconstructing recycled images, Lear approached Rolle with an opportunity that has received scant academic discussion: the role of Maude Findlay's domestic, Florida Evans, on Tandem Production's *Maude*. Lear offered her the character after witnessing Rolle in a Negro Ensemble production in New York. Created and staffed by Black artists who focus on original work and train Black actors in the fundamentals of theater acting, the Negro Ensemble Company sought to invoke an outspoken advocacy of dignity and agency through their art.[70] With Rolle's history in this space, she was coming from a context that did not encourage buffoonery, and her style of portraying Florida reflected that.

Rolle used the opportunity of playing a domestic on *Maude* to lay to rest previous portrayals of the docile and compliant Black maid. As addressed by L. S. Kim, "The importance of looking at the figure of the maid is that she is a recurrent and patterned image of and occupation for women of color, demonstrating a discourse on and revealing the nexus of race, class, and gender hierarchies in American culture."[71] Black women as domestics have taken various forms throughout television history. According to Sturtevant, "The image of the Black domestic as actress further illuminates the extent to which the culture of dissemblance allowed Black women to adopt not a second personality but a role, an act which was divorced, consciously and completely, from their private identity."[72] Though weary of playing a domestic, Rolle knew that her portrayal was simply an act. However, she used her influence to act in this role in a fashion different from her predecessors.

Maude

Bea Arthur as Maude Findlay was the 1970s popular television voice and image of white liberal feminism. The white woman who stands up to her husband rejects the role of the guardian of the hearth, has an abortion, and sees herself as the catalyst to changing many of the social ills of the moment. In response to the domestic worker that Esther Rolle was to play on *Maude*, writer and critic Eugenia Collier believed that portraying Black domestics was simply furthering a white agenda. Rolle wished to complicate that claim. Collier states, "Every Black domestic is an expert on white culture. But whites (most whites) have so seldom recognized the humanity of Black people and have had such a compulsion to rationalize their own inhumanity toward Blacks that an honest and compassionate look at Black culture has been virtually impossible. For this reason, I am convinced that there are very few—if, indeed, any—white writers who can portray Black characters in a realistic and believable manner."[73] In an early episode of the series, "Maude Meets Florida," Maude's politics are taken to task by the Black domestic she attempts to hire, Florida.[74] The episode begins with Maude scrambling to clean her home in preparation for her first meeting with the domestic she is seeking to hire. Maude's daughter (Carol) teases her because Maude's white guilt is a key factor in their inability of hiring a stable domestic.

> CAROL: I suppose we are getting another Black one.
> MAUDE: Well, yes, OK, I did ask for one.
> CAROL: You spoil them. You see Black, and you melt. A Black man says hello, and you say sorry.

Because of her white guilt, Maude believes it is her role to undo/redress histories of bigotry, and that one step toward that is to not make Florida feel "unwelcome" in their home. Upon Florida's entrance, Maude fawns over her, trying to make her comfortable. Rolle uses this moment as Florida Evans to redefine the Black domestic through her quick wit retorts. She uses Maude's fawning to her advantage and jokes with her, claiming her agency in the space of a white home as a Black domestic speaking for herself.

> FLORIDA: The first week is a trial basis to see if this arrangement can work.
> MAUDE: Florida, you're not on trial.
> FLORIDA: I know. You are.

Here, Florida is taking agency in her own decision of whom she chooses to work for, not the decision of her white employers. Obvious to Maude's husband and daughter that Florida simply wants to be there to work and not be berated by Maude's agenda, Maude argues to them that it's her job to change Florida.

> MAUDE: Florida is not your modern Negro. She hasn't found that new sense of
> self-respect and militancy. Let's face it. Florida is your preliberation Southern
> Black. . . . I intend to treat that woman as an equal. To teach her a new sense
> of self-respect.

As her first week progresses, Florida deals with the guilt that Maude continues to throw at her. From insisting that she call her Maude instead of Mrs. Findlay and not allowing Florida to enter and exit through the back door of their home, even when the back door is more convenient. Florida simply complies throughout the first week, even calling Maude the "NAACP." This joke points to yet another moment in which Tandem is addressing its conservative viewership as it allows the viewer to identify with a Black character who not only is distinctively nonpolitical but mocks and makes fun of the white woman for being like the NAACP. When the week draws to a close and Florida announces that she is not returning, Maude is in utter disbelief.

> MAUDE: I have been trying to prove that a Black woman can be just as self-
> respecting and proud as a white woman, but you are too darn dumb to
> know it.
> FLORIDA: And for one week, I have been trying to do my work as a Black woman
> who is just as proud and self-respecting as any white woman, and you are just
> too darn dumb to know that!

Maude then accuses Florida of bigotry and not treating *her* as her equal. Although these words were written for her, Rolle's performance is what crucially stands out in this scene. In standing up to Maude, Florida doesn't break eye contact with her while raising her voice. In fact, Florida holds her head high and moves closer to Maude with each word uttered. She shows that she is neither afraid nor intimidated by Maude's whiteness. With her hands on her hips and chest out, Florida takes control of the scene, leaving Maude speechless as Florida quickly exits the home. Explaining to Carol that she won't be returning, Florida is positioned to realize that it is her duty to construct her own identity to Maude and to educate her on the resilience of Black women specifically, and Black people in general. Here, Rolle frames Florida as preferring tradition, showing a more conservative stance while she chides white liberalism. Rolle also shows that she can be a source of comedy on the show in her conversation with Carol upon her not returning to work for them.

FLORIDA TO CAROL: I keep running into problems with white liberals that just
   won't quit.
CAROL: You're not telling me you rather work for a bigot?
FLORIDA: No, but at least they don't keep trying to change you. They just hate you
   . as you is.

Deciding to stay, Florida leaves Maude with an ultimatum and last bit of
advice regarding her remaining in Maude's employment.

FLORIDA TO MAUDE: You do what you do good and let me do what I do good,
   or that's that.
      (*Maude nods in approval.*) (*As Florida exits through the door*) Going out
   back doors, that's something I do *real* good.

From this opportunity, it's clear that Rolle had the intention of using
every casting choice as her avenue to enact change. This early performance
of Florida Evans was a catalyst in reclaiming the Black domestic and just
how much power they wield within a household. After scoring big as the
maid in *Maude*, Lear asked the writers Michael Evans and Eric Monte, two
young Black men, to create a starring role for her—from there, *Good Times*
was born.[75] With the opportunity for a leading role in her own show, Rolle's
advocacy for what she saw as a more just Black representation was in closer
reach. Before accepting the role, she asks Lear, "Am I going to have some say
about this [show]? Remember, I've been Black the longest."[76] From the start,
Rolle makes clear that she won't attach her name to a program if her voice
isn't heard.

   Esther Rolle, as Florida, played her farewell scene on *Maude*, shock-
ing Maude by announcing that she was quitting. Florida's husband, Henry
(John Amos), had been promoted, and they could afford for her to stay
home, scrub her own floors, and raise her own children.[77] The following Fri-
day (Feb. 8, 1974) in the debut of *Good Times*, Florida turned up one thousand miles away from Tuckahoe, New York, to a Chicago, Illinois, housing
project with her three children and her husband, still played by John Amos,
who was now named James. Although it branched off from another Tandem
show (like *All in the Family* begat *Maude*), other than the main character's
name, *Good Times* placed Florida Evans in an entirely different world, so it
is difficult to call it a spin-off. Even *Good Times* producer Allan Manings
admits to the fragility of the term "spin-off" in reference to *Good Times*. In
an interview, he states that "it [*Good Times*] wasn't really a spinoff. . . . It was

one character, and we have changed that character."[78] The Florida Evans that serviced the Findlay family on *Maude* is vastly different from the Florida Evans on *Good Times*. Rolle puts it simply that this new role is a different side of Florida, saying, "What I do in my madam's house is a façade, what I do at home is me."[79] These words from Rolle are critical as they debunk the domestic figure, speaking to and about dissemblance. Through *Good Times*, Esther Rolle believed that she now had the ability to show her true self, in a space where she is the focus of the family and the hearth.

Good Times

With Esther Rolle as the actor at the helm of *Good Times*, the series was one of three female-dominated shows at that time starring Black women, the others being *That's My Mama* (1974–1975) and *Get Christie Love!* (1974–1975).[80] However, these images of Black womanhood were not necessarily favorable to some television critics. Regarding the Black women on television in 1974, Sandra Haggerty of the *Los Angeles Times* commented that "after heightened efforts on the part of Black writers, sociologists and psychologists to shatter the image-degrading myths of Black womanhood (the primary stereotype being that she is super strong, overbearing, castrating, loud, fat, and funky), this season's television depiction of the Black woman is particularly scurrilous."[81] Finding these present images as "humorously insulting" throughout her article, Haggerty is lamenting for what Black American womanhood looks like. She believed that the only redeeming quality of Florida Evans in *Good Times* is that she is married to her man. Sadly, here the status of marriage seems to be the only symbol of legitimacy and respectability of the image of Black womanhood. Haggerty ends her critique pleading to see the "responsible, articulate, sensitive, soft-spoken, and vulnerable Black woman" on the tube.[82] I believe Haggerty's analysis of Esther Rolle in her portrayal of Florida Evans is greatly limited.

Portraying the Evans family matriarch, Rolle utilized her relationship with Lear to create an image that was originally her own. In countless episodes, Florida is responsible for the livelihood of her family and home, she is articulate in expressing her agency by speaking her mind and taking a stance on what she believes in, and as the show's center, she is the most vulnerable to the pains of the Evans' living circumstances. Rolle was determined to use her portrayal as Florida Evans to make it clear that money isn't everything to poverty-stricken Black families and that strong moral character and values are what will keep a home intact. In a newspaper article discussing her transition to *Good Times*, Rolle states, "I think that what the haves in this world don't realize is that all is not lost because you don't have money, there are other values—love, sharing, caring—and if you concentrate on them sometimes you'll ride out the storm."[83] This quote makes it evident that Rolle wanted to use this platform as a space to demonstrate resilience and hustle economics amid social conditions that are consistently pushing the Black poor to give up. She aimed to make it clear throughout the series that these familial values were what would keep the Evans afloat through difficult times. However, the ability to portray such a wide-ranging and impactful character is credited to Rolle's resistance and negotiations at Tandem.

What may seem like a mainstay in television today, the simple act of a Black woman having a husband on-screen was revolutionary in 1974. Long before her protests of J.J.'s character mentioned earlier in the chapter, before production of the series, Rolle had to fight for the representation of a "complete" Black family. When Lear approached Rolle with the opportunity for her own show, Rolle commented that she was happy to do it (*Good Times*) because she had long wished to redeem the recycled image of the Black woman only being able to portray a domestic worker. She wanted to be a part of a new characterization.[84] Even in her role as a domestic on *Maude*, Rolle knew that her purpose was to redeem that image to open new avenues for Black women on television. After looking at the first script of *Good Times*, Rolle questioned where the children's father was, her husband.[85] Lear commented to her, "There is none, it was written for you and your three children."[86] Knowing that there was no show without her, Rolle took a stand against Lear and insisted that she had a husband. In response to not having a husband on-screen for her family, Rolle responded, "Find the actress who can do it, because I can't."[87] Such resistance at the start of the show establishes Rolle's position as the center of the show, and that it is, in fact, *her* show. This resistant act of hustle economics, using the star's agency to negotiate for more jobs and inclusive representation, prompted Lear to concede to the request, and John Amos was written into the pilot of *Good Times*.

Rolle saw that the inclusion of a Black father was necessary to combat a history of oppression against Black men in the home. Reading that *Good Times* was first written without a father, Rolle wasn't very surprised because she believed "the white man knows that if you castrate the Black man, you can handle the race. The Black man has a hard time getting a job, and his wife is told 'you can't get welfare with a husband in the home.' . . . This stings the Black man, so the wife has to spend a lot of time bolstering his ego because he is in such a shaky position. The myth is that she is the strong force in the family, when the truth is, she has had to be the breadwinner."[88] Rolle was well aware that accepting the absence of the father in the show would mean accepting how white executives, and the larger society, viewed Black men. She also believed that accepting the lack of a father took power away from the development of Black communities and their ability to speak for and define themselves. I must admit that this seeming disparagement of matriarchy may conform Rolle into a more conservative outlook on the Black family structure; however, embracing the "myth" of the Black woman as the strength of the Black family, Rolle points to how the myth became a popular understanding. Taking a stance on whether or not she believed in said myth had the potential to be intraracially divisive (between Black men and Black women). Rather, her goal here was to discuss the presence of a complete family unit on-screen. What I find of particular importance in her words is the matter-of-fact way in which she addresses a history of racial violence at the hands of white people in a popular white-controlled publication.

In addition to her battles with characters in the scripts, Rolle also sought drastic changes in the writing rooms at Tandem Productions. During table reads and live on set, Rolle exercised her power by often changing some of her lines through improvisation. She refused to be written out of context, and she claimed that "if I don't believe in a line, I change it. And I do. Often, the writer just doesn't have the right idiom."[89] Granted, although these interviews may be largely for the show and self-promotion efforts, I believe it is important to analyze what is said in these interviews as they can work to complicate Rolle's history of contention with Tandem. In making these comments and bringing these struggles to light in the press, Rolle risked her position on the show to hustle for varied Black imagery. It was necessary for Rolle to take control of her own voice rather than the one written for her in order to portray a more ambiguous representation of her character. While the concept of *Good Times* was created by two Black people (Eric Monte and Mike Evans) and it discussed the trials of a Black family, Rolle didn't feel there was an obligation for her to have an all-Black production staff. Rolle believed above all that the production staff must be "human" and of good moral character.[90] However, once pressed, Rolle admits, "If I did feel any obligation, it would be to have some Black women writers. A man just can't give my point of view. I'm screaming louder and louder about it every day, and I've been actively contacting a couple of Black women. I'm pressing my point daily."[91] These daily screams were answered with the inclusion of stories written by Patricia Edwards.

Although never receiving full writing credit for her episodes, Patricia Edwards was credited with the story development of two episodes of *Good Times*, "The Debutante Ball" and "Florida's Protest."[92] Edwards, the former secretary to the writers of *Good Times* and former stage manager for Lear's *One Day at a Time* (1975–1984), developed two stories for Tandem that demonstrated not only Black activism temporally but also the strength of Black women in creating change.[93] This moment on *Good Times* and at Tandem was pivotal because, at this point, Edwards served as the first woman to ever receive writing credit on *Good Times* and the only Black woman to ever receive writing credit for any Tandem Productions sitcom in general. Rolle's consistent hustle to pressure the Tandem executives made such a feat possible. Hustle economics from the perspective of Black women is seen on-screen in "Florida's Protest."

In this episode, Florida becomes outraged when James and the kids receive food poisoning after eating meat from the local supermarket. In response, she organizes a group of concerned citizens, and they boycott the market. The protest brings effective results but not before Florida experiences her first trip to jail. The narrative of this particular episode deserves more analysis due to the conventions of Black womanhood, poor Black life, and activism that it addresses throughout. With the high price of meat, the Evans are overjoyed that Florida spent the few extra dollars at Borgan's Market to treat them to roast beef for dinner. However, wanting to offer her family this rare delicacy backfires when the next morning, the entire family wakes up with food poisoning. When the children ask Florida why she continues to shop at Borgan's given the quality of the products, she laments that it is the only market available to the neighborhood, as "the chain ran every other business out and is the only market around here that we can get to without a car." With the greater majority of the project community relying on public transportation or walking, they have no choice but to purchase groceries there. This speaks to the real-life food deserts that exist in poor urban communities throughout the United States.[94] Low-income families tend to be negatively affected by the lack of access to healthy foods because they lack the means to travel to better food options.[95] When prices are high and there is a lack of financial assistance, those living in places with limited grocery stores find themselves in a situation where they are unable to access the food they need.

Angry about what the spoiled meat has done to her family, Florida gathers her Women's Club to picket the market for their high prices and low quality of food. While throwing her apron to the ground, Florida stands bold and assertive, affirming that she and her group "are going to let Borgan's know that we care about our families too!" As the television viewers witness Florida's protest through the commentary of James and his children watching the television screen, viewers hear the group of protestors marching and chanting "We will not be moved!" while in front of Borgan's Market. Here, protests seem like a sort of spectator sport in which Florida is out of place from her normal domestic life and is now on the front lines fighting for change. The Evans are proud to see Florida on television fighting for what she believes in (a moment of self-reflexivity) until James rises to his feet with anger seeing his wife being dragged into a cop car and shipped off to jail. A peaceful protest is met with time spent in a jail cell. Upon bailing Florida out of jail, James and Florida are determined to address the individual who put her in jail. So the two head to Borgan's Market to confront the store manager. Much to their surprise, the manager is Black, and he attempts to use his Blackness to calm down the Evans while expressing that they are on the same side and that he is doing everything he can to change Borgan's Market as the inside man. All the while, the manager knows that he is feeding his community bad food and is lying to their faces.

Although you may share the same skin tone, "all skinfolk ain't kinfolk." Popularized by author and folklorist, Zora Neale Hurston, this phrase is simply a creative way of saying that not all people, who share the same racial identity as you are your family.[96] In other words, there is more to friendship and affinity than mere racial similarity. Often, such as in this case, the phrase is used when other Black people betray their own, and this is an important point of Black unity (or lack thereof) that Patricia Edwards highlights in her story of this episode. Upon exiting the office, Florida hears the manager on the phone with Borgan after he believed he foiled the protestors, so Florida concocts a plan for payback. Returning to the manager's office to thank him for his help in being on their side, Florida and James bring him a plate of dinner, the roast that got their family sick. Thankful for the gesture, the manager starts to eat until Florida comments that the friend they brought with them to the office is a representative of the Food Administration. In actuality, he is a friend of the Evans family that agreed to the payback that Florida intended against the manager. When they realize his resistance to eating the meat, the manager is caught in the act of purposely selling bad meat in front of a man whom he assumes to be a Food Administration representative. To save face, he takes a bite of the food and immediately runs out of the office to the restroom. Florida and James laugh with each other and embrace because they foiled the manager. However, Florida still isn't satisfied with the result of their trickery.

FLORIDA: You know Borgan ain't gonna change nothing because of that, don't you?

JAMES: Yea I know, but, Florida, we got even. Just for *once*, we got even!

With satisfaction, they embrace yet again about the very rare instance of the poor getting even with those who have continuously taken advantage of them. Knowing that their predicament of access to healthy and fresh foods won't change, Florida finds solace in the small victory that her protest led to. Through instances such as these in her role as Florida, and in real life, Esther Rolle practiced hustle economics by frequently negotiating the image of Black women's power, agency, and resilience on and off the screen. These various acts of redeeming (to gain possession of it and compensate for its faulty past) the Black image led to Esther Rolle departing from the entire fifth season of *Good Times* due to the writing and characterization of Jimmie Walker as the buffoonish son J.J. However, she returned to end the series with grace for the show's sixth and final season.[97]

Although the production history of *Good Times* is often written to focus primarily on the resilience and contention of Esther Rolle as a Black actress navigating her own voice, agency, and power in order to redeem Black characters on-screen, she was not alone in that fight at Tandem Productions. Rolle's costar and on-screen husband, John Amos, also fought with Tandem executives regarding a lack of Black writers and demeaning characterizations in the production of *Good Times*. These acts of contention led to John Amos's demise at Tandem. However, his fight should not go unaddressed as it adds to a larger history of Black artists' hustle economics: risking finances, careers, and livelihoods in the space of a white-controlled television industry for the sake of Black opportunity.

"A Disruptive Factor": John Amos versus Tandem Productions

When asked if he felt like he had "made it" by another press member, Amos said not until he can produce his own pictures and "do what I want to do in the TV industry."[98]

John Amos became nationally known in his first major TV role, playing weatherman Gordy Howard on *The Mary Tyler Moore Show* (1970–1977) until 1973. However, less known but important to this discussion, before

Mary Tyler Moore, Amos worked as a staff writer for the variety series *The Leslie Uggams Show* (Sept. 28–Dec. 14, 1969).[99] With this initial experience as a writer, Amos knew the industrial power that was held in controlling a narrative and imagery on television. In the early 1970s television, to be a writer and to perform was an abstract concept to producers. In reflection, Amos states, "They [Tandem Productions] weren't ready for somebody who thought they could act *and* write. I had to wait until my turn came."[100] Amos felt that his time to write and perform had come with *Good Times*; however, his efforts would face much contention with the executives at Tandem, which ultimately risked his role on the show. In this section, I intend to make it clear that through Amos's portrayal of James Evans Sr. on-screen—public dissent of Tandem Productions, consistent contractual disputes and negotiations, and writing a critically refocused *Good Times* episode outline—Amos performed multiple types of hustle economics to preserve a redeeming image of Blackness and family on television.

Amos's famed portrayal of James Evans Sr., the patriarch of the Evans family, was one that television had not yet seen. As *Good Times* chronicled the first Black nuclear family on television, it also meant the first Black mother *and* father. James was known for his tough demeanor and his strict approach to raising his children in the rough housing projects that the family lived in. Episode after episode, James can be seen walking into his home after working double shifts yet still barely making it by. Early in the series, the audience can identify the type of man James is. He is hardworking and compassionate yet strict and protective. At the heart of much of the Evans family's struggles was a tight familial unit that yearned to find the positive in situations, using laughter in times of pain. Through the many instances where James's double shifts just aren't enough financial support, Florida embraces him and apologizes, while James consistently forbids her from taking any blame. James's role is that of a protector and provider, while Florida is the nurturer and guardian of the hearth, normalizing traditional gender roles that all audiences can relate to. The connection between John Amos and Esther Rolle on-screen as James and Florida Evans is a partnership integral to the success of the show that the two colleagues established before the series even began.

Upon being offered the role of James Evans on *Good Times*, Amos was well aware that this series would in fact be Esther Rolle's show. Although Rolle and Amos were both such hits on *Maude* (1972–1978) as Maude's maid Florida and her husband, the performance of Rolle is what garnered spin-off appeal.[101] In an Emmy TV Legends interview with Amos, he even states that in his initial meeting with Norman Lear, it was made clear that he would be "reading with Miss Rolle, it'll be her show."[102] Through this same interview, Amos speaks of Rolle in such high esteem and what they wanted out of this show was a husband and a wife so as to not perpetuate the matriarchal family. They were well aware of the stakes that their roles in this show had on Black communities, and they took it as their collective duty to honor them.[103] They believed it to be their mission to stick together and make sure that what they felt about the characters and their integrity as a family became a bond between the two of them.[104] With this role, Amos and the rest of the cast were under the leadership of Rolle and her larger vision to redeem the Black image on-screen.

"The First Black Father of a Complete Family"

In addition to the documented contention of Amos with Tandem, his portrayal of James Evans Sr. worked to establish Amos as a catalyst for change in the television industry. Through the discussion of Rolle in the previous section, it's clear that the ways in which Amos and Rolle chose to redeem the Black image took different forms. In a recent interview with *Vulture*, Amos reminisces on his time with Tandem on *Good Times*. When asked about the importance of his role he states, "I was carrying the weight of being the first Black father of a complete family, and I carried that responsibility seriously. Maybe too much so. Norman [Lear] thought I was taking on too much of a burden with it. But it was my responsibility. I knew that millions of Black people were watching. I know that my own father was watching. My own children were watching. And I was not going to portray something that was less than redeeming."[105]

Here, Amos sought to use this role as an opportunity to create a larger message to the American viewing body regarding not only the potential of Black performance but also the message of fatherhood, family, and faith through unfortunate trials. This image was important in this historical moment as the social understanding of the Black family, largely influenced by the Moynihan Report, was that it was either matriarchal or otherwise facing destruction.[106]

Airing February 8, 1974, "Too Old Blues" was the first episode of *Good Times* on CBS. This episode is so important to Black protest and hustle economics because it discusses James's bouts with ageism in a government-funded workspace. In the episode, written by a Black television writer, Bob Peete, James is excited because he is sure that he is going to get a high-paying union job. While the bulk of the show's comedy stems from the one-liners and jabs between the Evans children, and Florida's sharp wit toward her children, James's character is much more serious, and his comedy is often self-deprecating. Although James plays a central role in this episode, from the start, the pause and applause that follows Esther Rolle (as Florida) as she first enters the setting reaffirm that she is the star of the show. Waiting anxiously for the mail to arrive to see his scores on the union aptitude test, James emits a positive outlook on what the Evans family's future will look like with this newfound wealth and decides to view the newspaper want ads for fun.

> JAMES: Let's see what the equal opportunity employers have for James Evans this morning. Computer designer. College graduate . . . hmm ain't that tender, I only missed that one by four years college, four years high school, and two years public school.
> FLORIDA: Don't they have anything for mechanics? You're a very handy man, James.
> JAMES: Now that's it right there, baby. When you're white, you're a mechanic; when you're Black, you're a handyman.

Through this dialogue in the first episode, James makes it clear that he hadn't made it past a junior high school education and how that impacts job acquisition. Also, he is aware of the subtle ways that job postings, titles, and descriptions are often raced. These forms of knowledge are learned over time through the hustle of the working class. Often, it's easier to make a joke of or laugh at these disadvantages rather than dwell upon them, and using laughter as a defense is consistently practiced by the Evans family. Upon receiving news that he has passed the exam, James is invited to an in-person interview. Full of hope, he tells Florida to throw a party in his honor for the good fortune they are soon to receive. With James soon acquiring this steady job, the family's financial security and well-being are more intact. Florida even comments to her best friend Willona about the lengths that James, or as she states, "Mr. Breadwinner," had to endure before they reached this milestone.

> FLORIDA: When you think of all the things this man has done to keep his family together . . . dishwasher, laundry helper, night watchman, floor sweeper, and all that was just last week!

The burden of many jobs is one that may resonate with the working-class Black poor, who have to take multiple part-time jobs to supplement income for family and housing. Having one steady job paying $4.25 an hour was a luxury, and hoping to see James as a Black man fight to reach that is part of the thrill of watching *Good Times*. However, after passing the physical and mental test, a government error in recording his age prevents James from eligibility for the job as it is for men ages eighteen to thirty-five, and James is forty-one. The pride James exudes as he stands up for himself to the job recruiter is a verbal testament to the larger poor communities and Black people being forced to adhere to discriminatory government practices and guidelines, in this case, age.

> JAMES: I got a family. They need food on the table, clothes on their backs. I gotta pay rent; I need that job!

In situations like these, James must often go to battle to provide for his family. Despite his proclamation, the recruiter refuses James a job. Aware that he is not going to win this fight, James exits, lamenting, "I'm a senior citizen that only has to wait twenty-four more years for his social security." James's age restricts him from a government-funded opportunity and prevents him from receiving other financial aid, putting him in a very precarious situation when it comes to securing employment. Further, this quote fits into the broader context of the show as it explains just one of the many situations of prejudice that the Evans are forced to endure throughout the entirety of the series. When he gets home, James is greeted by his family and friends all singing "For He's a Jolly Good Dude" in his honor. Much to his dismay, he has to admit to his loved ones that his age barred him from getting the job and apologizes for crushing their dreams.

Florida quickly nurtures him, and their bond on-screen works to show how love and support work in their family, above material means. Florida comforts him by saying, "James, you always see this family through; you can do it," and that faith is all he needs to pick himself up. The very next day, James starts a new week-long job at a car wash with a smile on his face. Episodes like these throughout the series point to James's unfortunate need for resilience. With consistent drawbacks and missed opportunities, leaning on his wife and family, he is able to muster the courage to keep going. They also speak to the hustle economics that poor Black communities must contend with, taking short-term employment and multiple jobs at once when they are often barred from formal economies. Seeing a Black father on television practice this weekly grit is inspiring to the potential of the working-class Black father. In this role, Amos helped imagine a father figure that refused to quit amid a social, cultural, and political system that often made it easy to. However, in order to complete his previously mentioned goal of redeeming the Black image on-screen, Amos felt that simply acting the role was not enough; his insertion into all aspects of the production was where he believed the true change could be made.

In contrast to its Tandem predecessor, *Sanford and Son*, the concept of *Good Times* was created and written by Black writers, Eric Monte and Mike Evans. As a young Hollywood hopeful, Monte hitchhiked to Los Angeles from Chicago, Illinois, to make his big break. Falling on hard times, Monte hustled, gambled, and even sold drugs to make ends meet until he was able to break into the television industry.[107] Hearing his name around town as a gifted poet, Mike Evans (who at this point played Lionel Jefferson on *All in the Family*) encouraged Monte to help him develop his character on the show. Submitting a script to Norman Lear with Evans's *and* Monte's names on it began Monte's career in television. Later, when the two came together with a shared interest in creating a show with a complete Black family set in Monte's hometown of Chicago, *Good Times* was born.

After the story of the Evans family was bought by Lear, it had the immense potential not only for Black representation on-screen but also as the first network prime-time television show crediting Black creators. As a by-product of 1970s television's turn to social relevance, *Good Times* was created to exist as an answer to lived Black realities that shows, like *Julia* for instance, were unable to do. Unfortunately, although a Black writer, Eric Monte scripted the original episode, and the following four scripts were by freelance Black writers; the majority of the scripts thereafter were written by white writers, which was objectionable to Amos and Rolle because they believed these writers were disconnected from the show's central issues.[108] This disconnect, they felt, was responsible for the enlarging of their television son J.J.'s more buffoonish characterization that Amos and Rolle believed detracted from the show's cultural depth for the sake of pure comedy.[109] The role of J.J., which was at first used as comic relief to soften the blow of the family's hardships, soon shifted to a characterization that disrupted the original social agenda the show first set forth. In the first few episodes written by Black writers, the series addressed issues that Black communities faced, such as discriminatory age restrictions in the workforce, relying on religious faith to get through harsh times, the threat of eviction, con artists using religion for financial gain, and protesting the whitewashing of American history taught in school.[110] Christine Acham helps understand these changes in scripts and content once white writers shifted characterizations of the Evans family. Acham describes "three types of episodes that arose from these internal conflicts and became evident in viewing the series: pedagogical, political and 'pure sitcom.'"[111] Like Rolle discussed in the previous section, Amos too reacted more vehemently toward some of the pure sitcom episodes.

The pedagogical episode described by Acham is one that attempts to teach the audience overtly about a particular issue often containing character monologues on topics like health care or education.[112] The political episodes assert themselves through the daily acts of racism and/or discrimination that the Evans face in their community.[113] More important to this discussion is in fact the "pure sitcoms," which often steer clear of any political agenda or moral purpose, usually with the character J.J. as the focal point. Although there may be a certain politics to the freedom of Black male expression that is characterized in the episodes that center on J.J.'s performance, much of these episodes soon outnumbered the ones that were blatantly socially and culturally relevant. The pure sitcom became the easy solution to *Good Times* writing and production over the socially relevant tone in which it was conceived. In some instances, Amos and Rolle were able to use their voices to impact the scripts and direction of the show; however, they were given no production credits.[114] When this did not work, Amos became absent from the production spaces at Tandem and used commentary in popular magazines as a form of protest. A large concern of his was that the scripts were putting too much emphasis on J.J. "putting on his chicken hat and saying Dy-No-Mite every third page."[115] Amos felt as though much more emphasis could have been put on the aspirations of the future careers of the other Evans children, Michael and Thelma, instead of drifting into the consistently droll humor of the slacker oldest son J.J. Much of Amos's contention to the show's direction foreshadowed early signs of him and Tandem parting ways.

Using an *Ebony Magazine* article as his hidden transcript for protest and negotiation in "Bad Times on the 'Good Times' Set," Amos makes clear his issues with the start of the third season 1975–1976.[116] While *Good Times* producer Allan Manings denied that the role of J.J. had been expanded for comedic value, he claimed that the next year of the show (season three) and its characters would have more depth.[117] Amos, however, was not very convinced about this claim until seeing it come to fruition. When it came time to renew contracts for the upcoming season, Amos's contractual dispute with Tandem Productions caused a week-long delay at the beginning of show tapings for the new season.[118] Although some of the difficulties Amos addressed involved salary, a source close to the negotiations confided, "There is more than money involved here. It goes back to how Black men have been treated in this country all along."[119] Amos was "very strong in asserting his position, not only for himself but for the whole *Good Times* cast. Black actors and actresses have to go beyond the call of duty."[120] Much like his Tandem predecessor, Redd Foxx of *Sanford and Son*, Amos took a direct call to action toward Tandem, calling for a change in production and direction because the treatment of how the show visualized Black men, specifically J.J., was a disservice. Amos makes it evident that Black actors and actresses had to go above and beyond simply their acting duty for changes to occur and uses the restructuring of his contract as an act of hustle economics to advocate for the changes he wished to see.

In order to have a structure to infiltrate production, Amos established his own production company.[121] Through the creation of John Amos Productions, Inc., Amos put into motion a business model that would allow him to be credited for productions and future artistic ventures within and outside of Tandem Productions. After holding out on renewing his season three contract, Amos drafted a new contract for Tandem to consider. In an interoffice communication letter from Tandem Productions' vice president Alan Horn to founder Norman Lear and *Good Times* producer Allan Manings, Horn explains, "The recent amendment to John Amos' contract incorporates several stipulations concerning Mr. Amos' writing services."[122] These new contract stipulations on writing services and Amos's right to script consultation were redlined for Tandem to consider. They are listed at length as such:

3. Producer (Tandem Productions, Inc.) hereby guarantees that it will engage Company (John Amos Productions, Inc.) to furnish to Producer the services of Performer (John Amos) to write one (1) script for the series during the Third and each succeeding Contract Year for which Producer exercises its option to employ Performer hereunder.

4. At Performer's request the individual producer or executive producer of the series shall consult with Performer at mutually convenient times with respect to the script delivered to Performer for each program of the series. In the event of any disagreement between Performer and the individual producer or executive producer of the series with regard to the content of any such script, the decision of said producer or executive producer shall be controlling. Producer's failure to consult with Performer as to the script for any program shall not constitute a material breach by Producer of the Employment Agreement.

5. (a) At any time hereafter, Company may submit to Norman Lear for approval original ideas for one or more new television series. Lear shall respond to such submission within thirty (30) days.

(b) In the event that Lear approves in writing an idea submitted to him pursuant to subparagraph (a) hereof, then with respect to such idea Company may draw upon the Development Fund in such amount as it deems advisable to a maximum of Ten Thousand Dollars ($10,000) for the purpose of developing said idea into an acceptable pilot script for a television series project.[123]

These three contract amendments truly represented transformative employment arrangements for Black artists. Hustling for a new economic and creative stake in production, Amos outlines his own terms and demands the opportunity to have agency in development at Tandem. The effects of this change extend beyond Tandem and are relevant to television at large. No other contract of *Good Times'* actors had such clauses written into them. Through Amos's contract holdout and amendments made through his employment agreement, he set the terms for the ways in which he sought best to utilize his position on television. Although Redd Foxx of *Sanford and Son* voiced similar concerns, the result was a court settlement (as mentioned in chapter 2) that was largely financial, resulting in Foxx receiving $25,000 per episode, plus 25 percent of the producers' net profits.[124] Through John Amos Productions, Amos drafted the opportunity for writing and production credit into his contract. With section 3, Amos calls for the ability to have at least one writing credit each contracted season. This amendment proves to be of grave importance to the Black sitcoms of Tandem that have been criticized when the majority of episodes by white writers have been accused of being disconnected from the Black cultural issues at hand. The inclusion of writing credit, even one, offers the ability of Amos to reclaim the social relevancy at the core of *Good Times* for himself and his fellow actors—in turn, giving Black artists the ability to speak for themselves through scripts.

Considering section 4 of the contract, through mandating script consultation, Amos has the ability to comment on the language, structure, authenticity, and impact that a proposed script may have on the depiction of Black communities through the Evans family. Although the final say is given to the producer, making this assertion contractually proves the efforts Amos felt necessary to infiltrate production and be involved in the full process from writing to taping and airing. Finally, in section 5, through the establishment of Amos's own production company, he feels he is actually able to "do what he wants in the television industry," as said in the introductory quote of this section.[125] As an independent company, Amos strategically writes into his employment agreement that his position as a performer and company owner is a package deal. Given an idea for a profitable television series, Tandem Productions was required to fund its initial development. Through these forms of protest and hustle, Tandem soon agreed to Amos's demands as he establishes himself as an actor, writer, and producer in the larger television industry.

With the help of costar Ja'Net DuBois, Amos soon used his contractual agreement in section 3 to write a *Good Times* story outline for Tandem with hopes for it to be written and produced. The potential of this written episode is important to the discussion of dissent because these two artists felt that their words better suited the narrative of *Good Times*. The writing of the episode is proof of the negotiations that Amos had to bring forth in a space where he felt his voice wasn't being heard. On January 27, 1975, Amos and DuBois wrote an outline for a prospective *Good Times* episode entitled "It's a Family Affair."[126] Although the episode was not received until December 15, 1975, Tandem Productions vice president Alan Horn makes it clear to *Good Times* producer Allan Manings that the outline should be treated as a priority and given close consideration with regards to Amos's contract stipulations.[127]

In summary, the story outline takes place amid a dispute between Florida and her best friend and neighbor Willona, leaving the Evans family in disarray. James is forced to be the mediator between the two, and once together, they realize that they actually have no reason to be fighting. During this joyous reunion, Willona's house is robbed, forcing her to move into the Evans household until the locks on her doors are fixed. From taking too long in the restroom, having all her phone calls forwarded to their home, turning the channels without notice, and so on, Willona is steadily becoming an unwelcome guest in Florida's eyes. With Willona doing the laundry and cooking dinner, Florida feels her maternal duties are being taken over and soon decides that Willona has to go back to her own home. The story concludes when Florida forces James to fix Willona's broken door, and they find that Willona was already in the process of fixing it. They both felt their friendship slipping away with their constant presence in each other's space. Although this story outline is mainly a "pure sitcom," as it tells a funny story about friendship and familial roles, it does not feel frivolous nor does it overextend the same jokes of previous episodes. Also, it utilizes J.J. for small bits of comic relief rather than overshadowing his character at the expense of others. This was an issue that even Norman Lear reflects was a problem with many episodes of this time when he states in a Television Academy interview, "We allowed him (J.J.), for the sake of getting those easy laughs, to repeat himself too much."[128] So although not political or particularly pedagogical in its content, the proposed story outline had a twofold potential. First, the story carefully handled a change in content structure while continuing to keep the relevancy of each character to the narrative. Also, and finally, it had the potential of bringing more Black writers to the show's production credits at Tandem and displaying the various talents of Black artists as a whole in television. Unfortunately, this episode was never produced nor written into a script, as Amos's combined hustle economy at Tandem soon led to his release from *Good Times*.

"Damn, Damn, DAMN!"

Upon the start of the third season, Amos was informed that he would not be in the show's taping on September 18, 1975 (season 3 episode 7 "The Baby") so he could have an extra week off after the show's season hiatus.[129] After he refused to be present for the table reading for the following episode the next day, Amos was formally suspended from the September twenty-fifth episode taping (season 3 episode 8 "Michael's Big Fall") for violating contractual obligations requiring him to be present at all table reads and rehearsals.[130] The last presence of John Amos as James Evans Sr. was in the season three finale, "The Rent Party" (season 3 episode 24, March 2nd, 1976). Ironically, as discussed in chapter 2, these parties were not merely "institutions of necessity" or economic survival but spaces for amusement and community amid the daily drudgery of labor exploitation and white oppression.[131] James Evans Sr.'s last presence on television was celebrating Black life and community, escaping an oppressive world of labor and racial discrimination outside. A world that actor John Amos had to fight head-on.

In a Television Foundation interview, during the hiatus and before the start of the fourth season, Amos reflects on a phone call he received from Norman Lear regarding Amos's future at Tandem and with *Good Times*. Amos recalls picking up the phone to talk to Lear and Lear sharing the news, "We got renewed for another season . . . but you won't be with us."[132] Amos responded, "It's your show, have a good life" and hung up the phone.[133] Discussing the circumstances around his firing, Amos admits, partly in jest, that he "wasn't the most diplomatic guy in those days and that they [Tandem] got tired of having their lives threatened over some jokes on the script, so they killed me off."[134] After Lear continued to deem Amos as a "disruptive factor," Amos reflects that the experience taught him the lesson that he "wasn't as important as he thought he was to the show and Norman Lear's plans."[135]

At the start of the fourth season, the *Good Times* story arc continues under the pretense that James is in Mississippi and is planning to move the family out there because of a great job opportunity. However, the next day, the family receives a telegram that James had died in a car accident—effectively killing off the character James Evans Sr. from the series. In what is often regarded as one of the most emotional scenes in television sitcom history, upon digesting the news of his death, Florida Evans shouts, "Damn, Damn, DAMN!" breaking down in tears over the loss of her husband.[136] The closing credits then appear in silence rather than with the usual applause.[137] Without Amos, the show continued for three more seasons but was never quite the same. J.J.'s character was heightened even more, and the show's political and pedagogical roots became more veiled through consistent pure sitcom episodes, eventually leading to a season-long departure of Esther Rolle in season five, leaving Jimmie Walker (as J.J.) as the show's star. Although Amos and Lear mended their relationship twenty years later through the *All in the Family* spin-off *704 Hauser Street* (April 11th–May 9th, 1994), which Lear created and Amos starred in, the show lasted a mere six episodes, failing miserably in comparison to Amos's *Good Times* role. Albeit his hustle economics led to the downfall of his tenure with a groundbreaking sitcom, the efforts of John Amos prove to be a radical shift in television history that is rarely discussed. The push to hold executives accountable to the images and the narratives on-screen, fighting for his space in the writer's room, and taking a stand for redeeming Black images are important examples of opposition and hustle economics that John Amos initiated against Tandem Productions and are integral to understanding Tandem's history of Black sitcom production. Unfortunately, the efforts of hustle economics to scratch for better conditions sometimes fall short.

Although employment was lost, the dissent at Tandem in regard to *Good Times* was productive in terms of inspiring artists to fight for more; dissent was also acted on in production. As stated earlier in this chapter, Eric Monte (the cocreator of *Good Times*) faced his own battles with keeping a seat at the production table, a battle that soon had legal ramifications. In an interview with NPR in 2006, Monte reflects on his consistent discontent with Norman Lear, ABC, and CBS.[138] Sharing Esther Rolle and John Amos's continuing concern with the scriptwriting, because Monte sided with the actors, he noticed that he was consistently demoted, while the white writers were promoted. Monte even states that while in the writer's room, "the one note I got every meeting without fail, was 'you've got to get rid of the father. A strong Black man in a sitcom doesn't work.'"[139] From Monte's perspective, the strength in the image of Black fatherhood wasn't supported by his white colleagues at Tandem. A year after Monte took a leave to work on the box office hit film inspired by his real life, *Cooley High* (Schultz, 1975), Tandem got rid of John Amos as the father, James Evans.[140]

Through the interview, it becomes clear that Monte's impact on Tandem was much more expansive than the cocreation of *Good Times*. In addition to *Good Times*, Monte claims that he is the individual who found Redd Foxx and convinced Lear to cast Foxx as Fred Sanford in *Sanford and Son*.[141] Also, Monte claims to be responsible for pitching the idea to Lear that an entrepreneurial Black man, named George Jefferson, should be added to the *All in the Family* cast; subsequently, George and Louise Jefferson later appeared on *All in the Family*.[142] Other than the firing of John Amos, while Monte was on leave, Lear developed a show starring George and Louise Jefferson that was a spin-off of *All in the Family*, *The Jeffersons* (1975–1985). Norman Lear took the credit and billed himself as the creator of the show. Outraged at the actions that took place and the lack of recognition that Monte received for his work, in 1977, Monte successfully sued ABC, CBS, and Norman Lear for using his ideas in these sitcoms without giving him his credit.[143] Calling Lear a "racist, a hypocrite, thief, and a liar," Monte sued the parties for $185 million.[144] However, due to Monte's acute business acumen and legal representation, he only received a $1 million settlement, 1 percent ownership of *Good Times*, and no royalties for the other show ideas that he created.[145] It can be argued that the decision to settle out of court proves that Monte's claims have legitimacy. However, his "successful" lawsuit was actually a loss in comparison to the larger revenue that these shows brought to television over time.

Unfortunately, the worst was yet to come for Eric Monte. As soon as he filed the lawsuit against Lear and the company, all of his writing offers dried up. Monte stated that "nobody in Hollywood would talk to me, I was blacklisted."[146] It was the beginning of the end of his career as Hollywood marked him as a scriptwriter who was "difficult to work with."[147] When NPR asked Norman Lear to comment on these claims, he declined.[148] The blacklist that he was put on for calling out those in power led to Monte losing everything. Later in the 1990s, Monte is credited with the writing of a few popular Black sitcoms; however, his name never reached the heights that it had with *Good*

Times and *Cooley High*. As of 2022, Monte is living in an assisted living facility. Monte's story demonstrates the stakes these actors, writers, and producers faced when challenging white television executives. When Monte took agency to fight for what he was owed through his creations, his life came crashing in; his hustle economics risked everything. With his claims of various creative rights, Monte is in fact a creative mind within every Black sitcom produced at Tandem; however, his name is consistently written out of the histories of the impact that these sitcoms had on society at large. Of Monte's claims outside of *Good Times*, he states that he suggested hiring Redd Foxx on *Sanford and Son* and that he created Archie Bunker's neighbor on *All in the Family*, George Jefferson.[149] With George Jefferson, Monte's claim in the creation of a character so unapologetic about Black ascension and his own rearticulated form of hustle economics was so attractive that it spawned its own series, *The Jeffersons*.

The Jeffersons

"Movin' on Up?"

Much like the theme song for *Good Times*, the introductory verse for *The Jeffersons* works to remind the audience of the plot before every episode.

> To a deluxe apartment in the sky.
> We're movin' on up
> To the east side.
> We finally got a piece of the pie.[1]

Whether through a hip-hop remix of the sitcom's theme song in the St. Lunatics' "Batter Up" (which featured a guest cameo of Sherman Hemsley in the music video) or the character Ace being dubbed the "George Jefferson of the projects" for working at a dry cleaner in the film *Paid in Full* (2002), *The Jeffersons* has sustained a lasting impact in Black popular culture.[2] As the second longest-running Black sitcom in history, *The Jeffersons* stands as the first sitcom centered on a Black familial experience of financial upward mobility.[3] In this chapter, I will address the cultural significance of *The Jeffersons* (1975–1985) through the topics of (1) economic displacement, interrogating the show's theme of "movin' on up" rearticulating hustle economics; (2) Isabel Sanford's hustle in the televisual space before *The Jeffersons* and her stake in narrative production; (3) finally, with regard to dissent, audience reception to and how the Black artists (specifically Roxie Roker) perform interracial conflict and marriage. This chapter contributes to the overarching argument of *Scratchin' and Survivin'* as it traces the racial development of Black families in Tandem shows and how these Black artists had to practice resilience in their efforts of infiltrating the television landscape to tell a myriad of Black stories. In sum, I discuss how *The Jeffersons* and its cast's comedic portrayal of the American dream of Black financial ascension, amid the confines of discrimination, offered a new vision of Blackness on-screen. Popular reception of *The Jeffersons* highlights the show's focus on Black wealth and its interracial elements, which were the major issues that produced public response.

As noted in the conclusion of chapter 3, the claims to authorship of *The Jeffersons* have been historically complicated between Eric Monte and Norman Lear; however, there was no debate about this show's impact in casting a new vision of Black life. In a Television Academy interview, Lear comments on the creation and legacy of this hit CBS Black sitcom, claiming that "after a year and a half of *Good Times*, we [Tandem Productions] began to read, 'why are they [Black characters in these shows] all working 2–3 jobs, why can't they be fairly affluent, why can't there be another slice of Black life?'"[4] When asked if these concerns were valid, Lear responds that he doesn't necessarily believe they were valid for Tandem but valid for television generally.[5] Lear claims that through this general concern and "media spanking," he decided that his company should create a show about an upwardly mobile Black family, an idea that came to fruition in *The Jeffersons*.[6] Before he was bought out of his interest in Tandem by company president Jerry Perenchio, Bud Yorkin gave a significant comment on the company's intent in making *The Jeffersons*. Lear, he said, "had the idea of putting a Black man in a white man's world."[7] Note that Yorkin does not say they are putting "a poor man into a rich world." Instead, his phrasing suggests a certain conflation and slippage. To Tandem, poor is Black, and rich is white. Yorkin's racialized (and gendered) phrasing makes it clear that although upward mobility is a focus, Blackness and masculinity were central selling points for *The Jeffersons*. The show worked to tell the story of Black class mobility, making the phrase "movin' on up" internationally known.

"Movin' on up" is the tune that rings loudly throughout the introductory theme song of *The Jeffersons*. To "move up" inherently means to succeed at whatever you are trying to pursue, usually referring to making more money, getting a great job, or simply doing better. Movin' on up, in the case of *The Jeffersons*, also meant moving spatially (into a high-rise apartment) and into a fundamentally white world. Although reaching a greater economic stratosphere, Courtney R. Baker reminds us that "Black movement in the 1970s must therefore be viewed for all of its complexities and contradictions as the ability to move did not necessarily register as freedom."[8] "Movin' on up" requires hustling to a new economic status by varying means, and in the case of the Jefferson family, it is implied that their hustle economics has paid off. As the theme song lyrics state, it "took a whole lotta tryin', just to get up that hill," and the Jeffersons hustled through hard times to get up the hill to financial ascension. As a show, *The Jeffersons* complicates the promotion of upward mobility through the comedic "fish out of water" insertion of Black characters into the upper middle class, a space on television previously exclusive to white communities. I use the term "upper middle class" because there is a clear distinction between the Jefferson family's social class in comparison to the working-class identification of the characters in *Sanford and Son* and *Good Times*.

In Elizabeth Higginbotham's *Too Much to Ask*, she cites various definitions of how class has historically been discussed. I align my definition with her claim that "members of the middle class are involved in the accumulating capital by designing and controlling the work of others, even though they themselves receive wages and/or salaries. In contrast, members of the working class execute tasks designed by others and in many aspects have lost control over the work process. They are more likely to lack power in the workplace and be supervised by others, often doing work defined by members of the middle class."[9] Because George Jefferson runs a chain of successful dry cleaning stores, he is responsible for the managerial work of others while gaining a controlling salary. I see his class status as "upper" because not only is he responsible for the managerial work; he actually owns these stores. That ownership of a successful business franchise helps him transcend from simply being middle class. The definition used to describe the working class is clear for the predicament of the Evans family in *Good Times*; however, it is complicated when used to describe the Sanfords in *Sanford and Son*. As previously discussed, Fred and Lamont Sanford own and operate their own business; however, their financial predicament does not allow them the designation of middle-class status. They have no employees working for them, so they must do the managerial and day-to-day labor to run their business, and in their failing business market of junk and antiquities, they lack the financial capital to ever get ahead.

On one hand, *The Jeffersons* challenges the historical whiteness of an upper-middle-class space. On the other, although they are financially well off compared to Tandem's other Black families, the Jeffersons' Blackness and working-class origins required them to engage in alternative forms of hustle economics. Watching and studying *The Jeffersons*, their practice of hustle economics on-screen is reimagined from those on *Sanford and Son* and *Good Times*. Since the Jefferson family is meant to symbolize financial success, their hustle economics is practiced through an "economics of displacement," a term I am using to define the particular economic situation that the Jeffersons face as they are Black nouveau riche and must perform to the standards of their new class status. *The Jeffersons* constitutes a new category for the American sitcom of the 1970s, one defined by Blackness *and* wealth. This status often leaves the characters in precarious situations. Still, each week, the show gathered more than 30 percent of the national TV audience.[10] According to Herman Gray in *Watching Race*, series like *The Jeffersons* fall into the category of "Separate but Equal" discourse, "where Black characters live and work in hermetically sealed social milieus that are approximately equivalent to their white counterparts."[11] However, *The Jeffersons* complicate Gray's claim because although the show features a Black family's home at its center, the Black characters interact with and contest the cast of white characters daily, challenging whether their nouveau riche circumstances are actually equitable.

Although *The Jeffersons* received generally high Nielsen ratings, Lear faced continuing backlash from social groups in response to this show. This forced Lear to hire a full-time assistant whose key role was to negotiate with pressure groups.[12] In one instance, Lear purchased three scripts written by CORE-approved writers because CORE (the Congress of Racial Equality) believed Lear was stereotyping "Black matriarchs and emasculating their husbands."[13] Through it all came a show that flipped the script on the ways Black people had been seen and spoken for on television. Because of who they are, and where they came from, the Jeffersons could never feel like they fully belonged in the Upper East Side of Manhattan. The past pulled on them, and although neither ever *fully* forgot where they came from, the longer George, Louise, and Lionel stayed away from the old neighborhood, the less they knew of their old selves as their hustle economics meant keeping up appearances. However, reminders of where they came from consistently appeared in different forms. Because there are few academic discussions of

The Jeffersons, this chapter attempts to map the ground of the series through textual analyses of episodes, interviews from actors and producers, trade journal and magazine coverage, and production notes of *The Jeffersons*.[14]

As the introductory theme song suggests, through its upbeat tempo and lyrics, *The Jeffersons* is meant to portray a success story of a working-class family moving up and finally grasping the American dream, "a piece of the pie." Movin' on up also meant moving away from what you know. During the opening credits (played along with the theme song), every week the audience is reintroduced to the plot and setting as they see the image of Louise Jefferson (Isabel Sanford) wiping away her tears in fear of the change that is to come with their newfound wealth, while George Jefferson (Sherman Hemsley) grips her hand and in contrast wears a large grin, excited about leaving his past behind. The audience follows the car as George and Louise leave the old neighborhood for the new, crossing over from Queens into Manhattan, and following the couple as they walk into their new high-rise building while the camera tilts and literally moves up in accordance to their new "deluxe apartment in the sky."

The family consists of the arrogant patriarch and main source of comedic relief George Jefferson, the kind-hearted yet stern matriarch Louise "Weezy" Jefferson, and their son Lionel Jefferson (*Good Times* cocreator Mike Evans [seasons 1, 6–11] and Damon Evans [seasons 2–4]). Also, the main cast features neighbors Helen (Roxie Roker), Tom (Franklin Cover), and Jenny Willis (Berlinda Tolbert), the Jefferson's interracially married couple and their daughter, as well as Harry Bentley (Paul Benedict), the British U.N. translator. As a Black viewer of this show, it's hard to not feel a sense of pride while watching. Evidenced through Robin Means Coleman's work on Black viewers and their responses to Black sitcoms, her respondents often read *The Jeffersons* as "positive" because "it assigns a higher class status, and in turn elevates the race, which is often seen as not self-sufficient, or failing to be economically contributory to society."[15] Black audiences by extension could feel that they too, with a bit of hustle, can make it to "the big leagues" and be on the same playing field with their white counterparts, at least in the realm of sitcoms.

To be clear, I am not claiming that *The Jeffersons'* focus on an upper-middle-class family makes the show aesthetically better or worse (in terms of quality) than its predecessors *Sanford and Son* and *Good Times*. However, it is evident that through the subjects it addressed, *The Jeffersons* entered a terrain never before traveled on television, and that in itself is a transformative act. The costume designer at Tandem, Rita Riggs, states that in working

FIGS. 4.1 AND 4.2 *The Jeffersons* "Movin' on Up."

on *The Jeffersons*, she had the ability to "show exactly what was happening in America—Blacks were beginning to work and were becoming a force in the economy."[16] Her comment makes evident that costuming *The Jeffersons* was dressing the part of Black ascension. With *The Jeffersons*, Riggs was able to style the image of Black "success," much different than the Black sitcoms she costumed at Tandem Productions prior. Riggs also comments that the production atmosphere of *The Jeffersons* was "always funny, and very civilized," in contrast to her experience regarding the often more rebellious and resistant cast members in *Sanford and Son* and *Good Times*.[17] The respectability of the subject matter in *The Jeffersons* created less production resistance from this particular Black cast in relation to others.

Discovered during his stint on the all-Black Broadway play *Purlie*, Hemsley came from a space in which Black writers, directors, and actors had the authority in artistic content. When Lear cast Hemsley to play the reoccurring role of George Jefferson on *All in the Family*, Hemsley was introduced to a system of production vastly different from his theater role. *All in the Family* had no Black writers, and its spin-off, *The Jeffersons*, also had no Black writers or producers until the end of the second season, and even then, the Black presence behind the scenes was sparse.[18] When asked if he participated in the writing at all, Sherman Hemsley commented, "No . . . every once in a while, I would come up with a funny joke. We all would take chances at rehearsal by saying something that wasn't written, and if it was funny, it would make it."[19] Coupled with producer George Sunga's commenting that "the diversity behind the camera was nothing to talk about, we should've done better," it's clear that the lack of cultural specificity in the production of the show made the Black actor's performances (rather than scripted dialogue) fully responsible for portraying this nouveau riche Black image to television.[20]

With the premiere of *The Jeffersons* in 1975, it's crucial to note how trade journals and magazines chose to discuss the show. For instance, *TV Guide*—which provides television program listings information, television-related news, and interviews—is written mostly from a white perspective for a universal audience. In this regard, *TV Guide*'s initial coverage of *The Jeffersons* discussed Sherman Hemsley's poor upbringing in Philadelphia while highlighting that "George Jefferson, is the Black equivalent of Archie Bunker" because of his aversion to white people.[21] To see these two as equivalent is an overly simplistic racial logic that ignores the history of oppression against Black people that might have created George's antiwhite sentiments, while Archie's racism is a tool of oppression rather than a reaction to it. In contrast to *TV Guide*, *JET*'s coverage of *The Jeffersons* delivers a more personal account of the pride that Black people felt about this show's portrait of a wealthy Black family. *JET*, a magazine marketed to Black readers, described *The Jeffersons* as the hottest new TV family.[22] Discussing the show's plot, *JET* interviews two Black women in media from their perspective. Gloria Vinson and Patricia Edwards, who worked in production for various shows at Tandem, felt as though *The Jeffersons* was a show that was needed to further represent the race holistically. They commented that "none of these shows [Black sitcoms] represents in themselves, the total Black perspective, but they do represent aspects and facets of reality."[23] *The Jeffersons*' focus on Black financial ascension helps offer a diversity of the Black image on television, countering the frequently monolithic portrayal of the Black community.

In contrast, in *JET*'s sister magazine, *Ebony*, the reception of the sitcom is not as favorable. Here, Louie Robinson describes George Jefferson as "loud and aggressive, and if there ever was a vexation to the spirit, he is it."[24] In response, Sherman Hemsley states that the character he plays is simply "scared" and that "he uses his boastfulness to cover up a lot of things."[25] Although this article offers an important interiority to the mind of its main character and his insecurities in his new space of wealth, Robinson labels *The Jeffersons* as a show without social significance. Robinson claims, "For those who may still be looking for deep and satisfying social significance in Black shows on television, the wait goes on. Although *The Jeffersons* portrays Blacks on a different socioeconomic level than other Black TV shows, it is nevertheless, like the others, broad comedy and has to be accepted as such. But this is true, in one form or another, for most white shows, and thus TV must be realized, if not accepted, for what it is."[26] Given the sitcom's particular focus on the struggles inherent in Black upward mobility—namely, the fear about acceptance into a historically white cultural setting—to say that it lacks a social significance misreads the critical conversations and themes that exist throughout *The Jeffersons*. Further, in response to the above quote, what is so fascinating about the Jefferson family and their ascension to the upper middle class are the various changes it creates in their social lives. This new wealth requires the Jeffersons to practice a different form of hustle economics to stay afloat and not be cast as outsiders. They must emulate the lifestyle of the financial elite: perform, look, talk, and act rich. The dramatic shift in culture from the Jeffersons' once working-class beginnings is often at the center of episodic conflict throughout the sitcom's tenure. The new financial capital held by the family changed their cultural capital from a proletariat to a pseudobourgeoisie identity. I use the term "pseudo" because again, this identity is performed to prevent exclusion. George often attempts to use his money to maneuver his way into the lifestyle of the white and almost always fails. Quoting *JET*'s Louie Robinson further, he asserts that "George Jefferson is often the victim of his own acts: a put-down that backfires, a contrivance that goes astray, an ego-filled balloon suddenly deflated."[27] As he attempts to reject his working-class past, his existence as a Black man in this historically white space is often harshly recounted to him.

Unlike his white counterparts who come from money, George is self-made, and his hustle through poverty is what fuels him to reject his past. He makes this point known immediately in the show's first episode while talking to his wife, Louise. He argues, "We're gonna have a real maid, with a uniform, one that fits my position. Remember, I worked my way from the bottom up to the top."[28] After growing up poor in what he terms the "ghetto" of Harlem, George and his family moved to Queens, New York. As *The Jeffersons* is a spin-off of Tandem's parent sitcom *All in the Family*, merging the viewing of the two shows together, it is explained that the moving of George, Louise, and Lionel Jefferson to the Upper East Side (creating their own sitcom) is put in motion when George launches his dry cleaning business with money from a car accident settlement. This eventually leads to a chain of dry cleaners.[29] With his quick wit, fast-talking ability, hustler's mentality, and maybe just a little financial luck, George was able to establish an empire of his own.

George's eagerness to leave his past behind him is made evident early in the series through a discussion with his wife, Louise.[30] After Diane (Paulene Myers), a Black maid in their new building, mistakenly believes Louise is also a maid (since she is Black and spending time in a high-rise), an embarrassed Diane runs out of the Jefferson home. Diane's uncomfortable facial expressions and her immediate code-switching from a casual conversation with the Jeffersons to calling them "Mr." and "Mrs." make clear that social status inherently places a divide between those who live in a high-rise and those who clean one, regardless of race. While Louise is hurt that she is losing a friend, George grins at the respect that his new status has given him.

LOUISE: Diane is my friend.

GEORGE: No, she's not; she's a domestic.

LOUISE: You make it sound like a disease.

GEORGE: Fact of life, Louise, you own an apartment in the building, and she's a maid.

LOUISE: Now hold it right there, Buster! Ain't you forgetting where you came from?

GEORGE: It ain't the question of where I came from; it's the question of where I am. . . . You are East Side and she is West Side; I don't want no crosstown traffic in my kitchen.

Here, George asserts that he doesn't want any remnants of his past living on the West Side to coincide with the identity he is performing.

As much as George attempts to push his Blackness and economically disadvantaged upbringing away from memory, he is consistently dragged back into embodying it. A working-class Black cultural tradition often comes to play when George argues with his frequent nemesis, Helen, similar to the beloved riffs between Fred and Aunt Esther on *Sanford and Son*. In defense of herself or her white husband, Helen often engages George in a game of "the dozens." Through Robin D. G. Kelley's definition, whether it's called "capping," "snapping," "ranking," or "busting," "the dozens" is a kind of game or performance.[31] "The dozens" is a game of spoken words between two people, common in Black communities, where participants insult each other until one gives up. It's customary for "the dozens" to be played in front of people who act as an audience. Commonly used to talk about somebody's mother, "the dozens," more than anything, was an effort to "master the absurd metaphor, an art form intended to entertain rather than to damage."[32] In "Jenny's Low," Helen initiates the start of "the dozens" by pushing everyone back into a circle, leaving herself and George at the camera's center. Like a boxing match, she throws rhyming verbal blows toward George.[33] Through her initiation, George must choose whether or not to engage in this specific cultural tradition. Too proud to let himself be insulted, George states, "Uh-oh! Gimme room!" making space for himself to jab back into the battle. Situations such as this scene show George's ability to break away from his performed status as high society and hail back to his street roots when prompted.

George's wife, Louise, acts as a foil to his character by constantly reminding him to remember where he came from and to be modest about his spending as she attempts to hold on to the friends of her old neighborhood. George encourages Louise to be a stay-at-home wife and assume the identity of the rich by casting away their impoverished roots, shopping daily, having brunch, and hiring a housekeeper. To oblige, she frequently forces herself to "fake it till she makes it" by joining in on the performance, causing her visible discomfort in the episode "Former Neighbors."[34] In this episode, George aims to impress a high-society Black businessman (Coleman Harris) he hopes to do future business with by hosting an extravagant dinner. However, when Louise invites their old friends from Harlem, Roy and Natalie Simms, to have dinner the same night, George schemes to hide his past to close the deal with Coleman Harris.

When George receives the news that Louise has invited their old friends to dinner as well, he attempts to cancel the Simms' invitation. Making his case to Louise, George claims that Coleman Harris is the top dog in Black society, "one of the four hundred" of the financially and socially worthy of New York society, while the Simms are just common, everyday folk: "Roy and Natalie are meat and potatoes. Coleman is the upper crust." After the Simms arrive, the class differences between them and the Jeffersons are almost immediately shown. Wearing a baggy brown plaid sports coat with tuxedo pants, it's evident that he attempted to put together his very best to see his old friends in their "fancy new digs."

Portraying the Black poor in this manner was all too familiar to the Tandem Productions costume designer Rita Riggs, who styled the families of

FIG. 4.3 Clothing on *The Jeffersons*.

Sanford and Son and *Good Times*. With *The Jeffersons*, she got to "finally do 'high-style' fashion, pretty and fancier clothes for Blacks," and she states that she very much enjoyed making George a "dandy" in his three-piece suits.[35] Rita Riggs's identification of styling George as a "dandy" can't be overlooked as it is critical to his identification and class status. A "dandy," historically from British traditions, is a man who places particular importance upon physical appearance, refined language, and leisurely hobbies, pushed with the appearance of nonchalance in a cult of self. In the case of dandyism, clothes work to perform and spectacularize identity. For Rita Riggs, as a white woman, to describe *making* George a dandy without acknowledging his Blackness ignores the complex facets that the Black dandy encompasses. As a cosmopolitan figure, George wants his wealth to be accepted in every circle; the image of the Black dandy often crosses and recrosses boundaries of class, race, and nation, cleverly manipulating Western bespoke fashion, menswear in particular, through their usage of fine fabrics, colors, and patterns.

As Monica L. Miller notes in her book *Slaves to Fashion: Black Dandyism and the Styling of Black Diasporic Identity*, "Black dandyism is a strategy of survival and transcendence."[36] The styling of his attire is essentially a part of George's tactics of hustle economics. Although he is not a Black dandy in the sense that Miller intends, George is a pastiche of it. With wealth, George is able to control the dress and appearance of his body, counter to when fine fabrics were unattainable to the Black masses due to slavery and poverty. Ironically, George's business is in clothes and making them orderly and pristine. The aim of many Black dandies, similar to George, is to use their attire for "self and cultural (re)presentation aiming to subvert the provincialism of the color line."[37] George often attempts to blend these lines with his new rich, and mostly white, community via his attire and presentation. The Black dandy allures because of his slipperiness.[38] Through attire and adhering to the fashion moment, the Black dandy has challenged the way his body has been read by the dominant white European and American cultures while wearing the very garments produced by those cultures. As a result, Monica L. Miller argues, "Black dandyism serves as both liberation and a mode of conformity."[39] Through obtaining his wealth and altering his attire, George both liberates himself from the look of Black poverty and negotiates how to sustain an image of respectability and status. In many episodes, this attire seems to be his gateway to respect and acceptance as he makes concessions for the white elite in his building for access to their network.

With George's hustle to negotiate a more refined image in mind, in contrast to Roy's appearance, George opens the door wearing a navy three-piece suit tailored to fit. As they enter the home, the Simms are exuberant and break into song while greeting their old friends. As Louise joins in, George remains unfettered, not indulging in their excitement. From the Simms' talk of muggers, rats, muscatel, and run-down buildings to them being almost starstruck at the Jeffersons' new home, it's apparent that the Simms' living situation is much less fortunate and a reminder of where the Jeffersons came from. Talking about old times brings Roy and George to reveal painful parts of their upbringing, pain that is masked by their laughter.

> GEORGE: I can never forget how poor we were. Things were so hard when my father came home *with* a job, we didn't even know what that was! (*Crowd laughter.*)
>
> ROY: I know! A job is something that the white dude *behind* you just got! (*Crowd laughter.*)

This scene is much more poignant because although they both laugh about the struggles that being poor brought them, Roy was still in that class status but remains proud of George's financial success.

> ROY: George, as long as one of us was going to make it, and it wasn't me, I'm glad it was you.

To protect George and not ruin his business plans with Coleman Harris, Roy pretends to be the owner of a chain of successful restaurants, while Louise vehemently disagrees with faking it for George's sake.

> ROY: What am I supposed to do when this man asks me what line I'm in, and I gotta say the *unemployment* line? How's that going to make George look?
>
> LOUISE: Like a man who chooses their friends for what they are and not for what they've got. (*Crowd applause.*)

Regardless of Louise's stance, George agrees to Roy's idea of lying and begins to coach him on how to act rich when Roy asks, "What do rich people talk about?"

> GEORGE: Rich people don't talk about the three R's: Roaches, Rats, and Rent. They also don't talk about welfare, being broke, and being unemployed.... Money. They talk about how to make more money.

After this exchange, Roy straightens his posture, flattens his tie, and begins to talk in a high posh accent. As Coleman Harris arrives, his style and demeanor are immediately read as Black wealth. In talking with Roy, whom he believes to be a restaurateur, Coleman Harris seems impressed that he is in the vicinity of another Black elite like himself. His comfort in this safe space of Black wealth drives Coleman Harris to begin discussing business with Roy.

> HARRIS: You know, Simms, the trouble with the working class is that they don't want to work anymore. I don't know about you, but I'm having a lot of trouble getting *colored* help.

Harris begins to demean the Black working class because he believes he is in a space where the opulent share a common understanding about the "have-nots." When Roy questions how much Harris is paying his Black workers, Harris takes offense.

> HARRIS: A lot of *our* people aren't answering the door when opportunity knocks. . . . What difference does it make what I pay them? With all the people out of work, you think they'd be glad to get anything, but no, they rather sit at home living lazy on welfare.

Offended by Harris's pomposity and his views on the Black working class, the hustle has failed and is halted as Roy and his wife, Natalie, can no longer hold their tongues. His ties to the Simms ultimately force George to choose their side at the episode's conclusion. Yet George makes sure to still express his disappointment of losing out on the business opportunity that would've been granted to him if he had sided with Harris.

The hustle economics that the Black working-class practices is not only performed by George in his efforts to make sense of his economic displacement in his new space of wealth but also often used against him. When George interacts with his childhood friend in the episode "George's Skeleton," he sees that his wealth doesn't wash away his past hustling and its repercussions.[40] When an old friend threatens to expose embarrassing secrets from George's past unless he's paid in full, George quickly considers paying him. This form of hustle economics, blackmail, is different than ones previously discussed, but nevertheless, it is a form of informal business and staying financially afloat. When George's old friend Monk enters his home, George is noticeably agitated as if he has gone through this shakedown before. The audience learns that Monk has blackmailed George for years because when they were kids in Harlem, the two robbed a department store and spent a year in jail. George talks to his neighbor Mr. Bentley:

> GEORGE: My buddy is in town, and you can bet he's out to hustle me. He did it once before. The day Louise and I got married, he threatened me. Cost me eleven bucks, plus my argyle socks, and my Speidel watchband!

With George's present status as a successful businessman, he doesn't want his past incarceration exposed to his wife, son, and new neighbors. For Monk, this secret was his meal ticket, a way to always have money at the expense of his old friend keeping his reputation intact. Upon Monk's entrance, he immediately reveals that he is there to collect. Although a crook, Monk represents the life that George left behind when he became wealthy. From the mismatched clothes to the talks about the "old days in Harlem," Monk represents a scraping and impoverished community where one may resort to even conning a friend to make a buck. When George signs a check for only $200, Monk pressures him to extort him for more.

> MONK: I hate to take advantage of a brotha', but I got no choice. You got your family, you got your business, you got all of this, but most of all, you got your pride. I figure your pride is worth a thousand dollars to start.

This episode concludes with George putting his pride aside and confessing his past incarceration to his family. To his surprise, his family already knew about his time in jail. With a violent exit, Monk tells George that it's people like him, "the blabbermouths," that ruin the blackmail business. While George has a legitimate business operation, he is very much in the minority of this level of Black financial success in the 1970s. Though his business is legitimate, people that look like him, living just ten minutes west, are forced to contend with often shady and illegal business practices that have become normalized. No matter his wealth, George is unable to escape his cultural background and the hustle economies he often was forced to engage with.

Although much of George's dealings with his past force him to confront economics head-on in unfavorable ways, many of his dealings with status and money work to teach moral lessons to *The Jeffersons*' audience and to George himself. In "George Won't Talk," George is anxious to be a guest lecturer at a college until he realizes the school is in his old Harlem neighborhood.[41] Receiving the news that he was asked to be a guest lecturer, George thinks to use this platform to discuss his rise from the ghetto to the small business mogul he became.

> GEORGE: I started out with three strikes against me. Living in the ghetto, strike one. No education, strike two. Being Black, strike three, four, five, six, and a hundred.

In essence, George wants to use this speaking opportunity to "inspire" them, but really, he intends to boast about his rags-to-riches story and to publicize his stores. Much to George's disbelief, the community organizer who has asked George to speak informs him that he was actually asked to speak in a basement to a community group of young business hopefuls in Harlem. Receiving pressure from Louise, George attends the talk. However, while there, his van and work supplies are stolen, further cementing his views on making it out of the ghetto and never coming back. When the community organizer brings the thief to confront George and apologize, George is reluctant to forgive him and immediately seeks physical retaliation and to call the police. When the thief faces Lionel, the two embrace, and we see that they are friends from the old neighborhood who used to wreak havoc together. In fact, the thief (Train) calls Lionel "Diver" because he was known to be the one in the crew to "take a dive." In hustling terms, taking a dive was meant to be an act of deception where an individual would cause a distraction, usually faking an illness so that someone is distracted while others rob them. This interaction brings the two worlds of the Black haves and the have-nots together. As Lionel is now well off in the Upper East Side due to his father's business success, Train is still in Harlem where they both started and had to hustle, lie, and cheat to make ends meet. To prevent George from calling the police on Train, Louise and Lionel confront him with a harsh truth about their present class status, reminding him where they came from and the predicaments their community still faces just blocks away.

> LOUISE: If you [George] hadn't had the drive and the luck to get ahead and get us out of the old neighborhood—Lionel would be the crook.
> LIONEL: The other day, the biggest problem I had was finding the right shirt to wear. Train's problem every day is trying to find a way to stay alive.

Some viewers of the show wrote to Tandem expressing that this episode is in fact "condoning theft" as well as supporting the idea that the people who have not gotten out of a poverty-stricken Harlem are all criminals and will end up like Train.[42] However, in this case, I believe the episode has been misread. This story acts as a reminder to George that although he has made it, his times in the old neighborhood have shaped his family, their resilience, and his own drive to make it out. Because of this, he has a duty to help those that are still there who sometimes are forced to resort to illegal methods to survive daily—because regardless, those people are still *his* people. George shakes Train's hand, forgives him for his actions, and continues his commitment to speak to the community business class so that they too can have the opportunity and option to make it financially and "move up." This episode is so crucial to the larger story arc because although the plot often attempts to distance the Jeffersons from this direct contact with their past, they are reminded of their own times of scratching for survival and proves that no matter where you may be financially, the spirit of hustling to make ends meet is inherently a part of the poor Black culture that is within them. This hustle is a mode of survival that is essential to surviving and thriving as they maintain their opulence.

There are few moments across the series' tenure that challenge George's financial stability. In an episode ironically titled "Movin' on Down," the audience is finally introduced to George in fear of returning to poverty.[43] As a spin on the popular "movin' on up" line in the series' opening credits, this episode places the Jeffersons in the midst of a supposed financial ruin, counter to the ascension that the series is based on. This throws the arrogant George off-balance as he reflects on returning to the lifestyle of scratchin' and survivin' like the families of *Sanford and Son* and *Good Times*, a living condition he has hoped would remain a distant memory.

In "Movin' on Down," George's excitement about spending money is halted when his business makes 50 percent less profit than it did in the previous year. Additionally, George loses ten thousand dollars on shoddy cleaning equipment, and his confidence is completely lost when he attempts to receive a business loan from the bank and is given the runaround. On the brink of plans to open a new store, George laments to his wife, "Weezy, we gonna have to face it, we movin' on down." Fearing financial ruin, he describes a nightmare that he had the previous evening where cockroaches were waving to him and saying, "Welcome back, George!" As he wakes up screaming, he believes the dream is foreshadowing going back to the ghetto. The opulence that his new lifestyle has afforded him has literally caused his past life to be one of his deepest fears, one that drives his work ethic and financial prowess.

As George is faced with self-doubt, his son, Lionel, continues to ask for money in order to settle a bet with a schoolmate. This interaction with Lionel works to refuel George's confidence when George teaches Lionel a hustling ploy to help him win his money back. George teaches Lionel this trick, which involves having people bet with two pairs of playing cards and one pair of dollar bills. George tells Lionel to pick the best pair, and when Lionel picks up a pair of cards, George picks up the pair of dollar bills. He reminds Lionel that he didn't say specifically "a pair of cards." George explains to Lionel to "always be the one to set the stakes," so in turn, you are the one who can control your own destiny. Coded as a lesson, this card trick is also a hustle, as George literally obtains something in an underhanded way through purposeful misinformation. Amazed by "an old trick" George has taught him, Lionel expresses how much he values these "smarts" that George has picked up along the way in his life through his times in the ghetto and in his legitimate business. Again, although George attempts to distance himself from working-class sensibilities, he is reminded that he wouldn't be where he is without them.

Thus far, I have focused on the character George Jefferson and how hustle economics doesn't simply go away when financial success is reached, its tactics for survival still exist in coded ways. However, a discussion of *The Jeffersons* would be incomplete without an analysis of the actress Isabel Sanford as Louise Jefferson and her hustle throughout Tandem Productions negotiating her role as a Black woman. Isabel Sanford embodies the tension between a working-class upbringing and an upper-middle-class lifestyle. From the fan mail received at Tandem Productions, praising Sanford for her portrayal of Louise Jefferson as "elegant," "bold," and a "fierce Black woman," many viewers (male and female) supported her role.[44] Like Esther Rolle of *Good Times* before her, Isabel Sanford as Louise Jefferson on *All in the Family* came before Sherman Hemsley as George Jefferson. It was up to Sanford to make Hemsley comfortable and welcomed into the already established Tandem space. According to Hemsley, the two "instantly clicked, and it was as if she knew him all along."[45] While on *The Jeffersons*, again much like Esther Rolle of *Good Times*, Hemsley exclaims that his working relationship with Sanford was great, and the entirety of the cast respected her as she was the leader and always held herself with dignity and pride. In an interview, Hemsley laughs as he states, "We [*The Jeffersons* cast] called her the Queen, we bowed to her." Although viewers are more likely to recognize Hemsley as *The Jeffersons* star due to his loud and boisterous behavior, Sanford was the initiating and driving force that propelled the show's long success.

"Isabel Was Our Queen . . . and That's What We Called Her": Isabel Sanford and Tandem Productions[46]

As the only Black woman to win a Primetime Emmy Award for Outstanding Lead Actress in a Comedy Series, Isabel Sanford's portrayal of Louise Jefferson is vital not only to the history of Tandem Productions but to the history of Black women's roles on television in general. Although acting in a sitcom, Louise's comedic lines were few and usually came at the expense of George and Mother Jefferson. This is a point many fan letters highlighted in requesting Louise be given more of a voice on the show and even a leading role in another program so that she was "no longer confined behind George."[47] Where she shone was in her ability to weave laughter with a state of relatability, humility, grace, and high moral character. As discussed in previous chapters, the hustle economics of Black women at Tandem Productions negotiating their identity as Black *and* female took various forms. Some of the characterizations, like the more prominent Esther Rolle's portrayal of Florida Evans on *Good Times*, caused discontent from the actress toward Tandem and CBS, often putting her star power on the line to advocate for change. LaWanda Page (as Aunt Esther in *Sanford and Son*) used her role in the television space to create a subversive identity of Black women, counter to her stand-up persona. Isabel Sanford, it seems, traversed her time at Tandem in a space of both expressed discontent as well as simply being present for a new vision of Black women's embodiment of wealth. Isabel Sanford's hustle economics of negotiating the image of Louise Jefferson across television shows deserves greater scholarly scrutiny. Thus, I rely on interviews, a few academic citations, limited production notes, and textual readings to analyze not only the character Louise but also Isabel Sanford and her creation of said character—making it clear that *The Jeffersons* was in fact *her* show.

Robin Means Coleman describes Louise Jefferson as a "Sapphire characterization."[48] A "Sapphire" is what Deborah Gray White defines as a domineering female who consumes men and usurps their role and whose assertive demeanor makes them devoid of maternal compassion and understanding.[49] However, Louise's mixture of assertive and passive reactions to her rambunctious husband along with her protective attitude toward her son complicates the characterization of her as simply domineering. By contrast, Christopher J. P. Sewell in his brief discussion of Louise describes her as a Black Mammy, despite being the mother and wife.[50] Sewell claims, "Due to her large size and expressive face, she was often the person in the show who came off as the nurturer and as being domestic. She acted as the voice of reason, as her husband George often acted hastily, she was nurturing to her son Lionel . . . and Louise often served the role of mediator between Blacks and whites."[51] In Sewell's account, Louise is reduced to a very specific archetype. It is difficult to agree with Sewell's classification of Louise as a Mammy because Mammy historically served a white family and a white home. Although she mentions having been a domestic in her younger years, on the show, Louise is never seen working for white people in any sort of domestic capacity.[52] Moving from *All in the Family* to *The Jeffersons*, Louise's character develops intertextually, and I believe that identifying her solely as the Sapphire or Mammy is to misread the complexities the character's identity possesses as well as the actress hustling to perform this role while maintaining employment. Patricia Hill Collins believes that "self-definition has been essential to U.S. Black women's survival . . . by advancing Black women's empowerment through self-definition, these safe spaces help Black women resist the dominant ideology promulgated not only outside Black civil society but within African American institutions."[53] Self-definition allows Black women to speak freely and resist fixed societal identifications, an act that Sanford mastered in her role as Louise in the early seasons of the series.

From her beginnings, hustling through minor Hollywood appearances as a semiregular on the *Carol Burnett Show* (1967–1978) to her guest role in the acclaimed film *Guess Who's Coming to Dinner* (1967), Isabel Sanford knew early on that popular media was a business, and she treated it as such. Before Tandem reached its empire status, Sanford auditioned for the role of Louise Jefferson's sister on *All in the Family*. After her audition, *All in the Family* director, John Rich, called her back for the role of Louise Jefferson.[54] In a Television Academy interview, Sanford commented that the bigotry and crass humor of the character Archie Bunker never offended her because she had consistently seen it in real life.[55] When Sanford was introduced to Louise as a character, she made it clear what she felt Tandem had wrong in their writing of her character and Black women in general. In Sanford's interview, she states, "I said to John, I wouldn't come running to George asking him how his day was. Black women don't do that. I wouldn't go running into the kitchen to get him anything—we don't do that."[56] John Rich conceded and adjusted the character. Sanford claimed that she truly modeled Louise Jefferson after herself and patterned Louise how she worked with her husband in real life. Although the scripts did not credit any Black writers until many seasons later, when asked about her input into Louise's story lines, Sanford claims that Tandem allowed any cast members who didn't think that the line was right for them to say so.[57] With this opportunity, Sanford imagined Black women on television in a different light, counter to the often docile and compliant characterizations of Black women toward men on television.

When she felt her character wasn't vocal enough, Sanford made clear to the producer Bernie West, "You know I can memorize more than six lines, right? Can't you write me in a bit more?"[58] Her relationship with Norman Lear was so close and mutually respectful that Sanford skipped over the other producers and spoke directly to him. She consistently pressured him about the opportunity for more work. Sanford stated that whenever a new Tandem show came to fruition, she always fought to be on it. Never satisfied with the precarity of one job, Sanford performed her hustle economics by consistently negotiating other roles directly with Lear to keep herself financially afloat: "When *Maude* came up, I asked can I do *Maude*? When *Good Times* came up, I asked can I do *Good Times*?"[59] However, Lear responds, "No, you're identified in *All in the Family*."[60] To which Sanford retorts, "Six lines carried me for four years, and that's how I'm identified?"[61] It seemed Sanford could not catch a break and was growing tired of the role as she considered moving on from it.

When Carroll O'Connor (Archie Bunker in *All in the Family*) walked off *All in the Family* for weeks at a time in contract disputes with Lear, Sanford finally got those extra lines and screen time.[62] While smirking, she mentions how she loved when O'Connor was on strike as it was one of the best times of her early career because more lines were written for her.[63] Sanford remained outspoken with the show's producers about choices they made—even the choice of Sherman Hemsley to play her husband. Being twenty-one years Hemsley's senior, Sanford was initially unsure about the pairing. In her first interaction with him, Sanford described Hemsley as a "little man that I could've squashed like a bug." She goes further to say, "I don't know how Norman and John could think we looked like a good couple. But apparently, they had something right that I couldn't see."[64] No matter the magnitude of the change requested, if Sanford had a concern with her character's direction, she voiced it.

In the discussion of an all-Black spin-off from *All in the Family*, Sanford was first very reluctant. As the only cast member who objected, she claimed, "I didn't want to do the spinoff because *All in the Family* was a success. So, I initially turned *The Jeffersons* down. I didn't know what would come of it."[65] However, when Tandem casting director, Jane Murray, contacted her, Sanford was faced with a challenging career decision. Murray told Sanford that if the spin-off passed muster, Tandem would write Louise off *All in the*

Family and move her to *The Jeffersons*, with or without Sanford in the role.[66] Sanford was forced to take a role in this precarious new production or face being left behind. Although Sanford was the influence for the show's creation and the character, she was deemed expendable.

After initial talks of *The Jeffersons* being a spin-off, Lear approached Sanford to discuss her clear dissatisfaction with the move.[67] Sanford shared that she was "scared to death" regarding this leap to her new series. She had fear because, on *All in the Family*, she had very few lines for laughs every now and then, but now it was up to her to carry a show, lamenting, "I'm out in front."[68] This fear worked to drive Sanford through the transition, knowing that if she refused, she would be out of a job. The hustle had to go on. This built relationship with Lear was how Sanford was able to negotiate her terms and have the ability to speak freely as the person carrying the show.

The final episode of *All in the Family* that featured the Jeffersons before their spin-off foreshadows how this newfound wealth will impact George and Louise Jefferson. In "The Jeffersons Move Up," George and Louise prepare for their move from Queens to Upper East Side Manhattan due to George's business success.[69] With both Louise and George being from humble working-class beginnings, the move impacts them vastly differently. George is overjoyed to leave the past behind, while Louise fears moving to Manhattan's East Side with "all those fancy folks." After a heartfelt embrace with her long-term neighbor Edith Bunker (played by Jean Stapleton), which brings the two to tears, we see that Louise isn't prepared for the new person she must become in the new white and rich space she will be occupying. She knows how to live, work, and scrape to make ends meet, but she doesn't know how to perform as a rich housewife, and the possibility of losing herself and her values as a working-class Black woman strikes fear in her. She makes these fears clear to George who, throughout the series, minimizes her concerns while encouraging her to simply bask in the success.

LOUISE: I'm afraid of going where I don't belong.
GEORGE: When you got the money—you belong.
LOUISE: George, we are just plain folks.
GEORGE: Not anymore. We were plain folks $47,000.50 ago.

This verbal exchange between Louise and George Jefferson on their last appearance of *All in the Family* directly parallels the emotions displayed in the opening credits of every episode of *The Jeffersons*. As mentioned earlier in this chapter, during the opening credits, the audience sees Louise wiping away her tears while George grips her hand in support, excited about leaving his past behind. The tears represent a longing for a much simpler past that is transferred intertextually from *All in the Family* to *The Jeffersons* and reiterated to the viewer every time they watch an episode of *The Jeffersons*. This works to make Louise Jefferson's feelings of displacement a leitmotif throughout the series. As George attempts to make himself a part of high society, Louise rejects it to not lose her sense of self. In Sanford's portrayal of Louise, the writers push her to embody recycled traits of femininity, such as gentleness, empathy, sensitivity, and compliance. She was characterized as the voice of reason, while George is able to express his arrogance, power, and pompous sensibility.

These wholesome and virtuous attributes of Louise quickly became bothersome and limiting to Sanford and her abilities as an actress. Rather than recoil, as her character might, Sanford expressed her contention with the writers and producers. Sanford claims that she would complain to them, "You got me pure as the driven snow, isn't there something I can say that would spice it up?"[70] Sanford asserts that far too often, the writers would simply respond, "George can say things like that, Louise can't," and her inquiries were usually pushed to the side.[71] It's clear here that the writing of Louise's character is gendered, as the male writers often craft her in exhaustive tropes of docility. Although Louise's (and Sanford's concurrently) feelings are usually silenced, she often battles George to make sure she is heard, an action scarcely seen by Black wives and women on television at this moment. With a smile on her face, Sanford reflects on a moment where she is listened to, and her character Louise is given more color.[72] In "Like Father, like Son," when the money-flashing and lavish-spending George buys their son Lionel a fancy watch, Louise is in utter disbelief about such a sumptuous gift for no occasion.[73] Louise asks about the price of the watch, and her reaction is met with a two-minute-long laugh from the studio audience.

LOUISE: That watch must be at least $100.
GEORGE: $350.
LOUISE: $350 for a watch?! NIGGA PLEASE!

Sanford relished being able to add this shock value in unexpected moments as comedic relief. These moments were so pivotal because they were out of character with the quotidian mannerisms and reactions of Louise, this loud, combative, and very Black, culturally specific response was much more in line with lines written for George. Although moments like these were fleeting, Sanford's expressed contention with the simplicity of Louise's character incited these writing changes. These juxtaposing reactions to Black upward mobility and fiscal responsibility make for a compelling tension that drives a great deal of the episodic plots in *The Jeffersons*.

In the pilot episode of *The Jeffersons* "A Friend in Need," Louise is obviously tense, lost, and uncomfortable in her efforts to make a home out of her new life in a luxurious high-rise.[74] In order to combat her feelings of displacement and nostalgia, Louise attempts to spark a friendship with a Black maid (Diane) in the building. When Diane is surprised to find out that Louise is actually a tenant and not a maid like herself, Diane storms out in embarrassment. The money that Louise's family now possesses has changed the way that people view her, rendering her image out of her control. Working-class people, like Diane in this instance, are often cast in opposing social circles with the wealthy, regardless of if they share the same race. Louise laments over the fact that someone whom she once shared a class status and even an occupation with (as Louise mentions her past as a part-time maid for white families) has cast Louise as "other," as a friendship between a maid and a homeowner is seen to be unimaginable. This works to further Louise's already strong sense of isolation and nonbelonging through being hoisted into high society.

Amid these feelings, George urges her to accept her new status and the rights of passage and privilege it affords her. She remains steadfast in attempting to remind George of where they come from and that they are still just "plain folk." However, her efforts are to no avail as George grabs firmly to the lapels of his suit and demands that Louise hires a maid because it's what rich families do. Not just any maid, George says, a Black one. This exchange leads to a deeper insight into Louise's history and her morals around domestic servitude.

> LOUISE: Remember when Lionel was growing up and I did domestic work twice a week to help out? Remember the folks I worked for? It was "Yes, Ma'am, No, Ma'am." Now how can I ask Diane to say "Yes, Ma'am" to me?
>
> GEORGE: Because now you're the Ma'am. Some people gotta be the Ma'ams, and the rest gotta be the Mam'mies.

George urges Louise to realize that they have transcended from servicing others, and now they deserve to be the ones who are serviced. Continuing to groan over the money it would cost to hire a maid, Louise expresses how a "lifetime of being poor" leads her to constantly reject what she sees as frivolous spending. Eventually, she gives in and finds a maid (Florence, played by Marla Gibbs). Even after acceding to George's wishes, Louise expresses her discomfort with having another person picking up after them in her arguments with George and discussions with her neighbors, the Willises. Much of her grief comes from the realization that while she was poor, she assumed the money would solve their problems; however, George and Louise's opposing reactions to having wealth are what really causes their strife.

Louise's identity constantly shifts from compliant to self-willed when she expresses her continuous troubles with adjusting to "the good life" throughout episodic texts following the pilot. In "Louise Feels Useless," these troubles of assimilation drive Louise to discomfort in her own home.[75] With her son, Lionel, in school, George always at work, and their new maid cleaning up after them, Louise expresses, "Nobody needs me anymore, I got no reason for getting out of bed in the morning." In order to feel useful, Louise asks George if she can work part-time in his cleaning store that exists in the lobby of their building. Firmly against "these honkies" seeing his wife working, George takes a firm stance against the request.

> GEORGE: I don't want you to work; you've worked long enough. You've earned the right to do what all other high-class New York ladies do. Nothing.

George wanted Louise to fit into a mold of what a high-society wife was supposed to do. Using the Willises as her sounding board, Louise can't help but express her displeasure that George is attempting to make her someone she's not. When Louise meets a man desperate for part-time help at his store, despite George's feelings, Louise takes the reins of her own life and offers her assistance to work. Unbeknown to her, it is a job at a competing cleaning store. Taking the job, we see Louise smiling and singing, finally happy in her home as she has a reinvigorated purpose that exists outside the performance of wealth. Similar to the ways white women characters like Lucy in *I Love Lucy* (1951–1957) felt a sense of freedom and purpose when they left their homes and went to work.[76] Louise is able to reject the stay-at-home posh lifestyle that is being forced on her. However, the secret of her job does not leave room for as much liberation and agency as Louise had hoped for. Resisting in silence takes away from the larger stand that Louise intended to make because she now feels guilty for hiding something from her husband. When she is forced to come clean about her new job, George demands she quit. After space and reflection, Louise adheres to George's disapproval of her working for the competition; however, she finally takes a stand against George when she exclaims, "I am going to work downstairs, and that's that!" George's response is simply a blank stare of approval into the camera as it fades to black on the scene.

Through these early examples of Louise's character development, I believe that although Sanford as Louise may have often acted on tropes of the Sapphire or the Mammy, to classify her role in such a reduced matter is reductive. As Patricia Hill Collins states, "U.S. Black women as a group live in a different world from that of people who are not Black and female," and this world comes in various forms.[77] Louise ambiguously plays in the arenas of submissive, posh, domestic, and nurturing, yet she can also assume agency, travail, and command respect. Although Louise's character embodies identification beyond the historical Sapphire figure, she often shares traits with the character Sapphire in *Amos 'n' Andy*, as many claimed the role of Sapphire was stereotypical of shrewish Black bossy wives. Sapphire in *Amos 'n' Andy* only scolded her husband when he deserved it, but most often, her character was a kindly, loving, and loyal wife—much like Louise. This ambiguous imagery of Black womanhood is more evident throughout *The Jeffersons* than in any other Tandem Black sitcom. Through the identities of Black domestic servitude (Florence and Diane), the nouveau riche (Louise), and old money (Helen Willis), the very first episode of *The Jeffersons* alone makes way for a new diversity of Black women's identities blended into one television show. This negotiation of the ambiguous Black female form marks these actresses on *The Jeffersons* as auteurs who are radically performing hustle economics. This transformative image is highlighted vividly by the Jeffersons' new maid Florence in the final scene of "A Friend in Need." With Florence and Diane standing in between Louise and Helen in the Jeffersons' doorway, Florence looks at the group of women and is perplexed.

> FLORENCE: You folks mind if I ask something? (*To Louise*) You live in this apartment, right? (*To Helen*) And you got an apartment in this building too? Well, how come we overcame, and nobody told me?!

A clear nod to a rallying cry of resistance movements, "We Shall Overcome," this line caused a hysterical laugh from the characters on-screen as well as the studio audience.[78] The comedy in this line comes from the delivery of Florence and the way she is able to discuss a pivotal moment of change in an amusing tone. However, reading deeper into the line, it seems the laughter is conjured more out of a space of discomfort, as the domestic workers look to the Black women who have obtained wealth, while the domestics have seemingly missed their opportunity. Marla Gibbs (the actress who played Florence) says that this line is memorable to *The Jeffersons'* fans to this day.[79] To "overcome" meant to prevail over various injustices that the civil rights and other movements fought against. Injustices such as racial discrimination, sexism, and unfair working conditions caused protestors to shout these words as a declaration for better days to come. To Florence, seeing a Black woman—not a domestic—living in a high-rise demonstrated "overcoming," which is not so uplifting to her and Diane, as they still work to serve others. This symbol of "overcoming" seen on *The Jeffersons* exists as just one example of the ways this show worked against popular understandings of Black life. Making this proclamation directly to the audience was making it clear that this show was unlike any other, and its representation of Black women would follow suit. Probably the least subtle of these resistances to the norm is the sitcom's discussion of racial passing and its depiction of the first ever interracial (specifically Black and white) marriage on television.

FIG. 4.4 "How come we overcame, and nobody told me?"

"Zebras, Honkies, and Niggas"

The Jeffersons, arguably more than in any other Tandem Black sitcom, places Black and white racial controversy front and center in its narrative arc. It is seen in the early and consistent use of the words "Nigga" and "Honkey" throughout the first and second seasons, the instances of racial passing, and most vividly in the interracial intimacy and marriage of Helen and Tom Willis (portrayed by Roxie Roker and Franklin Cover, respectively). Unlike other Black sitcoms of Tandem, *The Jeffersons* places white characters in recurring supporting roles, which is consistent with the show's theme of placing a once poor Black man into a space of majority white wealth.[80] Through episode analysis, interviews, newspaper articles, and audience reception, a compelling discussion emerges about the intersection of Black and white identity and the individuals of Tandem Productions who helped contribute to it on television in *The Jeffersons*. With these contributions, the artists on the show, the Black artists in particular, performed characters and situations that a great percentage of America was not ready to see on prime time. Amid threats of violence and media backlash, these artists engaged in hustle economics by risking their lives and the longevity of the show to remain employed and contribute to growing Black visibility on-screen.

Although the history of the "miscegenation issue" is dated much earlier, the *Loving v. Virginia* case is important to discuss here in regard to interracial marriage.[81] In 1958, Mildred and Richard Loving (a Black woman and a white man, respectively) traveled to Washington, D.C., to marry, evading their home state of Virginia's Racial Integrity Act of 1924, which made marriage between whites and nonwhites a crime.[82] After multiple arrests in Virginia for their marriage, Mildred wrote letters to the American Civil Liberties Union, who aided in filing motions that the Virginia state laws on interracial marriage violated the Fourteenth Amendment's Equal Protection Clause.[83] The matter then made its way to the Supreme Court. In 1967, the Supreme Court ruling in the case *Loving v. Virginia* established marriage as a fundamental right for interracial couples and struck down all U.S. state laws that prevented this right.[84] Although laws such as these were generally upheld in the American South, which often adhered to strict Jim Crow segregation laws, 72 percent of the public opposed the court's decision at the time, and many decried it as judicial overreach, resisting its implementation for decades.[85] It's no coincidence that this case impacted the reception of the film *Guess Who's Coming to Dinner* (1967). Starring Sidney Poitier and Katharine Hepburn, the film was one of few at the time to depict an interracial relationship leading to marriage, as interracial marriage historically had been illegal in most states of the United States until *Loving v. Virginia*, just six months prior to the film's release. *Guess Who's Coming to Dinner* was an attempt to normalize interracial relationships by spreading a liberal consciousness against a backdrop of civil rights movements.

Just eight years after this revolutionary Supreme Court decision, the Willises enter the public eye on prime-time television in *The Jeffersons*. Similar to the Lovings, the Willises (Helen and Tom) are a married Black woman and a white man. However, their placement in the more liberal urban North keeps them from much of the de facto segregation experienced by the former. The interracial marriage between Helen and Tom is consistently poked fun at by the show's protagonist, George Jefferson. Although a sitcom stands for a fictitious imagination of reality, the interactions of the Willises as the first interracial marriage on television represent a subset of America whose story was finally being told. Helen embodies a history of Black wealth, high society, and elegance. With a father who is a self-made banker, Helen had always been privy to financial stability and comfort. The Tandem Productions costume designer, Rita Riggs, even mentions her own excitement to finally do "high-style" fashion with Helen, who represents a Black woman with means.[86] Helen is often the character that helps Louise adjust to a life of means, encouraging her that she deserves to enjoy life and spend money. While Tom is the descendant of Northern politicians and is an executive at a publishing company, his whiteness seems to be a connection to historical wealth, as his past is talked about much less frequently than Helen's.

George, who is notably opposed to interracial relationships, has a deep loathing for interracial couples, standing in for many that carry this same angst in real life. George often plays his discontent and ignorance comedically at the Willises' expense. With his own history of dealing with bigotry, it seems George uses comedy in reference to the Willises' relationship as a defense mechanism so that he doesn't have to cope with the reality of a happy relationship existing across racial lines—especially between Black and white. Although the effect of the comedy draws laughter and becomes a running joke, George persists because it doesn't sway the Willises. George's son, Lionel, dates (and eventually marries) Jenny, the Willises' daughter, who is Black *and* white—and George's discomfort grows when the Willises are getting more deeply enmeshed in his family and social circle. George often calls Tom a honky and refers to the couple as the Zebras, vanilla and chocolate, day and night, and even buys them towel sets (His, a white towel with black lettering, and Hers, a brown towel with white lettering).[87] The ability of George as a Black man being able to freely use the terms "nigga" and "honky" on television without being reprimanded drew criticism from some, seemingly racist, viewers. Particularly in a letter addressed to Norman Lear, a viewer believed it to be discrimination that George can say the word "honky" while a white person can't, or doesn't, respond in a similar fashion. The viewer suggested a suitable tag that would equate would be allowing a white person to say "nigger" on the show, in response to the antics of George.[88] Nevertheless, through the writing of these scripts, George refuses to normalize interracial marriage, while Louise consistently comes to their defense and grows a strong friendship with Helen. Writing this opposition within George's character speaks to an imagined Black cultural discontent with interracial relationships, a perspective created by the white writers of *The Jeffersons*. Because she has married a white man, George often challenges Helen's Blackness, and their repeated banter becomes a running theme. Even when the Willises aren't present, George makes fun of their marriage. For example, in the series' first episode, while George is arguing with Louise about hiring a maid, Lionel comments about the Willises having one.

LIONEL: That's not a bad idea, Mom. Jenny's parents have an apartment like this. They have a maid.

GEORGE: Only one? I figured the Willises would have three maids.

LIONEL: Three?

GEORGE: Well, I figure a Black one for Mr. Day, a white one for Mrs. Night, and a plaid one for Jenny.[89]

Joking at their expense, George also centers himself between the two in an effort to pit Helen and Tom at odds. In an episode regarding a local election, Helen and Tom find themselves in disagreement when the opposing candidates they support need the endorsement of George's dry cleaners.[90] Assuming that Helen is supporting the Black candidate, George instantly approves her request. Much to his surprise, Helen is backing the white candidate, and Tom is backing the Black one. No matter the candidate's political agenda, George supports the Black one and sides with Tom, leaving Helen and Tom at odds publicly and in the home, much to George's enjoyment. Even directly in the first episode, George attempts to throw a wrench into the happy marriage of Helen and Tom.[91] While Louise and George argue in front of the Willises, Louise asks George why they fight so much, and why can't they talk things through like Tom and Helen do. "They don't fight," George responds in a very matter-of-fact way.

GEORGE: They don't fight because they're scared to fight.

HELEN: What does that mean?

GEORGE: You know damn well what it means! If you two ever started really going at one another, inside of five minutes, he'd be calling you . . .

HELEN: Don't say it!

GEORGE: Nigga!

This verbal exchange leads Helen to question why the words "honky" may cross her mind in an argument or if the word "nigga" ever crosses Tom's. No matter the instigation, the marriage of the Willises remained in the show's story line. Although the discussion of it is not always unfavorable (unless it's from George), the interracial nature of their marriage is something the Willises cannot escape because it's at odds with societal norms. In one of their frequent gripe sessions about George, Louise expresses her envy of Helen and Tom's marriage.[92]

LOUISE: You two seem to handle your problems so well.

TOM: What problems?

LOUISE: (*looks down nervously*) Well . . . uh you know . . . uh, you and Helen.

HELEN: Oh! The "biggie."

TOM: That's not *our* problem; it's other people's. They're the ones who can't handle it.

The "biggie" referred to here is the biggest problem that they deal with in their union: being different races. Helen goes on to explain that when they announced their marriage to their families, Tom's parents yelled, screamed, and even fainted over the news, while Helen's parents completely wrote her out of her family's inheritance. Through the years of family isolation and outside hatred, it is difficult to have optimism in a world that largely doesn't accept their union. However, they hold themselves up through it all.

Although Helen and Tom represent the first televisual foray into a Black and white interracial marriage, their presence adds to a complicated history of interracial intimacy on television. In the original popular science fiction series *Star Trek* (1966–1969), despite science-fiction conventions that privilege metaphor and allegory, network decision-makers attempted to curtail and control the creative staff's liberal-humanist project.[93] Perhaps the most popular example of this struggle surrounds the production of season 3, episode 10, "Plato's Stepchildren," which calls for the main protagonist Captain Kirk (a white man), manipulated by Greek-god-like aliens, to kiss his crewmember Uhura (a Black woman). According to most speculations, this would have been American network television's first interracial kiss between a Black and a white person. Apparently, NBC was concerned with the fallout of such a "first," especially among its affiliates in the South, and requested changes. A memorandum from Jean Messerschmidt of NBC's Broadcast Standards Department made the network's position explicit: "It must be clear there are no racial overtones to Kirk and Uhura's dilemma."[94] While many creative decision-makers resisted the network's capitulation to racism, NBC nevertheless continued with their aim of censoring the interracial "dilemma." Apparently, they even requested that Spock, the racialized alien half-breed, be the one to kiss Uhura.[95] Actress Nichelle Nichols (who portrays Uhura) explains, "Somehow, I guess, they found it more acceptable for a Vulcan to kiss me, for this alien to kiss this Black woman, than for two humans with different coloring to do the same thing." She continues, "It was simply and clearly racism standing in the door . . . in suits. Strange how a 23rd-century space opera could be so mired in antiquated hang-ups."[96]

The scene that was aired shows Kirk paired with Uhura and Spock paired with the spaceship's nurse. It begins with the telekinetic Greek gods controlling the physical movements of these characters, making them walk and dance in contorted and humiliating ways for the pleasure and amusement of their captors.[97] Soon, a large group of the Greek gods watches as their leader forces Spock to kiss the nurse several times. In this scene, the audience can *see* Spock kiss the nurse as their lips are visibly touching on-screen in multiple shots. The group also watches Kirk and Uhura resist their *forced* coupling. These shots are also drawn out, dramatizing the extratextual racial tension surrounding their pairing.[98] Since this is coupling a Black woman and a white man, it is taboo and met with much more resistance and a struggle between the two characters while they are in their trance. Unable to fight the trance, Kirk turns Uhura's body toward the camera, the back of her head taking up most of the bottom half of the screen, and forcibly presses his lips against hers while staring in anger at the group watching them. Although accounts from Nichelle Nichols explain that the two actually did kiss, the audience is restricted from the sight of their actual lips touching.[99] Nichols asserts that "NBC's Office of Broadcast Standards and the creative decision-makers compromised: the interracial kiss was only implied."[100] This implication complicates the reality of a Black and white person sharing the intimacy of a kiss on-screen. It is essentially forced upon the two characters, and even through force, this forbidden action is blocked from the audience's view.

In a Television Academy interview with *The Jeffersons* producer, George Sunga, he remembers vividly Lear saying to Roxie Roker and Franklin Cover before *The Jeffersons* pilot, "You must be able to kiss each other and mean it."[101] The presence of Roxie Roker on *The Jeffersons* reimagines her previous television identity. Roker first worked as a reporter for an NBC affiliate station in New York where her husband, a white man, Sy Kravitz was an executive. This local recognition, along with her career in the Negro Ensemble Company and appearances in off-Broadway theater, launched her career into the public affairs television space. As a host of one of the first Black public affairs television programs, Brooklyn's *Inside Bedford-Stuyvesant* (1968–1971), Roker firmly placed herself as an advocate and interlocutor for this Black community and Black culture. With the dual goal of showcasing the area's attractive buildings and public spaces and of highlighting both the possibilities and challenges faced by the predominantly Black community, *Inside Bedford-Stuyvesant* represented a microcosm of all Black communities and was a counternarrative to the "ghettoization discourses" of the Moynihan Report—Roxie Roker was at the center.[102] According to Devorah Heitner, "On the program, the hosts themselves transform with the times, starting as members of the civil rights generation who have 'made it.'"[103] As a college-educated Black woman speaking in support of the Black cultural beauty that this neighborhood possessed, Roker was a welcomed correspondent whom viewers engaged with. From trying on dashikis on-screen to later wearing an Afro, she engaged more and more with the prevailing moods of Black Power over the course of the broadcast.[104] Having Roker front and center as the ambassador speaking for this community on television was deliberate. The choice of Roker as a host, "with her middle-class linguistic styles and appearance, was a subtle nod at 'uplift,' as a strategy invoked by elite African Americans to counter racism by 'calling attention to class distinctions among African Americans as a sign of evolutionary race progress.'"[105]

Hustling through different television production spaces, Roker was able to negotiate a new vision of what Black women could be on the small screen. Her real-life presentation on *Inside Bedford-Stuyvesant* directly correlates with her fictional role as Helen on *The Jeffersons* as a financially well-off Black woman demonstrating a new television characterization. With Roxie Roker being married to a white man in reality, her role as Helen Willis can be imagined as a peek into her real life once she departs the cultural center of Bedford Ave. and Stuyvesant Ave. Performing Helen and the backlash that would ensue in portraying an interracial marriage was all too familiar to Roker's lived experience. Giving the producers and writers at Tandem credit for their courageousness, Tandem used the very first episode of *The Jeffersons* to put forth the reality of interracial intimacy, despite the possible negative responses that they may receive. Even the show's star, Sherman Hemsley, mentioned that everyone feared showing interracial intimacy on-screen. He was particularly fearful of the fact that an interracial marriage would get them cancelled, since "no one has done it before."[106] Yet in a very private moment on-screen between Helen and Tom outside of the Jeffersons' doorway, the audience intervenes to watch the two share a very passionate and obvious kiss. The camera oscillates from a wide over-the-shoulder shot to a medium shot of the two—center screen—with Helen's arms wrapped around Tom and their lips pressed in a firm embrace. There is no question that their kiss is real and within the characters' control. The kiss lasts until they are embarrassingly interrupted by their neighbor Harry coming out of the elevator, leading them to laugh and embrace even closer. Whether or not the forcible kiss of Kirk and Uhura was on their mind, Tandem defiantly made it clear that interracial intimacy on-screen was possible, and they risked the cancellation of their show to prove it. Even riskier, Roxie Roker, working within a precarious employment culture in Hollywood, engages in hustle economics by performing this action on-screen, amid the threat of job security, in order to negotiate a new depiction of Black women in prime-time television.

As a company producing five acclaimed shows at the time, Tandem Productions could afford the possible backlash toward them. Yet the actors portraying this interracial marriage, Roxie Roker and Franklin Cover, could not afford such repercussions. They in fact were the ones risking their careers to make an important stand. Although this interracial marriage and intimacy are accepted by *most* of the characters within the story line, some of the real-life audience met the sight of Helen and Tom Willis on-screen with abhorrence. In hate mail regarding *The Jeffersons*, audience members particularly chastised Lear for his "filthy shows." Specifically, in this case, the audience berated Lear for showing interracial marriages on television. A writer from Philadelphia claimed, "I don't know anyone married or going with a Negro so it just isn't real life."[107] Regardless of whether the letter writer knew any interracial couples in his circle of friends, a 1970 study of married couples that have a Black wife and a white husband total 51,420 couples combined in the north and west sections of the United States, a 66 percent increase since 1960—interracial marriage was very real.[108]

Other letters from many disgruntled Southern viewers were sent directly in attack of the actor Franklin Cover, whom some saw as a disgrace

FIG. 4.5 Helen and Tom Willis share a kiss.

to white people. One particular letter addressed to Cover remarked, "With about 90% of people strongly against Black and white interracial marriage, it's difficult to know whether or not you work-needy class-B actors are in cahoots with those goddam producers-selling miscegenation to the American people . . . preparing them to accept the Marxists' long-standing goal of mass-hybridization."[109] It's clear here that many believed that the existence of interracial marriage on-screen was no more than a plot to encourage interbreeding, much to the chagrin of many Southern affiliates. Collective social groups even wrote directly to CBS to push for *The Jeffersons'* cancellation. They claimed that the existence of the show "continued to insult the intelligence of the American public by insisting that all those who oppose miscegenation are bigots. Blacks are justly proud of their race as are whites. Miscegenation is true bigotry because it announces to the world that one believes there should no longer be racial differences as provided by nature and evolution. Nuts to CBS and 'The Jeffersons.' You are true bigots, doing your best to put an end to the races."[110] To Tandem and the actors of *The Jeffersons*, these letters made it clear that their presence on-screen was even more necessary.

Despite these letters of prejudice toward interracial marriage on-screen, *The Jeffersons* continued to be successful, and the presence of Helen and Tom Willis was integral to that success. However, interracial marriages in the United States experience numerous uncertainties and strains outside their union. As F. James Davis suggests, "A major problem is the way the community classifies and treats the children of such marriages. A great many inter-married parents, primarily white parents, apparently hope and believe that people will overlook the racial mixture and just treat the child as a human being. Even children who are well prepared to be defined as Black can experience some problems, but those who are not so well prepared are likely to get some rude shocks as they get older."[111] In a 1976 interview with the *Washington Post*, Roxie Roker is featured as a Black woman on the rise, reflecting on her accomplishments as Helen Willis on *The Jeffersons*.[112] In a conversation regarding the season one finale episode, "Jenny's Low," Roker discusses how she had strong objections to the original script and voiced her concerns to demand adjustments be made.[113] Roker commented that in this episode, "our [the Willises] son who had been abroad returned. He's fair-skinned and was able to pass, our daughter is dark-complexioned. Now, the script wanted me to show favoritism towards her because she is brown like me, but I couldn't. I am the mother; I wouldn't treat any child that way. More than anything I want the script to be believable." This particular episode handles a racial situation that was also never before seen in the prime-time sitcom, passing.

In this season one finale, the Willises' daughter, Jenny (Berlinda Tolbert), becomes jealous when her brother, Allan (Andrew Rubin), returns from Europe because he is able to pass for white while she can't. Racial passing occurs when a person classified as a member of one racial group is accepted as a member of a racial group other than their own, usually for the better treatment that one racial group has over the other. According to F. James Davis, "Those who pass have a severe dilemma before they decide to do so since a person must give up all family ties and loyalties to the Black community in order to gain economic or other opportunities."[114] Here, I am using passing to describe a Black person who is able to assimilate into white society due to their skin tone. In this particular case, the biracial (Black and white) children of the Willises, Jenny and Allan, each favor the opposing racial identifiers. Allan, who favors his father's whiteness, is able to use his racially ambiguous appearance in order to pass as white.

At the start of the episode, when Jenny receives news that her brother has returned home from a two-year retreat throughout Europe, Jenny grows stoic. She quickly runs off the scene to avoid the situation entirely. When

Lionel catches up to her, he addresses her odd behavior, and Jenny speaks indirectly about what's really bothering her as Lionel attempts to lighten the mood.

JENNY: The trouble is, my brother takes after my father.

LIONEL: What do you mean? He's white?

JENNY: That's exactly what I mean. . . . Well I mean he looks like he's white.

LIONEL: Well OK, one of you turned out white, and the other turned out lucky (*laughs uncomfortably*). Well . . . is it maybe that you feel your brother is the one who turned out lucky?

Seeing her brother Allan in the next scene, it is notable that he does in fact "take after his father." He is tall, lanky, and has a white skin complexion, yet he still has thick Black curls formed into an Afro, possibly the only physical sign of his Blackness. Even George and Louise find it odd how much more he appears as white. While Louise attempts to avoid the obscurity, George can't help but shout, "I thought a zebra was bad enough. Now we got us a palomino!"[115]

When Jenny and Allan finally come face-to-face, Jenny gives him the cold shoulder. In his own boisterous way, George sheds light on the uncomfortable tension and forces Allan to see some hard truths. When George calls Allan a honkey, the two engage in a face-to-face heated exchange.

ALLAN: You know, I knew there was something I missed in Europe, wasn't anybody to feed me those dumb racial cracks.

GEORGE: That's because you never showed them your family portrait.

Here, George is making reference to Allan being able to live without anyone questioning whether or not he is Black; they would only know if they happened to look at a family portrait. When Allan leaves the scene, George continues to force the last word: "If he had any guts, he wouldn't have hidden out in Europe. He would've been here, with his mother and his sister, with his own kind." Although through candor, George can immediately sense that Allan had escaped America so that he can pass. When Jenny confesses that George is right about Allan, the stage goes quiet as the camera zooms into a close-up of a hurt and disappointed Jenny on the brink of tears.

Later, Helen and Tom are also at a loss regarding their son's two-year hiatus and lack of explanation; however, they refuse to address it with him directly. When Jenny and Allan finally come face-to-face again, Allan questions if Jenny's anger is regarding her jealousy toward him and his ability to pass. Still unable to confront her truth, both families are led back into the Jefferson household. Being met with even more snide remarks from George, Allan becomes fed up and attempts to prove his Blackness by initiating "the dozens." As described earlier in this chapter, "the dozens" is a game of spoken words between two people, common in Black communities, where participants insult each other until one gives up. A pattern of interactive insults, "the dozens" is evident among all classes of Black people, among males and females, children and adults.[116] George smiles and engages in the challenge. As the two continue to throw verbal jabs at each other, Lionel and Jenny watch as an audience and are astonished by Allan's sharp retorts, and they comment from the side of the game.

LIONEL: Your brother can get down when he wants to. He can play some dozens.
JENNY: I didn't know he could do that.

Allan's initiation of the dozens is explained with clarity by Adrian Piper: "I have sometimes met Blacks who, as a condition of social acceptance of me, require me to prove my Blackness by passing the 'suffering test.'"[117] In an effort to prove that his Blackness is inherent regardless of his skin tone, Allan initiated the game in hopes of gaining respect regarding his cultural and ethnic roots. After the final verbal blow, George and Allan laugh and give each other a dap while an impressed George states, "You only half-white, so that makes you half all right," even if for a brief moment, Allan had secured George's respect and proved that his Blackness is within. With both families present on the screen and many still confused about the animosity between Jenny and Allan, again George is the voice of clarity that sheds light on the feud. George exclaims, "He [Allan] crossed the color line, he's passing for an ofay, and his sister don't dig it."[118] It is now clear to everyone that Allan has been passing for white and that Jenny envies him for it. Jenny's hurt stems from a belief that since Allan essentially disappeared so long it is because he has a strong repudiation of her and their family. Adrian Piper's words are useful again here in Jenny's confusion about why Allan would choose to pass. Piper writes, "What is harder for me to grasp is how they [people who pass] could want these things enough to sacrifice the history, wisdom, connectedness, and moral solidarity with their family and community in order to get them. It seems to require so much severing and forgetting, so much disowning and distancing, not simply from one's shared past, but from one's former self."[119] Part of Jenny's envy is that she felt forgotten or not good enough in the eyes of her brother, and with all the risks, is passing worth it?

Allan makes an important declaration regarding his ability to pass and why he does it. He poses a question to the entire room, asking, "Is there anybody here who hasn't wondered just once what it would be like to be white?" In a moment of self-reflection, everyone remains silent as all of the Black characters come to grips with the truth that the imagination of being white and the privilege that it garners has in fact crossed their minds. Allan has the ability to act on that imagination, so he admits to doing it as a way to escape the painful realities of Blackness in a racially prejudiced America and the treatment he receives once his Blackness is identified. In Allan's eyes, "passing in order to get the benefits you know you deserve may seem the only way to defy the system."[120] Jenny finally expresses the roots of her envy when she tells Allan, "You were the one who had it easy. You went anywhere you wanted. You did what you wanted. Why you?" The unfairness of their physical racial identifiers has festered into a deep-seated resentment of Jenny toward her brother. Albeit, her inescapable Blackness has brought Jenny countless forms of discrimination in her life, Allan's ability to pass often left him with a different sense of pain, losing a sense of self and a lack of belonging while juggling conflicting identities. Allan explains that in America he had to pass because everyone asked him who he was, while in Europe, no one asked him who he was, to a point where he lost himself and no longer knew.

The ability to pass is seen here as a space where one's identity can become lost or unknown—a crippling feeling and critique of a historic practice never before addressed (at this point) on a sitcom platform. Jenny and Allan embrace each other, as they finally feel heard and understood. Her envy and his lost sense of self require them to lean on each other as their shared biracial identity brings a politics of representation that only the two can understand. Asking yourself who you are, and what it means to be able to assume another identity, leaves for a self-reflection of every character on-screen, as well as the viewers watching the show. Through complicating the practice of passing and the confines of interracial marriage in the space of a situational comedy, the Black artists' performances worked to incite important discussions of identity politics and the Black community. This form of introspection played out on-screen and in public proves the power of the imagery and narrative of *The Jeffersons* as these actors risked social backlash, unemployment, and threat in order to negotiate arenas of Blackness that television had yet to bring to light. These numerous hustle economics of dissent and negotiation between Tandem, audiences, and the Black artists of *The Jeffersons* prove just how integral this show was to the racial arc of Black identity formation constructed by popular media.

Reflection

Through Tandem Productions, Black images proliferated on network television in the 1970s. The case studies discussed throughout this book (whether through various series, episodes, and/or individual Black artists) suggest many of these Black representations were achieved through resisting the mainstream cooptation of Blackness and are thus transformative in not just the content of these shows but the individuals employed in television. All of the sitcoms of Tandem Productions are integral in establishing an arc of the racial formation of Blackness in popular television. Before *All in the Family*, popular sitcoms were predominantly segregated and featured all-white casts. *All in the Family* slowly integrated race marginally through its inclusion of the Jefferson family as the Bunker's neighbors. *Sanford and Son* and *Good Times* represented a somewhat separate but (un)equal portrayal of a family, as they featured an all-Black cast, but their financial and social circumstances were unequal to their white counterparts. Finally, *The Jeffersons* represented an integrated-privileged model where although Black characters were in leading roles, *The Jeffersons* featured a racially integrated cast, all possessing financial privilege.

This arc of racial formation is evident in the chronological production of these shows and their spin-offs. Whether through a junkyard tale of a father and son struggling to make it, a loving family stricken with the ills of poverty in the projects, or a nouveau riche family fighting to balance the new lifestyle that wealth has afforded them, these Black sitcoms of Tandem and the artists within (creators, writers, actors) are intertextually connected through their hustle economics within the complex political backdrop of popular culture during the 1970s. Tandem's production of *The Jeffersons* slowly crept into what Christine Acham defines as "integrationist themed," as it depicts a Black family entering a space of upward mobility that is usually reserved for the white elite. *The Jeffersons* hinted at the end of an era of all-Black-casted sitcoms where the struggles and culture of Blackness are at the center.[121]

Conclusion

A Piece of the Pie

Although Tandem Productions grew much of its critical acclaim through its Black sitcoms, the last popular television show to feature Black characters at Tandem took a form counter to its predecessors. In 1978, Tandem Productions debuted *Diff'rent Strokes* (1978–1986). The series starred Gary Coleman and Todd Bridges as Arnold and Willis Jackson, respectively, two Black boys from Harlem who are taken in by a rich Park Avenue–living white businessman and widower named Phillip Drummond (Conrad Bain) and his daughter Kimberly (Dana Plato), for whom the boy's deceased mother previously worked for. Moving from a Watts salvage yard to the Chicago projects to an Upper East Side Manhattan high-rise apartment, the last sitcom of Tandem Productions placed Black boys in a penthouse on Park Avenue. The show was a parable of integration. But although *Diff'rent Strokes* starred two young Black actors, the leading character in the credits is a white man (Conrad Bain), whose vantage point the show often adopts. Bud Yorkin, in fact, describes how he conceived the idea for the show after seeing actor Beau Bridges's interactions with his newly adopted Black son.

Yorkin wanted the show to "put a Black child into a white man's world" (the same construction he used for *The Jeffersons*) and discuss the various woes the white father and Black child deal with in their daily lives.[1] Perhaps it is not a surprise that in a show featuring Black children, the resistance and agency from Black actors were less prominent than in previous Tandem sitcoms. *Diff'rent Strokes* was, like *All in the Family*, a mixed-cast show. But unlike *All in the Family*, there was a Black showrunner. Even with the inclusion of one of the first Black television showrunners and directors, Gerren Keith, overseeing all phases of production on *Diff'rent Strokes*, because of its efforts of racial integration and harmony, the show lacked the upfront Blackness portrayed in previous Tandem sitcoms. As the Black actors and writers discussed throughout this book, with his seeming position of power on the set, Keith himself bemoans his place in the television industry as still being a consistent struggle when he stated, "Because the vestiges of racism have not been erased from the entertainment industry . . . I'm not allowed to think I'm a *director*. I'm a *Black* director."[2] White executive power at Tandem and the larger television network still had the final say in all of Keith's productions.

As Keith hustled his way through the white-dominated television industry to become a showrunner, it may be assumed that he had reached the level of authoritative power in television that so many of the Black artists discussed throughout this book had fought for so diligently. However, Keith's quote contradicts this assumed power on set. Keith's quote clarifies that the age-old debate around Black representation on television, as addressed earlier in chapter 1, in Phillip Brian Harper's discussion of simulacral versus mimetic realism, is simply not enough.[3] Rather than being a battle of the number of Black people seen versus the authenticity in their characterizations, the true agency wielded through Black representations, what these Black artists practicing hustle economics sought to accomplish, exists with the merging of simulacral realism, mimetic realism, and what I call authoritative realism. The idea of authoritative realism exists when Black artists have a position and sense of ownership of their art, historicized as contributing auteurs. In terms of television, this authority of course has levels of hierarchy, for instance, a stake in the writing as opposed to production, directing, or even holding an executive position within a network. As seen with *Sanford and Son*, *Good Times*, and *The Jeffersons* possessing simulacral and mimetic realism, their shows were greatly received in their practice of hustle economics, Black women's embodiment, and in their address of social issues and dissent. However, without authority over these characters, the Black artists of these shows were often at odds with the white executive power, leading to lawsuits, cancellations, firings, and poor-quality episodes. In contrast, *Diff'rent Strokes*, having an assumed authoritative realism with

Gerren Keith at the helm of this show as its director and showrunner, had the potential of groundbreaking Black representation. However, through its integrationist themes, it lacked the familiar simulacral and mimetic realism of Blackness its predecessors had. This shift is possibly what forced *Diff'rent Strokes* to never break into the top ten in the Nielsen ratings, never matching up to the fame of the previous sitcoms featuring Black people at Tandem.[4]

Throughout *Scratchin' and Survivin'*, I chose to give voice to Black creators, writers, and actors and to put them at the forefront of the various politics of representation they were forced to contend with on-screen and behind the scenes at Tandem Productions, within the larger network system and in society. Through numerous practices, performances, and productions of hustle economics, these individuals faced racism and ill-treatment at the hands of Hollywood executives head-on, putting themselves and their careers on the line in order to contribute to the imagination of what Blackness can be on television. Chronicled throughout this book, the history of the Black sitcoms of Tandem Productions is one that takes different forms in each show. However, the situation in each show revolves around class, race, and gender in complex, layered formulations. Through hustle economics, the negotiated and racialized "under the table," "catch as catch can," and sometimes illegal methods working-class Blacks use to survive financially and the off-screen negotiations and risks that take place in the production of Blackness in these shows, *Scratchin' and Survivin'* illustrates how the Black artists of each of these sitcoms practiced agency and resilience to transform the television industry. Of course, some efforts were more successful than others, but the risks taken throughout this television tenure make clear that the Black artists within put their bodies on the line to rearticulate recycled imagery of their race. These Black artists should be historicized in discussions of television auteurs within the era of social relevance that so often only mentions white media players.

Sanford and Son makes clear the television industry's alignment of Blackness with the working-class poor. *Sanford and Son* became the first of Tandem's sitcoms to represent the Black domestic sphere, and at the same time, the Black actors and writers used the show to reframe how Black communities existed on television. *Sanford and Son*'s hustle economics was practiced and performed through the trickster narratives on-screen and the efforts of Redd Foxx fighting for better wages and to have a production stake in the show. Performing radical ambiguity, LaWanda Page worked to complicate and negotiate preconceived notions of Black women's identity. Through production dissent, Black television writers such as Ilunga Adell, Paul Mooney,

Richard Pryor, and Odie Hawkins were brought to the mainstream to tell Black stories from a culturally specific perspective. These acts of hustle economics aid in the understanding of this sitcom as more than a show but a redefining moment in television history as these artists set the tone for ways in which Black artists advocated for belonging in the television industry.

Through *Good Times*, the cast engaged with the Black press to speak about the changes they wished to see in the content they portrayed. As a sitcom that chronicled a Black family dealing with the woes of living in the projects, various forms of hustle economies were shown on-screen in an effort to keep their heads above water. Knowing that the Evans family stood for the Black family at large, in response, Esther Rolle continued to challenge Norman Lear to make changes in story content and dialogue that allowed for the family to be portrayed in a light that was less reliant on buffoonery and get-rich-quick schemes. Using her role to push past the history of Black women as "grinning domestics," Rolle demanded her on-screen family have a working husband and a family that is not dependent on white people. Also, her costar, John Amos, went to greater lengths of dissent against Tandem executives as he wrote a clause into his contract that required a higher wage and writing credit—so that he too could be at the table to write more dialogue that took advantage of the positive potential that *Good Times* had for television and America. This protest, unfortunately, led to Tandem executives writing Amos out of the show. On the production side, when cocreator and writer Eric Monte sought a greater stake in day-to-day show operations and a higher wage because he saw the degradation of the show's Black characters he created, he sued Tandem Productions. Although a settlement was made, Monte was essentially blacklisted from television jobs and credits.

Finally, in *The Jeffersons*, Black ascension is realized. With the introduction of white supporting cast members and the propulsion of Black characters into the financial elite, *The Jeffersons* drew less public dissent between their Black artists and Tandem executives compared to its predecessors. However, their particular predicament of being Black and nouveau riche within a mostly all-white social space left the Jefferson family in a conflicting state of economic displacement. They weren't Black enough for the ghetto, and they weren't white enough to be respected among the elite, a precarious position for George Jefferson, who was frequently placed between these conflicting identities. His hustle economy was to perform as rich so that one day he would be accepted. Yet *The Jeffersons* was transformative in its layered depiction of Black women. May it be the nouveau riche Louise, the old money Helen, or the streetwise maid Florence, *The Jeffersons* showed that Black women can occupy multiple spaces in America and on television. At the helm of the characterization of Black women on this show was Isabel Sanford, who denied the common Sapphire characterization and portrayed Louise as a woman who transcended traditional labels of Black womanhood. Although dissent from Tandem executives is seen the least on *The Jeffersons*, there were critical moments where the Black actors were able to add input into the dialogue, jokes, and direction of the shows. Largely, the conflict that received the most attention in the early seasons of the show was the interracial marriage of Helen and Tom Willis (Roxie Roker and Franklin Cover, respectively) and racial passing. Amid unemployment and fears of cancellation and in the face of ill-mannered comments and hate speech, Roxie Roker remained steadfast in her performance of a Black family archetype that television had resisted casting.

Although different in each show, these Black artists used their agency in multiple ways that are important to the history of television production, and it took the resilience of each of these artists to make way for artists of the future. These are individuals who sacrificed and often held their tongues to the system at Tandem Productions and the varying networks, in turn making these systems billions of dollars. However, these individuals continuously fade into the periphery in discussion of television history, auteurs, and media change-makers. Whether through a junkyard tale of a father and son struggling to make it, a loving family stricken with the ills of poverty in the projects, or a nouveau riche family fighting to balance their new lifestyle that wealth has afforded them, these Black sitcoms of Tandem are intertextually connected to describe a temporal politics that took place in television during the 1970s, and the Black artists who were a part of this vision deserve recognition. The work of these Black artists paving a new way forward was the impetus for future Black artists within the confines of network conventions on race and identity. The dissent of Tandem's Black artists of the 1970s, on-screen and off, are moments that must be highlighted in discussions of media history, as these Black artists and Black bodies have largely failed to be properly historicized in scholarly texts. The focus is often on the white executives who have won numerous awards and accolades for their production of Black images, but what about the Black artists responsible for performing these images and having the burden of defining their race?

Although Hollywood's system of awards is also historically racially biased, another topic that exists outside the scope of this work, even the exclusion of these 1970s Black sitcom artists from Hollywood's Walk of Fame was met with resilience.[5] As the inclusion on the Hollywood Walk of Fame is one of the most enduring and honored symbols of celebrity around, there is another, much smaller, and all but forgotten monument to another group of celebrities simply etched into the cement outside of the former office building of Redd Foxx Productions. Although this "Redd Foxx Walk of Fame" is not officially recognized by any commemorative markers, in front of a modern office building at 933 North La Brea in West Hollywood, California, exists signatures, dates, and hand/footprints left by Foxx, Lynn Hamilton, LaWanda Page, and other Black actors and comedians popularized in the 1970s. In a 1987 *JET* article, ten years after the cancellation of *Sanford and Son*, Redd Foxx is seen holding the hand of his former costar LaWanda Page as she presses her feet into the wet cement and smiles at this momentous occasion. Like the cover of this book makes clear, rejecting Hollywood's markers of validation, these Black artists hustled and scratched through years of industry discontent and silenced voices and survived a myriad of battles regarding a Black visual possibility to proudly historicize themselves, slicing their own piece of the pie.

Due to contemporary Black artists nodding to Black television's past, like the season two finale of *Black-ish* "Good-ish Times," which was mentioned in this book's introduction, we are reminded that the disruptive work of these Tandem Black artists and their sitcoms is integral to how we understand and watch television today. What drew me to reflect and focus on the content of shows and the dissent of Black artists in the 1970s for this book were the multiple instances that contemporary Black television programs self-consciously mine their roots and pay homage to this period of Black televisual transformation. Slowly given increased access to the power of authoritative realism, contemporary Black artists have reimagined and reintroduced Tandem's Black artists to the contemporary mainstream. Whether through Jordan Peele and Keegan Michael-Key's parody of *Sanford and Son* in the sketch comedy series *Mad TV* (1995–2009, 2016), the cast of *The Bernie Mac Show* being photographed in 2005 as a tribute to a 1974 *TV Guide* cover of *Good Times* characters, to Sherman Hemsley, Isabel Sanford, and Marla Gibbs crossing over into contemporary Black sitcoms portraying their characters from *The Jeffersons* in *The Fresh Prince of Bel-Air* and *Tyler Perry's House of Payne* (2007–2012), contemporary Black artists have consciously nodded to the Black actors and sitcoms of Tandem Productions and their inspirational legacy.[6]

On May 22, 2019, television personality Jimmy Kimmel and (then ninety-six-year-old) Norman Lear hosted and executive produced an ABC ninety-minute live production of *All in the Family* and *The Jeffersons. Live in*

Front of a Studio Audience: Norman Lear's "All in the Family" and "The Jeffersons" featured contemporary actors remaking one original script from each of the shows. The star-studded event stemmed from a two-year, first-look deal that Lear signed with the studio in July 2018.[7] Albeit a few mishaps in dialogue and exaggerations of characters, the live performance received great reception and of course tons of laughter. What was so great about this event is that the contemporary actors read original scripts from the 1970s—words that largely remain relevant today.

The Jeffersons' episode that Lear and company chose to remake is the very first episode of the series, one that I analyzed at length in chapter 4, "A Friend in Need." The episode featured Jamie Foxx as George Jefferson, Wanda Sykes as Louise Jefferson, Javon Adepo as Lionel Jefferson, Kerry Washington as Helen Willis, Will Ferrell as Tom Willis, Amber Stevens West as Jenny Willis, Stephen Tobowloski as Harry Bentley, Jackée Harry as Diane, and Fran Bennet as Mother Jefferson. With such a great ensemble, along with singer Jennifer Hudson doing a live rendition of the classic "Movin' on Up," it truly felt as though the audience was being transported back to 1975 and that deluxe apartment in the sky. What sparked controversy, however, was the initial casting of Latina actress Justina Machado as the Jeffersons' legendary maid, Florence Johnston (originally played by Marla Gibbs). In fact, due to the racial impact of the iconic line that Florence delivers at the end of this episode, "How come we overcame, and nobody told me?" the stars playing these roles, particularly Jamie Foxx, moved to have the role recast, as they felt it would be a disservice to not have a Black woman speak these words.[8] To the audience's surprise, during the live show, when the door was knocked at the Jeffersons' home, in walked eighty-eight-year-old Marla Gibbs, reprising her role as Florence Johnston. Being met with a groundswell of praise live in the studio and via social media, Gibbs's presence hearkened back to the dynamic impact she made forty-four years ago.

Following the success of their first live reenactment, on December 18, 2019, Jimmy Kimmel and Norman Lear hosted *Live in Front of a Studio Audience: Norman Lear's "All in the Family" and "Good Times"* on ABC. Introduced with the opening credit theme being sung by Patti LaBelle and Anthony Anderson, the live cast performed season 3, episode 9 of *Good Times*, "The Politicians" (11/4/75). The performance featured Viola Davis as Florida Evans, Andre Braugher as James Evans, Jay Pharoah as J.J., Corrine Foxx as Thelma, Asante Blackk as Michael, Tiffany Haddish as Willona, Jharrel Jerome as Jimmy Pierson, and finally, surprise guest star John Amos, the real James Evans, playing the role of the politician Fred Davis. At the end

of the episode, the audience gives a standing ovation to John Amos returning to his set over forty years later. The crowd roared even louder as, much
to the audience's surprise, Jimmie Walker, BernNadette Stanis, and Ja'Net
DuBois joined Amos on stage to take a bow in honor of their beloved show.

Paying homage to the legacy of *Good Times*, *The Jeffersons*, and their Black
artists, these contemporary actors not only participated in this live event
and used original scripts but used their agency to do their due diligence and
make sure that the performances were done right to honor those that led the
way for them. With events such as these and with talks of future remakes
on the horizon, it's evident that popular television is facing a reinvigorated
interest in Black popular culture and is attempting to mine its cultural roots
with the shows that redefined the medium. Similar to the work done by
these contemporary actors, I hope *Scratchin' and Survivin'* not only helps pay
homage to a legacy of Black artists whose hustle and resilience made way for
how we all see television today but also encourages scholars of Black popular
culture and media studies to rearticulate the canon and challenge recycled
broadcast histories that often push this Black labor to the periphery.

Acknowledgments

This journey has been a true test of resilience and faith, and I could not have done it without family. To my parents Michael and Cheryl, I thank you for raising me to not make excuses and to put my head down and simply do the work. My siblings: Raymond, T.J., Sean, and Brandon, I thank you for your constant encouragement. I can always count on you to cheer me on—that meant more to me than you could ever imagine. Jasmine and Sidney—you are my foundation, my biggest fans, and without you, I wouldn't have had the grit to make it through. Charles, Kendra, and Frankie, thank you for welcoming me and extending my family even further. To Alpha Phi Alpha Fraternity Inc., Gamma Xi Chapter, the Pack, the Wolfpack, and my North County Family (CR)—I couldn't ask for better people that continue to push me to my fullest potential. Victor Republicano, thank you for the early edits and encouragement. To Nicole Solano of Rutgers University Press, thank you for having faith that this book deserved to be seen.

As an undergraduate at UCLA, I struggled to find my voice and my purpose, and I have many people to thank for seeing something in me that I didn't. To Rhonda Hammer, Sharon Bays, and Aisha Finch, I am forever grateful to you for helping me realize that my voice has meaning and to use it. Thank you to the UCLA School of Theater, Film, and Television for opening my eyes to the power of visual storytelling. The idea for this book came from an undergraduate course, History of American Television taught by John Caldwell and my teaching assistant at the time, Benjamin

Sampson. Through this class, I was encouraged to use television as a way to understand and make sense of the world around me. I am grateful for the tools that you two bestowed upon me. During my time at Columbia University, being so far from home, I had to find a community. Alex Alston, Marsha Jean-Charles, Wilt Hodges, Tiana Reid, Ellen Louis, Matthew Morrison, J. T. Roane, Jarvis McGinnis, Julius Fleming, Sharon Harris, Farrah Jasmine Griffin, Carla Shedd, Natasha Lightfoot, and Marcellus Blount, I thank you for taking me in and helping me grow up in more ways than one.

During this journey, I was fortunate to gain awards that aided in the completion of this once dissertation-turned-manuscript. To the Mellon Mays Undergraduate Fellowship and the Social Science Research Council's dissertation development, writing retreat groups, and the PhD Professional Development conferences, thank you for the amazing networks they introduced me to, as well as the mentorship. The access to production documents and correspondence at the Pacific Title Archives, Norman Lear's Act III Productions, UCLA's Young Research Library Special Collections, and the University of California Santa Barbara Special Research Collections have been integral to my original research findings. A special and warm thank you to Saul Turteltaub for taking the time to meet with me and share his stories about working at Tandem Productions. I would be remiss to not thank Dr. John L. Jackson, the University of Pennsylvania's Annenberg School of Communication, the University of Pennsylvania Predoctoral Fellowship for Excellence through Diversity, the UC Consortium Intercampus Travel Grant, UCLA's Graduate Summer Research Mentorship, and UT Austin's Summer Research Assignment for the mentorship, time, and encouragement required to write this book.

I am forever indebted to many women who encouraged me daily to pick my head up and keep writing. Beatrice Choi, Chinbo Chong, Deshonay Dozier, and Anjanette Tack, you made Philadelphia a home for me when I had no one else, and you remained supportive in one of the most difficult years of my life. Ashleigh Fata, Jess DePrest, Laura Ha Reizman, Sozen Ozkan, Viola Ardeni, Emily Lord-Kambitsch, Tuyen Le, Sarah Hearne, and Rebecca Choi, whether through virtual or in-person weekly writing groups, I could always count on you to hold me accountable, cheer me on, and support me. You are forever my tribe, and I can't wait to see what the future holds for us. To my dissertation committee: Darnell Hunt, Denise Mann, John Caldwell, and Ellen Scott, I give my deepest gratitude. Drs. Hunt,

Mann, and Caldwell, thank you for taking the time to read my work, offer feedback, and give encouraging words when I needed it most.

To Ellen Scott, I simply don't have the words. From our first meeting when you came to UCLA, I knew that I had found my advisor and dissertation chair. You have brought me back up when I was low and discouraged, and you kept me energized and excited about my work and its potential throughout the entirety of my candidacy. With your guidance, I always knew that I had a mentor that would go to bat for me and always push for my best interest. I just hope to be an educator as dynamic, inspirational, and supportive as you for my future students. I would also like to give my profound appreciation to my dynamic colleagues at UT Austin. Noah Isenberg, Ya'Ke Smith, Jenn McClearen, Marisol Enríquez, Wenhong Chen, Kathryn Fuller-Seeley, Suzanne Scott, Curran Nault, Mary Beltran, Alisa Perren, Caroline Frick, Lalitha Gopalan, Shanti Kumar, Madhavi Mallapragada, Charles Ramirez-Berg, Cindy McCreery, Jennifer Wilks, Lee Sparks, Elana Wakeman, and Rachel Walker, your guidance and aid have been invaluable to my development as a scholar and professor. I thank you.

This book is also dedicated to the dynamic media scholars who have inspired me in all the work that I have done and intend to do: Herman Gray, Bambi Haggins, Ellen Scott, Beretta Smith-Shomade, Robin Means Coleman, Jacqueline Stewart, Allyson Field, Michael Boyce Gillespie, Christine Acham, Kristal Brent Zook, Kristen Warner, Samantha Sheppard, Racquel Gates, Jennifer Fuller, Alfred Martin, A.J. Christian, Brandy Monk-Payton, Andre Brock, A. E. Stevenson, Philana Payton, Brooklyne Gipson, Briana Barner, Daelena Tinnin, Lily Kunda, Ailish Elzy, Isadora DuMont, Avery LaFlamme, A.J. Walker, Kellen Sharp, Rachael Hatchett, and many more.

To Bud Yorkin and Norman Lear, I thank you for being courageous in your efforts to bring critical social discussions to television. Finally, to all of the inspiring Black artists of Tandem Productions that I discuss in this book and otherwise: Redd Foxx, Demond Wilson, LaWanda Page, Lynn Hamilton, Whitman Mayo, Don Bexley, Nathaniel Taylor, Hal Williams, LeRoy & Skillet, Ilunga Adell, Mark Warren, Syd McCoy, Stan Lathan, Richard Pryor, Paul Mooney, Esther Rolle, John Amos, Jimmie Walker, BernNadette Stanis, Ralph Carter, Ja'Net DuBois, Eric Monte, Mike Evans, Gloria Vinson, Patricia Edwards, Isabel Sanford, Sherman Hemsley, Marla Gibbs, Roxie Roker, Berlinda Tolbert, Zara Cully, Damon Evans, and Gerren Keith, this work wouldn't be possible without your legacy of resilience. I hope I made you proud.

Notes

Introduction The Hustle

1 To highlight its critical acclaim, *Black-ish* has been nominated for multiple Primetime Emmy Awards over its run. It received a Peabody Award in 2016 and a Golden Globe Award in 2017 for actress Tracee Ellis Ross.

  I use the term "Black" throughout as a means of identifying members of the larger African diaspora. I steer away from the term "African American" commonly used by other scholars primarily because I do not wish to assume that these actors and artists defined themselves as "African American," and racial markers of members of this diaspora have continued to change through the century due to various political influences and censuses. "Black" is a term that best encompasses a range of members of this diaspora.

2 Ingela Ratledge, "*Black-ish* Lets the *Good Times* Roll," *TV Guide*, May 9, 2016.

3 Ratledge.

4 Ratledge.

5 Daniel Holloway, "Kenya Barris Signs $100 Million Netflix Deal," *Variety*, August 16, 2018.

6 J. Fred MacDonald, *Blacks and White TV: African American in Television since 1948* (Nelson-Hall, 1983).

7 Lynn Spigel, *Make Room for TV: Television and the Family Ideal in Postwar America* (University of Chicago Press, 1992).

8 Darnell M. Hunt, *Channeling Blackness: Studies on Television and Race in America* (Oxford University Press, 2005), 269.

9 *Sanford and Son*, season 3, episode 15, "Fred Sanford, Legal Eagle," aired January 11, 1974.

10 Stuart Hall, "What Is This 'Black' in Black Popular Culture?," *Social Justice* 20, no. 1/2 (Spring–Summer 1993): 104–114.

11 Hall, 104.

12 Hall, 104.

13 Hall, 105.

14 Richard Iton, *In Search of the Black Fantastic: Politics and Popular Culture in the Post–Civil Rights Era* (Oxford University Press, 2008), 4–5.

15 Amanda D. Lotz, *The Television Will Be Revolutionized* (New York University Press, 2007), 85–86.

16 Robert S. Alley and Horace Newcomb, *The Producer's Medium: Conversations with Creators of American TV* (Oxford University Press, 1983).

17 Herman Gray, *Watching Race: Television and the Struggle for "Blackness"* (University of Minnesota Press, 1995), xiv.

18 Jane Feuer, "Genre Study and Television," in *Channels of Discourse, Reassembled: Television and Contemporary Criticism*, ed. Robert C. Allen (Routledge, 2005), 110.

19 Feuer, 110.

20 Darrell Hamamoto, *Television Situation Comedy and Liberal Democratic Ideology*, rev. ed. (Praeger, 2001), 9.

21 Glenda Carpio, *Laughing Fit to Kill: Black Humor in the Fictions of Slavery* (Oxford University Press, 2008), 1–2.

22 Herman Gray, *Watching Race: Television and the Struggle for "Blackness,"* rev. ed. (University of Minnesota Press, 2004), 89.

23 Gray, *Watching Race* (1995), 88. Also see Bambi Haggins, *Laughing Mad: The Black Comic Persona in Post-soul America* (Rutgers University Press, 2007), 8.

24 Robin Means Coleman, *African American Viewers and the Black Situation Comedy: Situating Racial Humor* (Garland, 1998), 21.

25 Horace Newcomb, *TV: The Most Popular Art* (Anchor Books, 1974), 28.

26 Christine Acham, *Revolution Televised: Prime Time and the Struggle for Black Power* (University of Minnesota Press, 2005), xv.

27 George Lipsitz, "The Meaning of Memory: Family, Class, and Ethnicity in Early Network Television Programs," in *Private Screenings: Television and the Female Consumer*, ed. Lynn Spigel and Denise Mann (University of Minnesota Press, 1992), 71–108.

28 Jonathan Gray, *Show Sold Separately: Promos Spoilers, and Other Media Paratexts* (New York University Press, 2010), 6.

29 Which was in line with the film and television industries at the time. Hollywood moved away from Black-cast films to the interracial buddy comedy by the end of the 1970s, and even 1978's *The Wiz* attempted to be a film with a Black cast that would appeal to white folks (achieved through casting—although the film didn't make back its production budget). Alfred Martin Jr., "Surplus Blackness," *Flow Journal*, April 27, 2021.

Chapter 1   Approaching Tandem Productions

1 Poor People's Campaign of 1968, "Why a Poor People's Campaign?," accessed January 2023, http://staging.poorpeoplescampaign.org/poor-peoples-campaign-1968/.

2 John F. Kennedy Presidential Library and Museum, "The Civil Rights Movement," https://www.jfklibrary.org/learn/about-jfk/jfk-in-history/civil-rights-movement.

3 John F. Kennedy Presidential Library and Museum.

4 John F. Kennedy Presidential Library and Museum.

5 University of Virginia, Miller Center, "Lyndon B. Johnson: Domestic Affairs," https://millercenter.org/president/lbjohnson/domestic-affairs.

6 Gordon Mantler, *Power to the Poor: Black-Brown Coalition and the Fight for Economic Justice, 1960–1974* (Chapel Hill: University of North Carolina Press, 2013), 19.

7 Mantler, 19.

8 Mantler, 19.

9 Poor People's Campaign.

10 Poor People's Campaign.

11 The Temptations, "Ball of Confusion (That's What the World Is Today)," *Gordy*, 1970.

12 Robin D. G. Kelley, *Yo' Mama's Disfunktional! Fighting the Culture Wars in Urban America* (Beacon Press, 1997), 5.

13 Daniel P. Moynihan, *The Negro Family: The Case for National Action* (Washington, D.C.: Office of Policy Planning and Research, U.S. Department of Labor, 1965), 1–46.

14 Moynihan, preface.

15 Moynihan, 75.

16 Moynihan, 14.

17 Moynihan, 7.

18 Moynihan, 15.

19 Moynihan, preface.

20 Kelley, *Yo' Mama's Disfunktional!*, 9–10.

21 Hortense Spillers, "Mama's Baby, Papa's Maybe: An American Grammar Book," *Diacritics* 17, no. 2 (1987): 64–81; and Roderick Ferguson, *Aberrations in Black: Toward a Queer of Color Critique* (Minneapolis: University of Minnesota Press, 2004).

22 Amanda Lotz, "What Is U.S. Television Now?," *Annals of the American Academy of Political and Social Science* 625, no. 1 (2009): 50.

23 Lotz, 51.

24 Lotz, 50.

25 Lotz, 51.

26 Erik Barnouw, *Tube of Plenty: The Evolution of American Television* (Oxford University Press, 1990), 326.

27 Barnouw, 326.

28 Barnouw, 327.

29 Lyndon B. Johnson, "The President's Address to the Nation on Civil Disorders," American Presidency Project, July 27, 1967, https://www.presidency.ucsb.edu/documents/the-presidents-address-the-nation-civil-disorders.

30 History Matters, "Our Nation Is Moving toward Two Societies, One Black, One White—Separate and Unequal: Excerpts from the Kerner Report," http://historymatters.gmu.edu/d/6545/.

31 James Ciment, *Postwar America: An Encyclopedia of Social, Political, Cultural, and Economic History* (Routledge, 2015).

32 National Advisory Commission on Civil Disorders, *Report of the National Advisory Commission on Civil Disorders* (1967), 210.

33 National Advisory Commission on Civil Disorders, 212.

34 National Advisory Commission on Civil Disorders, 212.

35 National Advisory Commission on Civil Disorders, 212.

36 National Advisory Commission on Civil Disorders, 212.

37 Acham, *Revolution Televised*, 41.

38 Acham, 42.

39 Devorah Heitner, *Black Power TV* (Duke University Press, 2013).

40 Heitner, 3.

41 Heitner, 54.

42 Phillip Brian Harper, "Extra-Special Effects: Televisual Representation and the Claims of 'the Black Experience,'" in *Living Color: Race and Television in the United States*, ed. Sasha Torres (Duke University Press, 1998), 62.

43 Harper, 62.

44 Harper, 70.

45 Harper, 69.

46 Harper, 71.

47 The Norman Lear Center, "50 Years after the Kerner Commission: Can Entertainment Inspire a New Will?," *USC Annenberg*, streamed on February 23, 2022, YouTube video, 1:26:35, https://www.youtube.com/watch?v=MQuKm4S70Xg&t=54s.

48 Television Academy Foundation, "Bud Yorkin," Interviews, streamed on 1997, video, 4:53, https://interviews.televisionacademy.com/interviews/bud-yorkin#about.

49 Lemack (Brad) Collection (PA Mss 58), *University of California, Santa Barbara Special Research Collections*, 2. Memo on company's history and business structure.

50 Lemack (Brad) Collection.

51 *Cold Turkey* is a 1971 satirical comedy film produced by Tandem Productions. It stars Dick Van Dyke plus a long list of comedic actors. The film was directed, coproduced, and cowritten by Norman Lear and is based on the unpublished novel *I'm Giving Them Up for Good* by Margaret and Neil Rau. Norman Lear, *Even This I Get to Experience* (Penguin, 2014), 177.

52 Norman Lear, *Even This I Get to Experience* (Penguin, 2014), 239.

53 Lear, 267.

54 Brad Lemack Collection, 2.

55 Brad Lemack Collection, 2.

56 Darrell Y. Hamamoto, *Nervous Laughter: Television Situation Comedy and Liberal Democratic Ideology* (Praeger, 1991).

57 Lear, *Even This I Get*, 235.

58 Michael Arlen, "Media Dramas of Norman Lear," *New Yorker*, May 10, 1975, 163.

59 Arlen, 164–165.

60 Arlen, 203.

61 Television Academy Foundation, "Norman Lear," Interviews, streamed on February 26, 1998, video, 1:40, https://interviews.televisionacademy.com/interviews/norman-lear.

62 Bruce Fretts and Matt Roush, "The Greatest Shows on Earth," *TV Guide Magazine*, December 23, 2013, 16–19.

63 Lear, *Even This I Get*, 223.

64 Todd Gitlin, *Inside Primetime* (University of California Press, 2000), 69.

65 Dick Adler, "Look What They Found in a Junkyard—the Spare Parts for a Comedy Series That Breaks Some New Ground," *TV Guide*, May 13, 1972.

66 Acham, *Revolution Televised*, 91.

67 Acham, 91.

68 Acham, 91.

69 Acham, 108.

70 Lear, *Even This I Get*, 267.

71 During its first full season on the air, 1974–1975, the show was the seventh highest-rated program in the Nielsen ratings, with more than 25 percent of all American households tuning into an episode each week. Three of the top ten highest-rated programs on American TV that season centered on the lives of African Americans: *Sanford and Son*, *The Jeffersons*, and *Good Times*. Tim Brooks and Earle Marsh,

The Complete Directory to Prime Time Network and Cable TV Shows 1946–Present, 9th ed. (Ballantine Books, 2007), 1687.

72 Lear, *Even This I Get*, 269.

73 TAT Communications was formed in 1974, when Norman Lear joined with former talent agent Jerry Perenchio, a year before Yorkin ended his partnership with Lear. Bud Yorkin was a part of *The Jeffersons* until Lear and Perenchio bought him out as Yorkin wanted to focus on making films. As a subsidiary of Tandem Productions, TAT Communications was established for financial reasons as creative principals had changed. Much like the other offshoots of Tandem Productions where Yorkin and Lear worked with other collaborators, like TOY and Bud Yorkin Productions.

74 In its first season (1974–1975), *The Jeffersons* ranked at number four, surpassed by its parent series *All in the Family* (which landed at number one for the fifth year in a row).
   Michele "Wojo" Wojciechowski, "The Norman Lear Experience: His Shows, His Honesty, and One Thing He Wanted to Do," *Parade*, July 28, 2015.

75 To "move up" inherently means to succeed at whatever you are trying to pursue, usually referring to making more money, getting a great job, or simply doing better.

76 Means Coleman, *African American Viewers*, 94.

77 Means Coleman, 94.

Chapter 2   *Sanford and Son*

1 John J. O'Connor, "TV View: Good Times for the Black Image," *New York Times*, February 2, 1975. The three sitcoms referred to in this quote are *Sanford and Son*, *Good Times*, and *The Jeffersons*.

2 Tandem Productions was popularly deemed the "Norman Lear factory" yet was founded by Bud Yorkin and Norman Lear.

3 Haggins, *Laughing Mad*, 4.

4 Clifford Alexander, interview 3 by Joe Frantz, Lyndon Baines Johnson Oral History Collection, June 4, 1973, transcript, 3.

5 Means Coleman, *African American Viewers*, 94.

6 Means Coleman, 94?

7 P. Williams, executive producer, *CBS Reports, Watts: Riot or Revolt?* (Columbia Broadcast System, 1965).

8 Maya Angelou, producer, "*Blacks, Blues, Black!* Episode 9 [Violence]," Bay Area Television Archive, accessed August 15, 2018, https://diva.sfsu.edu/collections/sfbatv/10287.

9 Acham, *Revolution Televised*, 93.

10 The informal sector is the part of the economy that is neither taxed nor monitored by any form of government, unlike the formal economy. The informal economy is often stigmatized as troublesome and unmanageable; however, it often provides critical economic opportunities for the poor. Kristina Flodman Becker, *The Informal Economy: Fact Finding Study* (Sida, 2004).

11 LaShawn Harris, *Sex Workers, Psychics, and Numbers Runners: Black Women in New York City's Underground Economy* (University of Illinois Press, 2016), 2.

12 Lipsitz, "Meaning of Memory," 73.

13 Michael Seth Starr, *Black and Blue: The Redd Foxx Story* (Applause Theatre and Cinema Books, 2011), 1.

14 Starr, 5.

15 Starr, 18–20.

16 Acham, *Revolution Televised*, 87.

17 Acham, 87.
18 Terrence T. Tucker, *Furiously Funny: Comic Rage from Ralph Ellison to Chris Rock* (University of Florida Press, 2018), 71.
19 Mel Watkins, *On the Real Side: A History of African American Comedy* (Lawrence Hill Books, 1999), 458–476.
20 Tucker, *Furiously Funny*, 86.
21 Redd Foxx and Norma Miller, *The Redd Foxx Encyclopedia of Black Humor* (W. Ritchie Press, 1977), 239.
22 Tucker, *Furiously Funny*, 88.
23 Acham, *Revolution Televised*, 86.
24 Mel Watkins, *On the Real Side: Laughing, Lying and Signifying—the Underground Tradition of African-American Humor That Transformed American Culture, from Slavery to Richard Pryor* (Simon and Schuster, 1994), 167.
25 Cynthia James, "Searching for Ananse: From Orature to Literature in the West Indian Children's Folk Tradition—Jamaican and Trinidadian Trends," *Children's Literature Association Quarterly* 30, no. 2 (2005).
26 Lawrence Levine, *Black Culture and Consciousness: Afro-American Folk Thought from Slavery to Freedom* (Oxford University Press, 1977), 90.
27 Trudier Harris, "The Trickster in African American Literature," National Humanities Center, accessed March 16, 2017, http://nationalhumanitiescenter.org/tserve/freedom/1865-1917/essays/trickster.htm.
     Brer Rabbit, as the primary African American trickster, may have been an adaptation of the African cunnie rabbit, a small deer, and/or of Anansi, the well-known African spider trickster. Animals that appear frequently in the tales about Brer Rabbit, such as elephants and lions, are also believed to be African transplants, since these animals are not native to the United States. From these adaptations, enslaved African Americans created worlds in which animal actions mirrored human actions during and after slavery. Their kinship to fables thus enabled the seriousness of the tales to be overlooked at times.
28 Harris quoting Lawrence Levine in "The Trickster in African American Literature."
29 Harris.
30 Mel, *On the Real Side*, 167–168.
31 Mel, 168.
32 *Sanford and Son*, season 1, episode 8, "The Great Sanford Siege," directed by Aaron Ruben, aired March 3, 1972.
33 Carpio, *Laughing Fit to Kill*, 1–2.
34 *Steptoe and Son*, season 4, episode 4, "The Siege of Steptoe Street," directed by Alan Simpson and Ray Galton, October 25, 1965.
35 *Sanford and Son*, season 2, episode 3, "The Dowry," directed by Richard Pryor and Paul Mooney, September 29, 1972.
36 Harris, *Sex Workers, Psychics*, 20.
37 Haggins, *Laughing Mad*, 147.
38 Beretta E. Smith-Shomade, *Shaded Lives: African-American Women and Television* (Rutgers University Press, 2002).
39 Acham, *Revolution Televised*, 110–142.
40 Bonnie Dow, *Prime-Time Feminism: Television, Media Culture, and the Women's Movement since 1970* (University of Pennsylvania Press, 1996), xix.
41 Dow, xvi.
42 Dow, xvi.

43 To be clear, I am speaking in particular about women's representations on network prime-time television. More broadly, through the Black Arts Movement happening concurrently, Black women were visible in multiple public affairs and local television shows such as *Soul!* These public affairs programs were made by and for Black people, and they featured Black women as performers, artists, and even hosts. These fluid representations are evidenced in Heitner's *Black Power TV*.

44 Dow, *Prime-Time Feminism*, xvii.

45 Lynne Joyrich, "Critical and Textual Hypermasculinity," in *Logics of Television*, ed. Patricia Mellencamp (Indiana University Press, 1990), 161.

46 Joyrich.

47 In *Julia*, Carroll played widowed single mother Julia Baker (her husband, Army Capt. Baker, an O-1 Bird Dog artillery spotter pilot who had been shot down in Vietnam), who was a nurse in a doctor's office at a large aerospace company.

48 Marlon Riggs, dir., *Color Adjustment*, Signifyin' Works, 1991.

49 Aniko Bodroghkozy, *Equal Time: Television and the Civil Rights Movement* (University of Illinois Press, 2013), 185.

50 Bodroghkozy.

51 Acham, *Revolution Televised*, 112.

52 Bill Davidson, "Trouble in Paradise," *TV Guide*, April 6, 1974, microfilm.

53 Davidson.

54 Hunt, *Channeling Blackness*, 270. National Black Feminist Organization, quoted in U.S. Commission on Civil Rights, *Window Dressing on the Set: Women and Minorities in Television* (1977).
    The National Black Feminist Organization (NBFO) was founded in 1973. The group worked to address the unique issues affecting Black women in America. One of two earliest organizations formed in the Black feminist movement, the National Black Feminist Organization clearly reflected the goals put forth in the Combahee River Collective Statement, which was being developed at around the same time by some of the same women. The 1973 Statement of Purpose for the NBFO declared the organization was formed "to address ourselves to the particular and specific needs of the larger, but almost cast-aside half of the black race in America, the black woman." K. Wada, "National Black Feminist Organization (1973–1976)," BlackPast, accessed September 3, 2018, https://www.blackpast.org/african-american-history/national-black-feminist-organization-1973-1976/.

55 Christine Gledhill, "Pleasurable Negotiations," in *Female Spectators: Looking at Film and Television*, ed. E. Deidre Pribram (Verso, 1988), 68.

56 Harris, *Sex Workers, Psychics*, 2.

57 Blue comedy is a style of comedy that is off-color, risqué, indecent or profane, or largely about sex. It often contains profanity and/or sexual imagery that may shock and offend some audience members.

58 Bill Davidson, "The World's Funniest Dishwasher Is Still Cleaning Up: But for Redd Foxx, It Has Been a Long Trip from the Kitchen to 'Sanford and Son,'" *TV Guide*, March 17, 1973, 27.

59 Adrien Sebro, interview by Saul Turteltaub (coexecutive producer on *Sanford and Son*), May 30, 2018.

60 Davidson, "World's Funniest Dishwasher," 27.

61 A nightclub act, which included Page eating fire and lighting cigarettes with her fingertips. This talent can be seen in *Sanford and Son*, season 5, episode 15, "The Greatest Show in Watts."

62 Darryl J. Littleton and Tuezdae Littleton, *Comediennes: Laugh Be a Lady* (Applause, 2012).

63 *Sanford and Son*, season 2, episode 15, "The Big Party," directed by Odie Hawkins, aired January 5, 1973.

  A "Holy Roller" is a popular Black colloquial term, describing a character who often quotes scripture, publicly shames acts of sin, and engages in dancing, shaking, or other boisterous movements in the church because they perceive themselves as being under the influence of the Holy Spirit.

64 Acham, *Revolution Televised*, 73.

65 Acham, 94–96.

66 *Sanford and Son*, "Big Party."

67 Davidson, "World's Funniest Dishwasher," 27.

68 Davidson.

69 Haggins, *Laughing Mad*, 2.

70 Darryl Littleton, *Black Comedians on Black Comedy: How African-Americans Taught Us to Laugh* (Hal Leonard Corporation, 2008), 117.

71 Norman Lear TV Shows / Production Box #S-274, "Correspondence-Sanford and Son," *Pacific Title Archives, Act III Productions*.

72 Haggins, *Laughing Mad*, 3.

73 Particularly, the only two Black women who performed party records for Laff Records were LaWanda Page and Tina Dixon.

74 Haggins, *Laughing Mad*, 2007.

75 Jennifer Fuller, "*Gimme a Break!* and the Limits of the Modern Mammy," in *Watching While Black: Centering the Television of Black Audiences*, ed. Beretta E. Smith-Shomade (Rutgers University Press, 2012), 118.

76 Tucker, *Furiously Funny*, 88.

77 Mel Watkins, "LaWanda Page, 81, the Aunt on TV's 'Sanford and Son,'" *New York Times*, September 18, 2002.

78 Exclusively through Laff Records, before starring in *Sanford and Son*, Page released two solo albums, *Mutha Is Half a Word* (1970) and *Pipe Layin' Dan* (1973). She also released an album with Skillet and Leroy, entitled *Back Door Daddy* (1972). Skillet and LeRoy would go on to also play characters of the same name as Fred Sanford's friends on *Sanford and Son*.

79 L. H. Stallings, *Mutha Is Half a Word: Intersections of Folklore, Vernacular, Myth, and Queerness in Black Female Culture* (Ohio State University Press, 2007), 115.

80 Stallings, 12.

81 A phrase she became renowned for using on *Sanford and Son*.

82 At the industry level, in 1958, the Recording Industry Association of America introduced its gold record award program for records of any kind, albums or singles, which achieved one million dollars in retail sales. For albums in 1968, this would mean shipping approximately 250,000 units; for singles, the number would be higher due to their lower retail price. Shannon L. Venable, *Gold: A Cultural Encyclopedia* (ABC-CLIO, 2011).

83 Christine Acham, "Sanford and Son: Televising African American Humor," *Spectator* 20, no. 2 (Spring/Summer 2000): 75–89.

84 LaWanda Page, *Watch It, Sucker!* (Laff Records, 1972).

85 Stallings, *Mutha Is Half a Word*, 140.

86 Brooks and Marsh, *Complete Directory to Prime Time*.

87 "Sanford's Comedy Black Writer's Work," *Sarasota Herald-Tribune TV-Work*, July 7–13, 1974, 11.

88 "Sanford's Comedy Black Writer's Work," 11.
89 *Sanford and Son*, season 3, episode 14, "Mama's Baby, Papa's Maybe," directed by Ilunga Adell, aired January 4, 1974.
90 Spillers, "Mama's Baby, Papa's Maybe."
91 Stallings, *Mutha Is Half a Word*, 116.
92 Davidson, "World's Funniest Dishwasher."
93 Eugenia Collier, "*Sanford and Son* Is White to the Core," *New York Times*, June 17, 1973.
94 Sebro, interview.
95 Acham, *Revolution Televised*, 103.
96 *Sanford and Son*, season 2, episode 17, "Lamont Goes African," aired January 19, 1973; *Sanford and Son*, "Fred Sanford, Legal Eagle."
97 *Sanford and Son*, season 6, episode 20, "Fred the Activist," February 25, 1977. Although outside the scope of Tandem Productions' partnership between Yorkin and Lear, this episode is relevant to numerous forms of activism seen on-screen.
98 Sebro, interview.
99 J. R. Young, "Include Him Out," *TV Guide*, October 5, 1974, 22.
100 Young.
101 "Foxx Goes, Wilson to Star in 'Sanford Arms,'" *JET Magazine*, January 27, 1977, 54.
102 Brooks and Marsh, *Complete Directory to Prime Time*.
103 Davidson, "Trouble in Paradise."
104 Davidson, 5.
105 Davidson, 5.
106 Louie Robinson, "Redd Foxx—Crazy like a Fox: 'Sanford and Son' Star Seeks a Piece of the Action," *Ebony Magazine*, June 1974, 158.
107 Gary Deeb, "Redd Admits Trying to Outfox NBC," *Chicago Tribune*, March 11, 1974.
108 Norman Lear TV Shows, "Correspondence-Sanford and Son."
109 Norman Lear TV Shows.
110 Letter received and time-stamped on March 15, 1974, Norman Lear TV Shows.
111 A pure sitcom, defined by Christine Acham, often steers clear of any political agenda or moral purpose. Acham, *Revolution Televised*, 133.
112 Letter received and time-stamped on March 15, 1974, Norman Lear TV Shows, "Correspondence-Sanford and Son."
113 Kay Gardella, "If NBC Keeps Promises, I'll Be Back, Says Foxx," *New York Daily News*, March 15, 1974, 272.
114 Gardella.
115 Gardella.
116 Norman Lear TV Shows, "Correspondence-Sanford and Son."
117 Letter received and time-stamped on March 28, 1974, Norman Lear TV Shows.
118 Letter received and time-stamped on April 5, 1974, Norman Lear TV Shows.
119 Norman Lear TV Shows.
120 "Fear Redd Foxx Has Blown His Wife, TV Show," *JET Magazine*, May 9, 1974, 14–16.
121 "Fear Redd Foxx," 14–16.
122 "Fear Redd Foxx," 14–16.
123 Sebro, interview.
124 Brooks and Marsh, *Complete Directory to Prime Time*.
125 Sebro, interview.
126 "Fear Redd Foxx," 14–16.

127 *Sanford and Son*, season 4, episode 18, "The Masquerade Party," January 31, 1975; *Sanford and Son*, season 5, episode 23, "Sergeant Gork," March 12, 1976.
128 Young, "Include Him Out," 24.
129 Young, 26.
130 Bob Lucas, "Grady Bids for TV Stardom on His Own Show," *JET Magazine*, December 25, 1975, 58.

Chapter 3   *Good Times*

1 "Good Times," performed by Jim Gilstrap and Blinky Williams, composed by Dave Grusin, 1974.
2 Dolores Hayden, *The Power of Place: Urban Landscapes as Public History* (MIT Press, 1995), 18.
3 Courtney R. Baker, "Movin' on Up—and Out: Remapping 1970s African American Visual Culture," in *Black Cultural Production after Civil Rights*, ed. Robert J. Patterson (University of Illinois Press, 2019), 101.
4 Baker.
5 Television Academy Foundation, "Norman Lear."
6 Television Academy Foundation.
7 Television Academy Foundation.
8 Soyini D. Madison, *Acts of Activism: Human Rights as Radical Performance* (Cambridge: Cambridge University Press, 2010), 6.
9 Felicia D. Henderson, "*South Central*: Black Writers and the Responsibility and Burden of Creating Black Characters for a Black Audience," *Emergences* 11 (November 2, 2001): 241.
10 Bob Lucas, "A 'Salt Pork and Collard Greens' TV Show," *Ebony Magazine*, June 1974, 53.
   The show never specifically states that the Evans live in the Cabrini-Green Homes. However, because of the establishing shots in the opening credits and the show's cocreator Eric Monte being born and raised in the North Side of Chicago and the Cabrini-Green Homes, the show's location is inferred to be based within Cabrini-Green and confirmed via interviews with Norman Lear.
11 Louie Robinson, "Bad Times on the 'Good Times' Set," *Ebony Magazine*, September 1975, 36.
12 Robinson.
13 Letter from Lilla Capers to Perry Lafferty, August 12, 1975. Norman Lear TV Shows, "Correspondence-Good Times."
14 Lynn Spigel, *TV by Design: Modern Art and the Rise of Network Television* (University of Chicago Press, 2008), 71.
15 David R. Francis, "How the 1960s' Riots Hurt African Americans," National Bureau of Economic Research, September 2004, https://www.nber.org/digest/sep04/w10243.html.
16 National Advisory Commission on Civil Disorders, *Report of the National Advisory Commission*, 115.
17 National Advisory Commission on Civil Disorders, 115.
18 National Advisory Commission on Civil Disorders, 115–120.
19 Peter Dizikes, "Chicago Hope," *MIT News*, March 3, 2003, http://news.mit.edu/2011/chicago-public-housing-0303.

20 Alana Semuels, "New York City's Public-Housing Crisis," *Atlantic*, May 19, 2015, https://web.archive.org/web/20160531234646/http://www.theatlantic.com/business/archive/2015/05/new-york-citys-public-housing-crisis/393644/.

21 Douglas S. Massey and Shawn M. Kanaiaupuni, "Public Housing and the Concentration of Poverty," *Social Science Quarterly* 74, no. 1 (1993): 109–122.

22 Massey and Kanaiaupuni, 109–122.

23 Susan Saulny, "At Housing Project, Both Fear and Renewal," *New York Times*, March 18, 2007.

24 Saulny.

25 Gray, *Watching Race* (2004), 89.

26 Steven R. Holloway, Deborah Bryan, Robert Chabot, Donna M. Rogers, and James Rulli, "Exploiting the Effect of Public Housing on the Concentration of Poverty in Columbus, Ohio," *Urban Affairs Review* 33, no. 6 (1998): 67–89.

27 Holloway, Bryan, Chabot, Rogers, Rulli, 67–89.

28 Cecil Smith, "Florida Moves to Chicago via CBS," *Los Angeles Times*, February 18, 1974.

29 Bruce Haynes, "Racial Order of Suburban Communities: Past, Present, and Future," *Sociology Compass* 2, no. 4 (2008): 1245–1251.

30 Terry Byrne, *Production Design for Television* (Focal Press, 1993): 18.

31 Edward Stephenson Papers (1956–1986), *Collection PASC 143* (University of California, Los Angeles Performing Arts Special Collections), figure 1. At this point in the development of the show, it does not have a name but rather nods to the central character, Esther Rolle, in her reprisal of Florida Evans from *Maude* (1972–1978).

32 Edward Stephenson Papers, figure 2.

33 Alice Evans Fields, *Hollywood, USA: From Script to Screen* (Vantage, 1952), 115.

34 Byrne, *Production Design for Television*.

35 Television Academy Foundation, "Rita Riggs," Interviews, video, 7:08, http://www.emmytvlegends.org/interviews/people/rita-riggs.

36 Television Academy Foundation.

37 Television Academy Foundation.

38 Television Academy Foundation.

39 Jane Gaines, "Costume and Narrative: How Dress Tells a Woman's Story," in *Fabrications: Costume and the Female Body*, ed. Jane Gaines and Charlotte Herzog (Routledge, 1990), 187.

40 Television Academy Foundation, "Rita Riggs."

41 *Good Times*, season 1, episode 1, "Too Old Blues," directed by Bob Peete, February 8, 1974.

42 Television Academy Foundation, "Rita Riggs."

43 Television Academy Foundation.

44 *Good Times*, season 1, episode 3, "Getting Up the Rent," directed by Eric Monte, February 22, 1974.

45 Gaines, "Costume and Narrative," in Gaines and Herzog, *Fabrications*, 181.

46 Television Academy Foundation, "Rita Riggs."

47 Television Academy Foundation.

48 Deidre Royster, *Race and the Invisible Hand: How White Networks Exclude Black Men from Blue-Collar Jobs* (University of California Press, 2003).

49 Royster, 17.

50 Royster, 17.

51 Carl T. Rowan, "Two 'Black' TV Shows: 'Good Times' and Bad," *Washington Post*, 1974.

52 Rowan.

53 Robinson, "Bad Times."

54 Robinson, 38.

55 Robinson, 35.

56 Robinson, 34.

57 Robinson, 40.

58 Robinson, 40.

59 Robinson, 42.

60 Robinson, 40.

61 Robinson, 34.

62 Lucas, "Salt Pork and Collard Greens," 53.

63 Victoria Sturtevant, "'But Things Is Changin' Nowadays an' Mammy's Getting' Bored': Hattie McDaniel and the Culture of Dissemblance," *Velvet Light Trap*, no. 44 (Fall 1999): 68–79.

64 Sturtevant, 68.

65 Sturtevant, 69.

66 Riggs, *Color Adjustment*.

67 Riggs.

68 Bodroghkozy, *Equal Time*, 182.

69 Acham, *Revolution Televised*, 113. To be clear, "hidden transcripts" is a concept developed by James Scott in his book *Domination and the Arts of Resistance: Hidden Transcripts*, and the broader reference of this concept is a discussion of public roles played by the powerful and powerless and the mocking, vengeful tone they display offstage—their public and hidden transcripts. Here, Acham has adopted the term to discuss Black television actresses voicing their activism.

70 Anthony Duane Hill, "The Negro Ensemble Company (1967–)," *Black Past*, February 13, 2008, https://www.blackpast.org/african-american-history/negro-ensemble-company-1967/.

71 Lahn Sung Kim, "Maid in Color: The Figure of the Racialized Domestic in American Television" (PhD diss., University of California, Los Angeles, 1997), x.

72 Sturtevant, "But Things Is Changin'," 9.

73 Collier, "*Sanford and Son*."

74 *Maude*, season 1, episode 3, "Maude Meets Florida," 1973.

75 Lucas, "Salt Pork and Collard Greens," 50.

76 Robinson, "Bad Times," 40.

77 *Maude*, season 2, episode 20, "Florida's Goodbye," aired February 5, 1974.

78 Robinson, "Bad Times," 34.

79 *Maude*.

80 Sandra Haggerty, "TV and Black Womanhood," *Los Angeles Times*, November 6, 1974.

    That's My Mama is a sitcom set in a middle-class African American neighborhood in Washington, D.C., and revolved around the character Clifton Curtis (played by Clifton Davis), a man in his mid-twenties who worked as a barber and his loving but opinionated mother Eloise "Mama" Curtis, who wanted him to settle down and find a nice wife.

81 Haggerty.

82 Haggerty.

83 Judy Klemesrud, "Florida Finds Good Times in Chicago," *New York Times*, May 5, 1974.

84 Riggs, *Color Adjustment*.

85 Riggs.

86 Riggs.

87 Riggs.

88 Klemesrud, "Florida Finds Good Times."

89 Klemesrud.

90 Klemesrud.

91 Klemesrud.

92 *Good Times*, season 2, episode 18, "The Debutante Ball," story by Patricia Edwards and teleplay by Jack Elinson and Norman Paul, February 4, 1975.

93 "People" *JET Magazine*, June 10, 1976.

94 A food desert is an area, especially one with low-income residents, that has limited access to affordable and nutritious food. The designation considers the type and quality of food available to the population, in addition to the number, nature, and size of food stores that are accessible. Mary Story, Karen M. Kaphingst, Ramona Robinson-O'Brien, and Karen Glanz, "Creating Healthy Food and Eating Environments: Policy and Environmental Approaches," *Annual Review of Public Health* 29 (2008): 253–272.

95 Caitlin E. Caspi, Ichiro Kawachi, S. V. Subramanian, Gary Adamkiewicz, and Glorian Sorensen, "The Relationship between Diet and Perceived and Objective Access to Supermarkets among Low-Income Housing Residents," *Social Science & Medicine* 75, no. 7 (October 2012): 1254–1262.

96 Zora Neale Hurston, *Dust Tracks on a Road: An Autobiography* (HarperCollins, 2010).

97 Lee Marguiles, "Esther Rolle Returning to 'Good Times,'" *St. Petersburg Times*, June 10, 1978.

98 Estyr P. Peak, "Actor Turned Work into 'Good Times' for Writer," *Twin Cities Courier*, January 31, 1975.

99 The series aired on CBS as part of its 1969 fall lineup and was the second variety series to feature an African American host since *The Nat King Cole Show* (1956–1957).

100 Josef Adalian, "John Amos on *Mary Tyler Moore*, Racism on Set, and Playing the First Black Family Man," *Vulture*, October 13, 2015, http://www.vulture.com/2015/10/john-amos-mary-tyler-moore-good-times.html.

101 Lucas, "A 'Salt Pork and Collard Greens' TV Show," *Ebony Magazine*, June 1974, 50.

102 "John Amos" *Television Academy Foundation Interview*, 12/02/2014, https://interviews.televisionacademy.com/interviews/john-amos#interview-clips.

103 Ibid.

104 Adalian, "John Amos on *Mary Tyler Moore*."

105 Adalian.

106 Moynihan, *Negro Family*.

107 Dara Starr Tucker (@Daratuckerb), "The Breakdown: Eric Monte vs. Norman Lear," Instagram, accessed July 1, 2022, https://www.instagram.com/reel/Ce_Jh2vg61V/?igshid=NmZiMzY2Mjc=.

108 Acham, *Revolution Televised*, 211.

109 Acham.

110 *Good Times*, "Too Old Blues," directed by Bob Peete, aired February 8, 1974; *Good Times*, "Black Jesus," directed by Kurt Taylor and John Donley, aired February 15, 1974; *Good Times*, "Getting Up the Rent," directed by Eric Monte, aired February 22,

1974; *Good Times*, "God's Business Is Good Business," directed by Roland Wolpert, aired March 1, 1974; *Good Times*, "Michael Gets Suspended," directed by Eric Monte, aired March 8, 1974.

111 Acham, *Revolution Televised*, 133.

112 Acham, 133.

113 Acham, 135.

114 Acham, 132.

115 "John Amos" *Television Academy Foundation Interview*, 12/02/2014, https://interviews.televisionacademy.com/interviews/john-amos#interview-clips.

116 Robinson, "Bad Times," 33–42.

117 Robinson, 40.

118 Robinson, 40.

119 Robinson, 40.

120 Robinson, 40.

121 Interoffice Communications and Contracts began to reference "John Amos Productions" in 1975 correspondence. Norman Lear TV Shows, "Correspondence-Good Times."

122 Letter received on July 28, 1975. Norman Lear TV Shows, "Correspondence-Good Times."

123 Contract written on July 10, 1975. Norman Lear TV Shows, "Correspondence-Good Times."

124 Sebro, interview.

125 Peak, "Actor Turned Work."

126 "It's a Family Affair" story outline written by John Amos and Ja'net DuBois January 27, 1975, Norman Lear TV Shows, "Correspondence-Good Times."

127 Interoffice Communication Letter December 15, 1975. Norman Lear TV Shows, "Correspondence-Good Times."

128 Television Academy Foundation, "Norman Lear."

129 Interoffice Communication Re: John Amos Suspension September 23, 1975. Norman Lear TV Shows, "Correspondence-Good Times."

130 Norman Lear TV Shows.

131 Harris, *Sex Workers, Psychics*, 20–21.

132 Television Academy Foundation, "John Amos," Interviews, streamed on December 2, 2014, video, 2:44, https://interviews.televisionacademy.com/interviews/john-amos#interview-clips.

133 Television Academy Foundation.

134 Television Academy Foundation.

135 Television Academy Foundation.

136 James Hill, "The Breakdown: Good Times—'Damn, Damn, Damn!,'" *TV One*, April 7, 2016, https://tvone.tv/31287/the-breakdown-good-times-damn-damn-damn/.

137 *Good Times*, season 4, episode 2, "The Big Move: Part 2," September 29, 1976.

138 Katia Dunn, "For Classic TV Producer, Good Times No Longer," *NPR Media*, July 29, 2006.

139 Dunn.

140 *Cooley High* is a 1975 American coming-of-age / drama film that follows the narrative of high school seniors and best friends, Leroy "Preach" Jackson (Glynn Turman) and Richard "Cochise" Morris (Lawrence Hilton-Jacobs). Written by Eric Monte, directed by Michael Schultz, and produced by American International Pictures (AIP), the film, primarily shot in Chicago, Illinois, was a major hit at the box offices,

grossing over $13,000,000. The lighthearted-turned-tragic story line captivated viewers with its comedic portrayal of carefree best friends, and its soundtrack featured many Motown hits.

141 Clarence Walker, "Screenwriter Eric Monte Fought Hollywood," *New Blaze* February 28, 2018.
142 Walker.
143 Dunn, "For Classic TV Producer."
144 Walker, "Screenwriter Eric Monte."
145 Dunn, "For Classic TV Producer."
146 Dunn.
147 Dunn.
148 Dunn.
149 Tucker, "Breakdown."

Chapter 4   *The Jeffersons*

1 *The Jeffersons* theme song / opening credits, written by Ja'Net DuBois and Jeff Barry, performed by Ja'Net DuBois, "Movin' on Up," Sony/ATV Music Publishing LLC, 1975.
2 St. Lunatics, "Batter Up," track 14 on *Country Grammar*, Universal, 2001, compact disc.
3 *The Jeffersons* was surpassed in 2012 by *Tyler Perry's House of Payne* (2007–2012) by one episode, though *The Jeffersons* ran for more seasons.
4 Television Academy Foundation, "Norman Lear."
5 Television Academy Foundation.
6 Television Academy Foundation.
7 Yorkin wanted to be bought out so that he can solely focus on making films. Television Academy Foundation, "Bud Yorkin."
8 Baker, "Movin' on Up," in Patterson *Black Cultural Production*, 96.
9 Elizabeth Higginbotham, *Too Much to Ask: Black Women in the Era of Integration* (University of North Carolina Press, 2001), 23.
10 Louie Robinson, "The Jeffersons: A Look at Life on Black America's New Striver's Row," *Ebony Magazine*, January 1976, 112.
11 Gray, *Watching Race* (1995). Also see Haggins, *Laughing Mad*, 8.
12 Harry F. Waters, *Newsweek*, June 2, 1975, 79.
13 Waters, 79. The Congress of Racial Equality (CORE) is an African American civil rights organization in the United States that played a pivotal role for African Americans in the civil rights movement.
14 To name a few, Lisa Woolfork, "Looking for Lionel: Making Whiteness and Blackness in *All in the Family* and *The Jeffersons*," in *African Americans on Television: Racing for Ratings*, ed. David J. Leonard and Lisa A. Guerrero (Praeger, 2013), 45–68. Darren Rhym, "An Analysis of George Jefferson and Heathcliff Huxtable," in *Journal of African American Men* 3, no. 3 (Winter 1998): 57–67.
   Gordon L. Berry, "Black Family Life on Television and the Socialization of African American Child: Images of Marginality," *Journal of Comparative Family Studies* 29, no. 2, Comparative Perspectives on Black Family Life: Vol. 2 (Summer 1998): 233–242.
15 Robin Means Coleman, *African American Viewers and the Black Situation Comedy: Situating Racial Humor* (Garland, 1998), 166.
16 Television Academy Foundation, "Rita Riggs."

17 Television Academy Foundation.

18 Other than Eric Monte's creative dispute over the creation of George Jefferson, as discussed at the end of the previous chapter, there existed no Black presence in *The Jeffersons'* production until season 2, episode 22, "Lionel's Problem" (February 22, 1976) with story credit given to Mia Abbott (Norman Lear's adopted Black daughter).

19 Television Academy Foundation, "Sherman Hemsley," Interviews, streamed on 2003, video, 2:08, https://interviews.televisionacademy.com/interviews/sherman-hemsley.

20 Television Academy Foundation, "George Sunga," Interviews, streamed on February 1, 2008, video, 3:27, https://interviews.televisionacademy.com/interviews/george-sunga#interview-clips.

21 Dick Hobson, "Up from the Ghetto," *TV Guide*, June 21–27, 1975, 21.

22 Robert E. Johnson, "The Jeffersons: Hottest New TV Family," *JET Magazine*, March 27, 1975.

23 Johnson, 60.

24 Robinson, "Jeffersons," *Ebony Magazine*, 112.

25 Robinson, 114.

26 Robinson, 115.

27 Robinson, 112.

28 *The Jeffersons*, season 1, episode 1, "A Friend in Need," directed by Barry Harman and Harve Brosten, aired January 18, 1975.

29 *All in the Family*, season 1, episode 3, "Archie's Aching Back," January 26, 1971; and *All in the Family*, season 5, episode 16, "The Jeffersons Move Up," aired January 11, 1975.

30 *Jeffersons*, "A Friend in Need."

31 Kelley, *Yo' Mama's Disfunktional!*, 1.

32 Kelley.

33 *The Jeffersons*, season 1, episode 13, "Jenny's Low," directed by John Ashby, April 12, 1975.

34 *The Jeffersons*, season 1, episode 11, "Former Neighbors," directed by Art Baer & Ben Joelson, March 29, 1975.

35 Television Academy Foundation, "Rita Riggs."

36 Monica L. Miller, *Slaves to Fashion: Black Dandyism and the Styling of Black Diasporic Identity* (Duke University Press, 2009), 8.

37 Miller, 191.

38 Miller, 1.

39 Miller, 16.

40 *The Jeffersons*, season 1, episode 6, "George's Skeleton," story by Erik Tarloff, February 22, 1975.

41 *The Jeffersons*, season 2, episode 9, "George Won't Talk," directed by John Ashby, November 8, 1975.

42 Norman Lear TV Shows, *Pacific Title Archives*.

43 *The Jeffersons*, season 2, episode 9, "Movin' on Down," directed by Ken Levine and David Isaacs, November 1, 1975.

44 Norman Lear TV Shows, *Pacific Title Archives*.

45 Television Academy Foundation, "Sherman Hemsley."

46 "Actress Isabel Sanford, 86, Starred as 'Weezie' on TV's 'The Jeffersons,' Dies," *JET Magazine*, August 2, 2004, 61–62.

47 Norman Lear TV Shows, *Pacific Title Archives*. (Over 10 fan letters available requested this).

48 Means Coleman, *African American Viewers*, 98.

49 Deborah Gray White, *Ar'n't I a Woman* (W. W. Norton, 1999), 176.

50 Christopher J. P. Sewell, "Mammies and Matriarchs: Tracing Images of the Black Female in Popular Culture 1950s to Present," *Journal of African American Studies* 17, no. 3, *Springer* (September 2013): 308–326.

51 Sewell, 320.

52 In "A Friend in Need," Louise reminds George that when they were a young married couple, she did domestic work a couple of times a week.

53 Patricia Hill Collins, *Black Feminist Thought: Knowledge, Consciousness, and the Politics of Empowerment* (Routledge, 2000), 98, 101.

54 Television Academy Foundation, "Isabel Sanford," Interviews, streamed on April 3, 2002, video 3:29, https://interviews.televisionacademy.com/interviews/isabel -sanford#interview-clips.

55 Television Academy Foundation.

56 Television Academy Foundation.

57 Television Academy Foundation.

58 Television Academy Foundation.

59 Television Academy Foundation.

60 Television Academy Foundation.

61 Television Academy Foundation.

62 Although the racial dynamics were a large dispute of Redd Foxx's walkout on *Sanford and Son*, O'Connor's walkout was comparable in its impact on *All in the Family* and its dedicated fan base. Like Foxx, O'Connor received a raise and appeared in the series until it ended.

63 Television Academy Foundation, "Isabel Sanford."

64 Television Academy Foundation.

65 Television Academy Foundation.

66 Television Academy Foundation.

67 Television Academy Foundation.

68 Television Academy Foundation.

69 *All in the Family*, season 5, episode 16, "The Jeffersons Move Up," January 11, 1975.

70 Television Academy Foundation, "Isabel Sanford."

71 Television Academy Foundation.

72 Television Academy Foundation.

73 *The Jeffersons*, season 1, episode 12, "Like Father, like Son," directed by Frank Tarloff, April 5, 1975.

74 *The Jeffersons*, season 1, episode 1, "A Friend in Need," story by Barry Harman and Harve Brosten, teleplay by Don Nicholl, Michael Ross, Bernie West, Barry Harman, and Harve Brosten, January 18, 1975.

75 *The Jeffersons*, season 1, episode 3, "Louise Feels Useless," directed by Lloyd Turner and Gordon Mitchell, February 1, 1975.

76 *I Love Lucy*, season 2, episode 1, "Job Switching," September 15, 1952.

77 Collins, *Black Feminist Thought*, 23.

78 Victor Bobetsky, "The Complex Ancestry of 'We Shall Overcome,'" *Choral Journal* 57:26–36.

79 Television Academy Foundation, "Marla Gibbs," Interviews, streamed on July 27, 2006, video, 4:19 https://interviews.televisionacademy.com/interviews/marla-gibbs #interview-clips.

80 Although *Sanford and Son*'s character Officer "Hoppy" Hopkins (portrayed by Howard Platt) is seen very often throughout the series, the characters Tom Willis and

Harry Bentley (portrayed by Franklin Cover and Paul Benedict respectively) exist in the majority of *The Jeffersons* episodes, are in the opening credits sequence, and even have story lines that revolve around them.

81 Further readings on the history: Susan Courtney, *Hollywood Fantasies of Miscegenation: Spectacular Narratives of Gender and Race* (Prince University Press, 2004); Glenda Gilmore, *Gender and Jim Crow: Women and the Politics of White Supremacy in North Carolina, 1896–1920* (University of North Carolina Press, 1996).

82 Jessica Viñas-Nelson, "Interracial Marriage in 'Post-racial' America," *Origins: Current Events in Historical Perspective* 10, no. 12 (September 2017), http://origins.osu.edu/article/interracial-marriage-post-racial-america.

83 The clause, which took effect in 1868, provides "nor shall any State . . . deny to any person within its jurisdiction the equal protection of the laws."

84 Viñas-Nelson, "Interracial Marriage."

85 Viñas-Nelson.

86 Television Academy Foundation, "Rita Riggs."

87 *The Jeffersons*, season 1, episode 2, "Georges Family Tree," directed by Perry Grant and Dick Bensfield, January 25, 1975.

88 Norman Lear TV Shows, *Pacific Title Archives*.

89 *Jeffersons*, "Friend in Need."

90 *Jeffersons*, "Like Father, like Son."

91 *Jeffersons*, "Friend in Need."

92 *Jeffersons*.

93 *Star Trek* is an American science-fiction television series created by Gene Roddenberry that follows the adventures of the starship USS *Enterprise* and its crew. The article referenced is Daniel Bernardi, "Star Trek in the 1960s: Liberal-Humanism and the Production of Race," *Science Fiction Studies* 24, no. 72, part 2 (July 1997): 216.

94 This memo, in the Gene Roddenberry Papers housed in Special Collection at University of California Los Angeles, attempts to censor any material of a sexual nature: "Caution on the postures and actions of our four principles so that no impropriety can be suggested. The embraces must not be such as would embarrass a viewer, and there must be no open-mouth kissing."

95 Bernardi, "Star Trek in the 1960s," 216–217.

96 Bernardi, 217.

97 Bernardi, 217.

98 Bernardi, 217.

99 Nichelle Nichols, *Beyond Uhura: Star Trek and Other Memories* (New York: G. P. Putnam's Sons, 1994): 195–198.

100 Nichols.

101 Television Academy Foundation, "George Sunga."

102 Heitner, *Black Power TV*, 20.

103 Heitner, 20.

104 Heitner, 20.

105 Heitner, 34.

106 Television Academy Foundation, "Sherman Hemsley."

107 Norman Lear TV Shows, *Pacific Title Archives*.

108 David M. Heer, "The Prevalence of Black-White Marriage in the United States 1960 and 1970," *Journal of Marriage and Family* 36, no. 2 (May 1974): 246–258.

109 Norman Lear TV Shows, *Pacific Title Archives*, December 26, 1975.

110 Norman Lear TV Shows, *Pacific Title Archives*, March 6, 1976.

111 F. James Davis, *Who Is Black? One Nation's Definition* (Pennsylvania State University Press, 2001), 144.

112 Jacqueline Trescott, "Roxie Roker: Moving on Up," *Washington Post*, March 1976.

113 *The Jeffersons*, season 1, episode 13, "Jenny's Low," directed by John Ashby, April 12, 1975.

114 Davis, *Who Is Black?*, 143.

115 A palomino is a genetic color in horses consisting of a gold coat and white mane and tail. The degree of whiteness can vary from white to yellow.

116 John Dollard, "The Dozens: Dialectic of Insult," in *Mother Wit from the Laughing Barrel*, ed. Alan Dundes (University Press of Mississippi, 1973), 278–279.

117 Adrian Piper, "Passing for White, Passing for Black," *Transition*, no. 58 (1992): 6.

118 An ofay is a slang term used to describe white people.

119 Piper, "Passing for White," 13.

120 Piper.

121 Acham, *Revolution Televised*, 171. "Integrationist-themed" shows indicate the integrating face of African American representation at the end of the 1970s. Shows in which Black casts integrate on-screen with White ones, as well as shows featuring Black characters in which their Blackness is somewhat muted, giving credence to the idea that racial divisions do not exist (i.e., *The Cosby Show* [1984–1992]).

Conclusion   A Piece of the Pie

1 Television Academy Foundation, "Bud Yorkin."

2 "Introducing: Gerren Keith, Dynamic Director Oversees All Phases of *Diff'rent Strokes*," *Ebony Magazine*, December 1982.

3 Harper, "Extra-Special Effects." Simulacral realism is a representation that "would improve the objective conditions characterizing daily life for the mass of African Americans living within the scope of television's influence." This term describes popular demands for greater representation of Blacks on TV, regardless of their roles, to improve their social status. On the other hand, he identifies the contradictory demand for relevance or "mimetic realism . . . whereby television would 'reflect' the social reality on which it was implicitly modeled." While problematizing each of these demands, Harper calls for the merging of the two.

4 Brooks and Marsh, *Complete Directory to Prime Time*.

5 Of all the Black artists discussed, only Isabel Sanford (2004) and Marla Gibbs (2021) of *Good Times* were given stars on the Walk of Fame.

6 *Mad TV*, season 11, episode 5, November 12, 2005; Photograph, *TV Guide*, cover, October 9–16, 2005; *The Fresh Prince of Bel-Air*, season 5, episode 17, "Will Is from Mars," February 20, 1995; *Tyler Perry's House of Payne*, season 8, episode 10, "Curtis Jefferson," November 18, 2011.

7 Lesley Goldberg, "Sony Eyes Other Norman Lear Reboots in New TV Deal with Iconic Producer," *Hollywood Reporter*, July 27, 2018.

8 Anonymous, Personal communication from source, May 23, 2019.

Bibliography

Acham, Christine. *Revolution Televised: Prime Time and the Struggle for Black Power.* University of Minnesota Press, 2005.

———. "Sanford and Son: Televising African American Humor." *Spectator* 20, no. 2 (Spring/Summer 2000): 75–89.

Adalian, Josef. "John Amos on *Mary Tyler Moore*, Racism on Set, and Playing the First Black Family Man." *Vulture*, October 13, 2015. http://www.vulture.com/2015/10/john-amos-mary-tyler-moore-good-times.html.

Adler, Dick. "Look What They Found in a Junkyard—the Spare Parts for a Comedy Series That Breaks Some New Ground." *TV Guide*, May 13, 1972.

Allen, Robert C., ed. *Channels of Discourse, Reassembled: Television and Contemporary Criticism.* Routledge, 2005.

Alley, Robert S., and Horace Newcomb. *The Producer's Medium: Conversations with Creators of American TV.* Oxford University Press, 1983.

Arlen, Michael. "Media Dramas of Norman Lear." *New Yorker*, May 10, 1975.

Baker, Courtney R. "Movin' on Up—and Out: Remapping 1970s African American Visual Culture." In *Black Cultural Production after Civil Rights*, edited by Robert J. Patterson, 94–116. University of Illinois Press, 2019.

Barnouw, Erik. *Tube of Plenty: The Evolution of American Television.* Oxford University Press, 1990.

Becker, Kristina Flodman. *The Informal Economy: Fact Finding Study.* Sida, 2004.

Bernardi, Daniel. "*Star Trek* in the 1960s: Liberal-Humanism and the Production of Race." *Science Fiction Studies* 24, no. 72, part 2 (July 1997): 209–225.

Berry, Gordon L. "Black Family Life on Television and the Socialization of African American Child: Images of Marginality." *Journal of Comparative Family Studies* 29, no. 2 (Summer 1998): 233–242.

Bobetsky, Victor. "The Complex Ancestry of 'We Shall Overcome.'" *Choral Journal* 54, no. 7 (2014): 26–36.

Bodroghkozy, Aniko. *Equal Time: Television and the Civil Rights Movement.* University of Illinois Press, 2013.

Brooks, Tim, and Earle Marsh. *The Complete Directory to Prime Time Network and Cable TV Shows 1946–Present*. 9th ed. Ballantine Books, 2007.

Byrne, Terry. *Production Design for Television*. Focal, 1993.

Carpio, Glenda. *Laughing Fit to Kill: Black Humor in the Fictions of Slavery*. Oxford University Press, 2008.

Caspi, Caitlin E., Ichiro Kawachi, S. V. Subramanian, Gary Adamkiewicz, and Glorian Sorensen. "The Relationship between Diet and Perceived and Objective Access to Supermarkets among Low-Income Housing Residents." *Social Science & Medicine* 75, no. 7 (October 2012): 1254–1262.

Ciment, James. *Postwar America: An Encyclopedia of Social, Political, Cultural, and Economic History*. Routledge, 2015.

Collier, Eugenia, "*Sanford and Son* Is White to the Core." *New York Times*, June 17, 1973.

Collins, Patricia Hill. *Black Feminist Thought: Knowledge, Consciousness, and the Politics of Empowerment*. Routledge, 2000.

Combahee River Collective. "Black Feminist Statement." April 1977.

Courtney, Susan. *Hollywood Fantasies of Miscegenation: Spectacular Narratives of Gender and Race*. Prince University Press, 2004.

Davidson, Bill. "Trouble in Paradise." *TV Guide*, April 6, 1974.

———. "The World's Funniest Dishwasher Is Still Cleaning Up: But for Redd Foxx, It Has Been a Long Trip from the Kitchen to '*Sanford and Son*.'" *TV Guide*, March 17, 1973.

Davis, F. James. *Who Is Black? One Nation's Definition*. Pennsylvania State University Press, 2001.

Deeb, Gary. "Redd Admits Trying to Outfox NBC." *Chicago Tribune*, March 11, 1974.

Dizikes, Peter. "Chicago Hope." *MIT News*, March 3, 2003. http://news.mit.edu/2011/chicago-public-housing-0303.

Dollard, John. "The Dozens: Dialectic of Insult." In *Mother Wit from the Laughing Barrel*, edited by Alan Dundes, 277–294. University Press of Mississippi, 1973.

Dow, Bonnie. *Prime-Time Feminism: Television, Media Culture, and the Women's Movement since 1970*. University of Pennsylvania Press, 1996.

DuBois, Ja'Net, and Jeff Barry. "Movin' on Up." *The Jeffersons* theme song/opening credits. Sony/ATV Music, 1975.

Dunn, Katia. "For Classic TV Producer, Good Times No Longer." *NPR Media*, July 29, 2006.

Ebony Magazine. "Introducing: Gerren Keith, Dynamic Director Oversees All Phases of *Diff'rent Strokes*." December 1982.

Edward Stephenson Papers (1956–1986). Collection PASC 143. University of California, Los Angeles Performing Arts Special Collections.

Ferguson, Roderick. *Aberrations in Black: Toward a Queer of Color Critique*. University of Minnesota Press, 2004.

Feuer, Jane. "Genre Study and Television." In *Channels of Discourse, Reassembled: Television and Contemporary Criticism*, edited by Robert C. Allen, 138–160. Routledge, 1992.

Fields, Alice Evans. *Hollywood, USA: From Script to Screen*. Vantage, 1952.

Fitzgerald, Ella. "Easy to Love." Written by Cole Porter. Warner/Chappell Music, 1956.

Foxx, Redd, and Norma Miller. *The Redd Foxx Encyclopedia of Black Humor*. W. Ritchie Press, 1977.

Fretts, Bruce, and Matt Roush. "The Greatest Shows on Earth." *TV Guide Magazine*, 2013.

Fuller, Jennifer. "*Gimme a Break!* and the Limits of the Modern Mammy." In *Watching While Black: Centering the Television of Black Audiences*, edited by Beretta E. Smith-Shomade, 118. Rutgers University Press, 2012.

Gaines, Jane. "Costume and Narrative: How Dress Tells a Woman's Story." In *Fabrications: Costume and the Female Body*, edited by Jane Gaines and Charlotte Herzog, 180–211. Routledge, 1990.

Gardella, Kay. "If NBC Keeps Promises, I'll Be Back, Says Foxx." *New York Daily News*, March 15, 1974.

Germany, Kent. "Lyndon B. Johnson: Domestic Affairs." University of Virginia, Miller Center. Accessed March 3, 2020. https://millercenter.org/president/lbjohnson/domestic-affairs.

Gilmore, Glenda. *Gender and Jim Crow: Women and the Politics of White Supremacy in North Carolina, 1896–1920*. University of North Carolina Press, 1996.

Gilstrap, Jim, and Blinky Williams. "Good Times" (theme song). 1974.

Gitlin, Todd. *Inside Primetime*. University of California Press, 2000.

Gledhill, Christine. "Pleasurable Negotiations." In *Female Spectators: Looking at Film and Television*, edited by E. Deidre Pribram, 64–89. Verso, 1988.

Goldberg, Lesley. "Sony Eyes Other Norman Lear Reboots in New TV Deal with Iconic Producer." *Hollywood Reporter*, July 27, 2018.

Gray, Herman. *Watching Race: Television and the Struggle for "Blackness."* University of Minnesota Press, 1995.

Gray, Jonathan. *Show Sold Separately: Promos Spoilers, and Other Media Paratexts*. New York University Press, 2010.

Haggerty, Sandra. "TV and Black Womanhood." *Los Angeles Times*, November 6, 1974.

Haggins, Bambi. *Laughing Mad: The Black Comic Persona in Post-soul America*. Rutgers University Press, 2007.

Hall, Stuart. "What Is This 'Black' in Black Popular Culture?" *Social Justice* 20, no. 1/2 (Spring–Summer 1993): 104–114.

Hamamoto, Darrel Y. *Nervous Laughter: Television Situation Comedy and Liberal Democratic Ideology*. Praeger, 1991.

———. *Television Situation Comedy and Liberal Democratic Ideology*. New ed. Praeger, 2001.

Harper, Phillip Brian. "Extra-Special Effects: Televisual Representation and the Claims of 'the Black Experience.'" In *Living Color: Race and Television in the United States*, edited by Sasha Torres, 62–71. Duke University Press, 1998.

Harris, LaShawn. *Sex Workers, Psychics, and Numbers Runners: Black Women in New York City's Underground Economy*. University of Illinois Press, 2016.

Hayden, Dolores. *The Power of Place: Urban Landscapes as Public History*. MIT Press, 1995.

Haynes, Bruce. "Racial Order of Suburban Communities: Past, Present, and Future." *Sociology Compass* 2, no. 4 (2008): 1245–1251.

Heer, David M. "The Prevalence of Black-White Marriage in the United States 1960 and 1970." *Journal of Marriage and Family* 36, no. 2 (May 1974): 246–258.

Heitner, Devorah. *Black Power TV*. Duke University Press, 2013.

Henderson, Felicia D. "*South Central*: Black Writers and the Responsibility and Burden of Creating Black Characters for a Black Audience." *Emergences* 11 (November 2, 2001): 237–248.

Higginbotham, Elizabeth. *Too Much to Ask: Black Women in the Era of Integration*. University of North Carolina Press, 2001.

Hill, Anthony Duane. "The Negro Ensemble Company (1967–)." Black Past. February 13, 2008. https://www.blackpast.org/african-american-history/negro-ensemble-company-1967/.

Hill, James. "The Breakdown: Good Times—'Damn, Damn, Damn!'" *TV One*, April 7, 2016 https://tvone.tv/31287/the-breakdown-good-times-damn-damn-damn/.

Hobson, Dick. "Up from the Ghetto." *TV Guide*, June 21–27, 1975.

Holloway, Daniel. "Kenya Barris Signs $100 Million Netflix Deal." *Variety*, August 16, 2018.

Holloway, Steven R., Deborah Bryan, Robert Chabot, Donna M. Rogers, and James Rulli. "Exploiting the Effect of Public Housing on the Concentration of Poverty in Columbus, Ohio." *Urban Affairs Review* 33, no. 6 (1998).

Hunt, Darnell M. *Channeling Blackness: Studies on Television and Race in America*. Oxford University Press, 2005.

Hurston, Zora Neale. *Dust Tracks on a Road: An Autobiography*. HarperCollins, 2010.

Iton, Richard. *In Search of the Black Fantastic: Politics and Popular Culture in the Post–Civil Rights Era*. Oxford University Press, 2008.

James, Cynthia. "Searching for Ananse: From Orature to Literature in the West Indian Children's Folk Tradition—Jamaican and Trinidadian Trends." *Children's Literature Association Quarterly* 30, no. 2 (2005).

JET Magazine. "Actress Isabel Sanford, 86, Starred as 'Weezie' on TV's 'The Jeffersons,' Dies." August 2, 2004.

———. "Fear Redd Foxx Has Blown His Wife, TV Show." May 9, 1974.

———. "People." June 10, 1976.

John F. Kennedy Presidential Library and Museum. "The Civil Rights Movement." Accessed February 2020. https://www.jfklibrary.org/learn/about-jfk/jfk-in-history/civil-rights -movement.

Johnson, Robert E. "The Jeffersons: Hottest New TV Family." *JET Magazine*, March 27, 1975.

Joyrich, Lynne. "Critical and Textual Hypermasculinity." In *Logics of Television*, edited by Patricia Mellencamp, 161. Indiana University Press, 1990.

Kelley, Robin D. G. *Yo' Mama's Disfunktional! Fighting the Culture Wars in Urban America*. Beacon, 1997.

Kim, Lahn Sung. "Maid in Color: The Figure of the Racialized Domestic in American Television." PhD diss., University of California, Los Angeles, 1997.

Klemesrud, Judy. "Florida Finds Good Times in Chicago." *New York Times*, May 5, 1974.

Lear, Norman. *Even This I Get to Experience*. Penguin, 2014.

Lemack (Brad) Collection. *Special Research Collections*. UC Santa Barbara Library.

Leonard, David J., and Lisa Guerrero. *African Americans on Television: Race-ing for Ratings*. ABC-CLIO, 2013.

Levine, Lawrence. *Black Culture and Consciousness: Afro-American Folk Thought from Slavery to Freedom*. Oxford University Press, 1977.

Lipsitz, George. "The Meaning of Memory: Family, Class, and Ethnicity in Early Network Television Programs." In *Private Screenings: Television and the Female Consumer*, edited by Lynn Spigel and Denise Mann, 71–108. University of Minnesota Press, 1992.

Littleton, Darryl. *Black Comedians on Black Comedy: How African-Americans Taught Us to Laugh*. Hal Leonard Corporation, 2008.

Littleton, Darryl J., and Tuezdae Littleton. *Comediennes: Laugh Be a Lady*. Applause, 2012.

Lotz, Amanda. *The Television Will Be Revolutionized*. New York University Press, 2007.

———. "What Is U.S. Television Now?" *Annals of the American Academy of Political and Social Science* 625, no. 1 (2009): 49–59.

Lucas, Bob. "Grady Bids for TV Stardom on His Own Show." *JET Magazine*, December 25, 1975.

———. "A 'Salt Pork and Collard Greens' TV Show." *Ebony Magazine*, June 1974.

MacDonald, J. Fred. *Blacks and White TV: African American in Television since 1948*. Nelson-Hall, 1983.

Madison, Soyini D. *Acts of Activism: Human Rights as Radical Performance*. Cambridge: Cambridge University Press, 2010.

Mantler, Gordon. *Power to the Poor: Black-Brown Coalition and the Fight for Economic Justice, 1960–1974*. University of North Carolina Press, 2015.

Marguiles, Lee. "Esther Rolle Returning to 'Good Times.'" *St. Petersburg Times*, June 10, 1978.

Massey, Douglas S., and Shawn M. Kanaiaupuni. "Public Housing and the Concentration of Poverty." *Social Science Quarterly* 74, no. 1 (1993): 109–122.

Means Coleman, Robin R. *African American Viewers and the Black Situation Comedy: Situating Racial Humor*. Garland, 1998.

Miller, Monica L. *Slaves to Fashion: Black Dandyism and the Styling of Black Diasporic Identity*. Duke University Press, 2009.

Moynihan, Daniel P. *The Negro Family: The Case for National Action*. Washington, D.C., Office of Policy Planning and Research, U.S. Department of Labor, 1965.

National Advisory Commission on Civil Disorders. *Report of the National Advisory Commission on Civil Disorders*. 1967.

Newcomb, Horace. *TV: The Most Popular Art*. Anchor Books, 1974.

Nichols, Nichelle. *Beyond Uhura: Star Trek and Other Memories*. New York: G. P. Putnam's Sons, 1994.

Norman Lear TV Shows / Productions Boxes. *Pacific Title Archives, Act III Productions*. Los Angeles, September 20, 2016.

O'Connor, John J. "TV View: Good Times for the Black Image." *New York Times*, February 2, 1975.

Page, LaWanda. *Watch It, Sucker!* Laff Records, 1972.

Peak, Estyr P. "Actor Turned Work into 'Good Times' for Writer." *Twin Cities Courier*, January 31, 1975.

Piper, Adrian. "Passing for White, Passing for Black." *Transition*, no. 58 (1992): 4–32.

Ratledge, Ingela. "*Black-ish* Lets the *Good Times* Roll." *TV Guide*, May 9, 2016.

Rhym, Darren. "An Analysis of George Jefferson and Heathcliff Huxtable." *Journal of African American Men* 3, no. 3 (Winter 1998): 57–67.

Robinson, Louie. "Bad Times on the 'Good Times' Set." *Ebony Magazine*, September 1975.

———. "The Jeffersons: A Look at Life on Black America's New Striver's Row." *Ebony Magazine*, January 1976.

———. "Redd Foxx—Crazy like a Fox: 'Sanford and Son' Star Seeks a Piece of the Action." *Ebony Magazine*, June 1974.

Rowan, Carl T. "Two 'Black' TV Shows: 'Good Times' and Bad." *Washington Post*, 1974.

Royster, Deidre. *Race and the Invisible Hand: How White Networks Exclude Black Men from Blue-Collar Jobs*. University of California Press, 2003.

Sarasota Herald-Tribune TV-Work. "Sanford's Comedy Black Writer's Work." July 7–13, 1974.

Saulny, Susan. "At Housing Project, Both Fear and Renewal." *New York Times*, March 18, 2007.

Sebro, Adrien. Interview with Saul Turteltaub (coexecutive producer on *Sanford and Son*). May 30, 2018.

Semuels, Alana. "New York City's Public-Housing Crisis." *Atlantic*, May 19, 2015. https://web .archive.org/web/20160531234646/http://www.theatlantic.com/business/archive/2015/05/ new-york-citys-public-housing-crisis/393644/.

Sewell, Christopher J. P. "Mammies and Matriarchs: Tracing Images of the Black Female in Popular Culture 1950s to Present." *Journal of African American Studies* 17, no. 3 (September 2013): 308–326.

Smith, Cecil. "Florida Moves to Chicago via CBS." *Los Angeles Times*, January 18, 1974.

Smith-Shomade, Beretta. *Shaded Lives: African-American Women and Television*. Rutgers University Press, 2002.

Spigel, Lynn. *Make Room for TV: Television and the Family Ideal in Postwar America*. University of Chicago Press, 1992.

———. *TV by Design: Modern Art and the Rise of Network Television*. University of Chicago Press, 2008.

Spillers, Hortense. "Mama's Baby, Papa's Maybe: An American Grammar Book." *Diacritics* 17, no. 2 (1987): 64–81.

Stallings, L. H. *Mutha Is Half a Word: Intersections of Folklore, Vernacular, Myth, and Queerness in Black Female Culture*. Ohio State University Press, 2007.

Starr, Michael Seth. *Black and Blue: The Redd Foxx Story*. Applause Theatre and Cinema Books, 2011.

Story, Mary, Karen M. Kaphingst, Ramona Robinson-O'Brien, and Karen Glanz. "Creating Healthy Food and Eating Environments: Policy and Environmental Approaches." *Annual Review of Public Health* 29 (2008): 253–272.

Sturtevant, Victoria. "'But Things Is Changin' Nowadays an' Mammy's Gettin' Bored': Hattie McDaniel and the Culture of Dissemblance." *Velvet Light Trap* 44 (Fall 1999): 68–79.

Television Academy Foundation Interviews. https://interviews.televisionacademy.com/.

The Temptations. "Ball of Confusion (That's What the World Is Today)." *Gordy*. Originally released in 1970.

Trescott, Jacqueline. "Roxie Roker: Moving on Up." *Washington Post*, March 1976.

Tucker, Dara Starr (@Daratuckerb). "The Breakdown: Eric Monte vs. Norman Lear." Instagram. Accessed July 1, 2022. https://www.instagram.com/reel/Ce_Jh2vg61V/?igshid=NmZiMzY2Mjc=.

Tucker, Terrence T. *Furiously Funny: Comic Rage from Ralph Ellison to Chris Rock*. University of Florida Press, 2018.

USC Annenberg. "50 Years after the Kerner Commission: Can Entertainment Inspire a New Will?" February 23, 2022. YouTube video, 1:26:35. https://www.youtube.com/watch?v=MQuKm4S70Xg&t=54s.

U.S. Commission on Civil Rights. *Window Dressing on the Set: Women and Minorities in Television*. A Report of the United States Commission on Civil Rights. 1977.

Viñas-Nelson, Jessica. "Interracial Marriage in 'Post-racial' America." *Origins: Current Events in Historical Perspective* 10, no. 12, Accessed September 2017. https://origins.osu.edu/article/interracial-marriage-post-racial-america?language_content_entity=en.

Walker, Clarence. "Screenwriter Eric Monte Fought Hollywood." *New Blaze*, February 28, 2018.

Waters, Harry F. "TV: Do Minorities Rule?" *Newsweek*, June 2, 1975, 78–79.

Watkins, Mel. "LaWanda Page, 81, the Aunt on TV's 'Sanford and Son.'" *New York Times*, September 18, 2002.

———. *On the Real Side: Laughing, Lying and Signifying—the Underground Tradition of African-American Humor That Transformed American Culture, from Slavery to Richard Pryor*. Simon and Schuster, 1994.

White, Deborah Gray. *Ar'n't I a Woman*. W. W. Norton, 1999.

Williams, P., executive producer. *CBS Reports, Watts: Riot or Revolt?* Columbia Broadcast System, 1965.

Wojciechowski, Michele "Wojo." "The Norman Lear Experience: His Shows, His Honesty, and One Thing He Wanted to Do." *Parade*, July 28, 2015.

Woolfork, Lisa, "Looking for Lionel: Making Whiteness and Blackness in *All in the Family* and *The Jeffersons*." In *African Americans on Television: Race-ing for Ratings*, edited by David J. Leonard and Lisa A. Guerrero, 45–68. Praeger, 2013.

Young, J. R. "Include Him Out." *TV Guide*, October 5, 1974.

Index

Page numbers in *italics* refer to figures.

About the Author

ADRIEN SEBRO is an assistant professor of media studies with a courtesy appointment in African and African diaspora studies at the University of Texas at Austin. He specializes in critical media studies and Black popular culture.